A HISTORY OF NYASALAND AND MALAWI FOOTBALL

VOLUME 1
1935 TO 1969

MARIO ANTOINE

authorHOUSE

AuthorHouse™ UK
1663 Liberty Drive
Bloomington, IN 47403 USA
www.authorhouse.co.uk
Phone: UK TFN: 0800 0148641 (Toll Free inside the UK)
*   UK Local: (02) 0369 56322 (+44 20 3695 6322 from outside the UK)*

Published by AuthorHouse   05/24/2022

ISBN: 978-1-6655-9840-8 (sc)
ISBN: 978-1-6655-9839-2 (e)

CONTENTS

FOREWORD BY PRESIDENT FOOTBALL ASSOCIATION OF MALAWI

Allow me to take time to appreciate the great work that Mario has put on compiling this volume and the subsequent ones that he plans on publishing in the coming years.

What Mario has achieved with this book is no mean feat and what it means for the game in Malawi is priceless.

But first, allow me acknowledge Mario's love and passion for Malawi football which transcends lip-glossed proclamations – he has actually done something that adds value to the management and administration of the game in the country.

As a country and as an association, we have fared badly in record-keeping, resulting in glaring gaps in the documentation of the history of the beautiful game in the country.

In football, as in other sports, statistics are a crucial component in the planning and execution of various development programmes. With no statistics in hand, the tacticians will be grappling in the dark. For one, instead of second guessing, stats help us to pinpoint specific areas of success in the history of the game in the country so that we can go back in history and draw success lessons from that period to help us grow and move forward.

For instance, what did we, as a footballing nation, do right during the success of 1977/78? What were the factors in and around the game that enables that success and what lessons can we draw from this specific period and team to enable us to raise the bar?

And one crucial element that we neglect to recognize about stats and indeed Mario's work is the fact that we, as an FA will now be able to recognize and acknowledge those players who have made great contributions to the game and to the national team.

While the debate of who has been, our greatest player is a foregone conclusion, with scores of fans and officials resting their case on the legendary Kinnah Phiri, debate in our areas of the field remain a touchy subject for the debate. For instance, the debate on who, over the years has been our greatest goalkeeper, defender or midfielder has been delicate ground for debate.

The existence of statistics will enable us to easily identify these individuals based on clean sheets, defensive records and so forth to enable us duly recognize and award these individuals based on facts and not on opinions or guesswork.

Over the above the attendant existence and easy availability of statistics from all our national team games since inception will enable us, as the FA, to avail these statistics to International broadcasters during international matches as we always fall short when those requests are made.

We can only hope that football writers in Malawi and beyond will take Mario's bait to add valuable literature to how the game has developed over the years.

For instance, autobiographics for some of the key figures in the sport are a must.

We recently launched one by Chancy 'Vinny' Gondwe but we need more for Ernest Mtawali, Kinnah Phiri, Lawrence Waya, Spy Msiska, Jack Chamangwana, Young Chimodzi and all the legends that have moved the game forward. These are stories that need to be told.

Mario has set the ball rolling; the ball is now in our court.

INTRODUCTION

This publication is intended to provide some information about football in Malawi, previously known as Nyasaland. Little is known about the humble beginnings of Malawi football and the two separate associations set up for the Europeans and the Africans. This may have been the trend in the early years, as some known separate associations also existed in South Africa, Southern Rhodesia, and Mauritius, to mention a few.

While the author has endeavoured to check all facts and figures, some inaccuracies will inevitably have crept in, particularly from the earlier years.

However, I trust that the publication will satisfy the many "Flames" and football enthusiasts' long-standing need. This project will be in three phases as follows: The first book from 1935 to 1969; the second book from 1970 to 1999; the third and final book between 2000 to date. It is hoped that after the first editions are released, enthusiast readers will be able to correct some facts.

I would like to express my sincere thanks to the people who have given material help and encouragement, among them my mentors the late Scott Cheshire and Ron Hockings (both authors of many Chelsea Football Club publications); the late Peter Khamisa (Football Association of Malawi (FAM) general secretary); Gomezgani Zakazaka, current FAM media director, members of Malawi's *Times* and *Nation* newspaper archives, particularly Peter Kanjere, Edson Kapito and Joy Ndovi; and also, those from the National British Library. Brian Griffin, who was a Malawi player-coach in 1967, provided much of his memorabilia from his time in Malawi, as did former national players Yasin Osman and Mustafa Munshi, Jack Chamangwana and Young Chimodzi. Another great assistant and provider is Neil Morrison from England. The information he has on minor countries is second to none, also Azhur Fajurdeen for the cover design.

I would be committing a grave mistake if I forgot my long-suffering "football widow," my wife, Liseby. Without the cooperation and her understanding, the production of this book would not have been possible.

Mario Antoine
June 2022

Mario Antoine: Very passionate of Malawi football's history

CHAPTER ONE
A BRIEF HISTORY OF MALAWI

History is a fascinating tale in our world. Today we are known as Malawi, but where did this name derive from? Well, our story begins in the eleventh century, when the Bantus began migrating into the area from the Congo to escape unrest and disease. The Amaravi people, who eventually became known as Chewa (possibly derived from a word meaning "foreigner"), founded the Maravi (thought to mean "flames") Empire in the 1480s. They were known to be ironworkers, and as such they introduced iron tools, weapons, and farming. They also attacked the Akafula tribes, who settled in small family clans. While many of the tribal groups in Central Maravi moved towards Centralisation, this was not true of the tribes in the northern area, known as Tumbuka, who were united around their culture and language. The Tumbuka lived under the rule of a Karonga (also spelt "Kalonga"), or a king. The Karonga ruled from his headquarters at Mankhamba, but his kingdom stretched from the south-western shores of Lake Malawi all the way into parts of modern-day Mozambique and Zambia. He appointed sub-chiefs to occupy and conquer new territory. The kingdom reached its peak between 1600 and 1650 under Chief Masula, who maintained good relationships with the Portuguese until the empire began to decline. It ultimately collapsed around 1700 as a result of infighting among the sub-chiefs and the weakening of the slave trade.

Sixteenth Century

The Portuguese reached the Maravi Empire, who sold slaves and ivory, and in return they brought maize, originally a crop from South America, to this part of Africa. The people from northern Mozambique, called the **Yao** raided Maravi and took captives to be sold to the Arabs as slaves.

Slave Trade

Mombasa was captured by Sultan Said of Muscat in 1824 and this brought great change in this part of Africa. The sultan's conquest ended Portuguese influence in the area as the Europeans and Americans moved inland, trying to abolish the slave trade. But under Omani rule, trade increased in 1839 as over forty thousand were sold through the Zanzibar slave market. Coastal trading centres at Karonga, Nkhotakota, and Salima became famous for slave trading as the Omani raiders attacked during the night.

Yao

In addition to the disastrous slave trade, the Yao tribes in the southern part of Malawi were converted to Islam by the Arabs, who armed them well to raid or offer rich prizes for slaves. The marauding Yao moved north, killing and capturing the local Chewas and Magangas, reigniting the Congo conflict of the past.

Mfecane

The Zulu tribe, located in the Eastern part of present-day South Africa, was under the rule of Shaka Zulu. He created three kingdoms—Ngwane, Ndwandwe, and Mthethwa—as a result of the militarisation of the Nguni culture in 1816. The Mthethwa Paramountcy fell under Shaka's rule, and two years later came the Ndwandwe Kingdom, and with this came an exodus to the north that was later known as Mfecane, as the Jere-Ngoni raided every village along the route and settled in the areas of Lake Malawi. There they inflicted terror on the Yao, who had settled near the lake, and the Tumbuka to the north.

David Livingstone

The Scottish explorer David Livingstone, who was a Congregationalist and a pioneer medical missionary, reached Lake Nyasa in 1859 at the age of forty-six after crossing the continent from west to east. Livingstone witnessed the brutality of the slave trade. His solution to the slave trade was the "three C's"—Christianity, commerce, and colonisation—which he believed was the only hope of Africans. Two Scottish Presbyterian missionary societies built missions in the area. Two more missionaries followed, and British merchants began to sell goods in the region. Livingstone died from malaria on 1 May 1873 in Chief Chitambo's village at Ilala, south-east of Lake Bangweulu, in present-day Zambia. Ten years later, Britain sent a consul to the area.

British Control

The Livingstonia Central Africa Company was formed in 1877 by local businessmen in Glasgow, Scotland, where its head office was located, to cooperate with Presbyterian missions in Nyasaland. Its first managers were two brothers, John and Frederick Moir. The company's original base in Blantyre, Mandala House, the oldest building in Malawi, still exists and is a national monument. It was renamed as the Africa Lakes Company Limited the following year, and then as the Africa Lakes Corporation Limited in 1894.

In light of an ongoing territory dispute with Portuguese East Africa as early as 1888, the British consul's deputy declared a Shire Highlands Protectorate and then changed the name to the Nyasaland Districts Protectorate in 1891. Following the 1890 British ultimatum delivered and accepted under duress to Portugal on 11 January 1890 and an 1891 Anglo-Portuguese treaty, the Southern Borders were fixed and renamed to The British Central Africa Protectorate in 1893. The date 6 July was to become a very significant date in the history of our country, as it was on that date in 1907 that the protectorate was given another name, this time the Nyasaland Protectorate. This was followed by independence in 1964 and establishment as a republic in 1966.

Meanwhile, the British South Africa Company united Mashonaland and Matabeleland as Southern Rhodesia in 1901, and North-Eastern Rhodesia and Western Rhodesia as the British Protectorate of Northern Rhodesia in 1911.

Nyasaland African Congress (NAC)

The North Nyasa Native Association (NNNA), consisting of mainly educated locals, was the pioneer of the existing Malawi Congress Party (MCP) when it was formed in 1912. During the

1920s and 1930s, numerous associations were formed, mainly spearheaded by Levi Zililo Mumba. By 1943, the leaders of the Nyasaland Native Association (NNA), influenced by Levi Mumba and James Frederick Sangala's proposal to work at the national level, formed the Nyasaland Educated African Council (NEAC). However, a few months later it changed to the Nyasaland African Congress (NAC), since the movement felt it should not be restricted to only the elite educated. Levi Mumba was elected as the first president general at their inaugural meeting in October 1944, but unfortunately he did not last long in his position, as he died three months later. Thamar Dillon Thomas Banda was the fifth president general, elected in 1957. He attended the Ghana celebrations in March 1957, and it was there that he met with Dr. Hastings Banda and urged him to return to Nyasaland to lead the national movement, which he did in July 1958.

Federation of Rhodesia And Nyasaland

The Federation of Rhodesia and Nyasaland, established on 1 August 1953, was a semi-independent federation of three Southern African territories, the self-governing British colony of Southern Rhodesia, and the British protectorates of Northern Rhodesia and Nyasaland. With the rulers of the new African states uniting to end colonialism in Africa, which saw most of the world moving away from it during the 1950s and early 1960s, the federation officially ended on 31 December 1963. The first country to gain independence was Nyasaland, on 6 July 1964, and its name changed to Malawi. It was followed by Northern Rhodesia on 24 October 1964, which was renamed Zambia. A year later, on 11 November 1965, Southern Rhodesia moved away from British rule and declared a unilateral declaration of independence. It was then known as Rhodesia until it gained its independence on 18 April 1980. It is now known as Zimbabwe.

Where We Are

Malawi is a landlocked country in South-East Africa and is bordered by Zambia to the north-west, Tanzania to the north-east, and Mozambique to the east, west, and south. The country is separated from Tanzania and Mozambique by Lake Malawi and is over 118,000 square kilometres (45,560 square miles) in area. The capital has been Lilongwe since 1975, and prior to that it was Zomba. The estimated population in July 2013 was just under 17 million.

Lake Malawi is sometimes called "the Calendar Lake," as it is 365 miles long and 52 miles at its widest. Malawi's highest mountain is Mulanje, at ten thousand feet.

CHAPTER TWO
THE EARLY YEARS OF GLOBAL FOOTBALL

Origins of Football

Football as we know it was most probably invented at least as early as 2500 BC by the Greeks, Egyptians, and Chinese, as has been mentioned in many articles. But the oldest and likely first rules were written and adopted in 1863 in England when the Football Association of England (believed to be the oldest association in the world) looked into previous ones written by Cambridge (1848), Sheffield (1855) and J. C. Thring (1862).

FIFA

As Football was spreading across the world, the Federation Internationale de Football Association (FIFA) was formed in Paris on 21 May 1904, and the following eight countries were affiliated: Belgium, Denmark, France, Netherlands (Holland), Spain (represented by Madrid Football Club, as their association was formed in 1913), Sweden, Switzerland, and Germany (who sent their proposed affiliation that same day). It is interesting to note that only the Europeans were affiliated to FIFA then. Afterward, the other confederations started to join, and to date, the numbers have grown to 211 and 12 associate members.

Non-FIFA Confederations

CAF: South Africa 1909 (withdrew in 1924 and rejoined in 1952 before being suspended in 1961, until such time as they were readmitted in 1992 under the newly re-formed association in 1992)
CONMEBOL: Argentina 1912
CONCACAF: Canada 1913
AFC: Japan 1921
OFC: New Zealand 1948
FIFA Confederations
CONMEBOL: Confederatia Sudamericano de Futbol **(1916)—10 members**
AFC: Asian Football Confederation **(1954)—46 members and 1 associate member**
UEFA: Union of European Football Association **(1954)—55 members**
CAF: Confederation Africane de Football **(1957)—54 members and 2 associate members**
CONCACAF: Confederation of North, Central American and Caribbean Association Football **(1961)—35 members and 6 Associate members**
OFC: Oceania Football Confederation **(1966)—11 members and 3 Associate members**

FIFA Presidents

FIFA has been in existence for 118, years and Mr Robert Guerin, a French National became the first ever president. He served for two years on the board and was the youngest president, elected at the age of twenty-seven years and eleven months. He retired at the age twenty-nine years, eleven months. The oldest president to be elected was Rodolphe Seeldrayers, at the age of seventy-nine, while Joao Havelange was the oldest to leave office, at eighty-two years of age. Jules Rimet is the longest-serving president, being in office for thirty-three years.

Unfortunately, three of the nine presidents passed on during their terms of office. They were Daniel Woolfall (1918), Rodolphe Seeldrayers (1955), and Arthur Drewry (1961). 2015 saw a president suspended for the first time ever when Sepp Blatter, who had been in office for seventeen years, was found guilty of misconduct. The full list and years of service is listed below.

Robert Guerin	France	23 May 1904–04 Jun 1906	2 yrs 12 days
Daniel Burley Woolfall	United Kingdom	04 Jun 1906–24 Oct 1918	12 yrs 142 days, (died in office)
Cornelis August Wihelm Hirschman	Netherlands (Holland)	24 Oct 1918–27 Aug 1920	1 yr 309 days (acting)
Jules Rimet	France	29 Aug 1920–1 Mar 1921	185 days (acting)
Jules Rimet	France	01 Mar 1921– 21 Jun 1954	33 yrs 112 days
Rodolphe Seeldrayers	Belgium	21 Jun 1954–07 Oct 1955	1 yr 108 days, (died in office)
Arthur Drewry	United Kingdom	07 Oct 1955–09 Jun 1956	246 days (acting)
Arthur Drewry	United Kingdom	09 Jun–25 Mar 1961	4 yrs 289 days (died in office)
Ernst Thommen	Switzerland	25 Mar 1961–28 Sep 1961	187 days (acting)
Stanley Rous	United Kingdom	28 Sep 1961–08 May 1974	12 yrs 222 days
Joao Havelange	Brazil	08 May 1974–08 Jun 1998	24 yrs 31 days
Sepp Blatter	Switzerland	08 Jun 1998–08 Oct 2015	17 yrs 122 days (impeached)
Issa Hayatou	Cameroon	08 Oct 2015–26 Feb 2016	141 days (acting)
Gianni Infantino	Switzerland/Italy	26 Feb 2016–present	6+ yrs (ongoing)

CAF Presidents

The Confederation of African Football (CAF) is the fourth-oldest confederation, as it was founded on 8 February 1957, only three years after both the European and Asian associations were formed. But they must be proud, as they have the most members in their list of fifty-six members, including two as associates, as compared to fifty-five from Europe. This confederation was formed in Khartoum, Sudan, beginning with four members from Egypt, Ethiopia, South Africa, and the host nation. Its first president was Abdel Aziz Abdallah Salem of Egypt, with Youssef Mohamad as the secretary general.

This followed their initial meeting held in Lisbon, Portugal, eight months earlier, on 7 June 1956, which three countries attended: South Africa, Egypt, and Somalia.

The office headquarters was first situated in Khartoum for several months until a fire broke out in the offices of the Sudanese Football Association, which then saw it move to Cairo, Egypt. In 2002, it changed venue again, and it is now situated in 6th of October City, near Cairo.

The six other affiliates to CAF are as follows:

- North Africa (2005): Union of North Africa Football Federation (UNAF)
- West Africa (1975): West African Football Union (WAFU-UFOA)
- Central Africa (1978): Central African Federations Union (UNIFFAC)
- East Africa: (1927) The Council for East and Central African Football Associations (CECAFA)
- Southern Africa (1997): Council of Southern African Football Association (COSAFA)
- Arab World (1974): Union of Arab Football Associations (UAFA)

Below is a list of all the CAF presidents:

Abdel Aziz Abdallah Salem	Egypt	1957–1958	0–1 yr
Abdel Aziz Moustafa	Egypt	1958–1968	9–10 yrs
Abdel Halim Muhammad	Sudan	1968–1972	3–4 yrs
Yidnekatchew Tessema	Ethiopia	1972–18 Aug 1987	15 yrs 229 days (died in office)
Abdel Halim Muhammad	Sudan	18 Aug 1987–10 Mar 1988	205 days (acting)
Issa Hayatou	Cameroon	10 Mar 1988–16 Mar 2017	29 yrs 06 days
Ahmad Ahmad	Madagascar	15 Mar 2017–23 Nov 2020	3 yrs 252 days
Constant Omari	Democratic Republic of Congo	23 Nov 2020–29 Jan 2021	67 days (acting)
Ahmad Ahmad	Madagascar	29 Jan 2021–12 Mar 2021	42 days
Patrice Motsepe	South Africa	12 Mar 2021–present	(ongoing)

The longest serving president was Issa Hayatou, from Cameroon. He was in office for twenty-nine years. Abdel Aziz Moustafa was the only president to be elected for two terms, but he spent the shortest time in office in his second term, as he served less than seven months.

CHAPTER THREE

EARLY FOOTBALL IN NYASALAND

As football was being introduced in many countries, mainly by the British, who travelled overseas for work, it was no surprise to learn that the British missionaries who came to Nyasaland, a British colony (the name of which was later changed to Malawi after the nation attained its independence in 1964), to spread the word of God, introduced football to the nation in the late 1800s. However, there are no records proven to verify this statement.

Zomba Gymkhana Club (ZGC) (9 April 1896) and Blantyre Sports Club (BSC) (31 July 1896) are two of the oldest clubs in the country. However, Mandala Athletic Club, supported by the African Lakes Corporation and Kubula Recreation Club of Kubula Hill, sponsored by E. H. Sharrer of Kubula Hill, preceded these clubs, whose early activities were shooting, cricket, tennis, and billiards.

Research shows that the first known football match took place in Zomba in 1896, when ZGC lost 2–0 to BSC. Two more results were recorded in 1911 and 1929, where BSC won both games 5–2 and 11–5. Friendly games were then taking place in the South, mainly as a source of entertainment amongst the European expatriates of Cholo (now known as Thyolo), Mlanje (Mulanje), Country Club Limbe (opened in 1923), and Zomba. The highlights of the regular friendly scene took place three times a year, namely on Christmas Day, New Year's Day, and King George's birthday, 3 June. Matches were predominantly between the Scottish community and either the English or others. In my research, I found no mention of any football activities in the central (Lilongwe) and northern (Mzuzu) regions.

As the years went by, apart from the selected matches, the games were played on a regular basis amongst the Southern Region clubs, which also formed the Indian Sport Club in 1920, followed by the Goans Club in 1928.

Some of the families that pioneered the formation of the European association known as Nyasaland Football Association still grace the shores of this land today. The Royle family, whose patriarch Jack was once on the English club Stoke City's books, sponsored both the league and a knockout trophy until that association was dissolved. Roger Royle played for Cholo in the '50s with two caps, and that family is well known in the Cholo/Mulanje area.

Nicholas Trataris, who owned one of the finest bakeries in Central Africa at the time, was another member that sponsored an international trophy that was played for between Nyasaland and Alexandra FC of Southern Rhodesia between 1954 and 1961, and three of his children, Costas, George, and John, all played for Nyasaland. His grandchildren still live here at tobacco companies.

Another family that comes to mind is the Hayes family. Lionel Hayes, who won nine caps in the '30s and '40s, scored 1 goal. Their family business was Antipest, which was run by Peter and is now run by his grandson David. The Saunders family has seen two generations play for the NFA between the '30s and '50s. Saunders won six caps in the '30s and '40s, and Pat Saunders won one cap in 1957.

The Phillips family had Malcolm Alexander Phillips, who won three caps in the '30s and '40s, but Brian Phillips was a star in the '50s and '60s with forty-one caps and 15 goals. His son, Malcolm, now lives in the United States.

The Cottinghams started late in the fifties, and once again, three brothers, Jackie, Jim, and Archie, all played for Nyasaland. The late Jackie created some history, as he represented all three federation teams: Southern Rhodesia, Northern Rhodesia, and Nyasaland. He is also one of only eleven players to have played for both the Nyasaland and Malawi team or Select XI, the others being James Kaminjolo, Allaudin Osman, John Brown, Ikram Sheriff, Costas Trataris, Bob Power, Januaro de Maghalaes, Joaquim Cunha, Franco Bregger, and Phillip Bradley.

CHAPTER FOUR

THE DIFFERENT BODIES

Records highlight two racially segregated football bodies that were in existence: namely Nyasaland Football Association (NFA), which catered to expatriates; and Nyasaland African Football Association (NAFA), which looked after the indigenous Malawians. This all changed after independence in October 1964, when the amalgamated body became known as the Malawi Football Association (MFA). Two years later, in August 1966, the name changed to Football Association of Malawi (FAM), as it is known today.

NFA

Despite the first known international fixture taking place in 1935 (that's as far as my research has gone; players were selected from the southern region teams that only played friendly games, but it is unclear whether any league was known to be in existence at that time), the NFA was formed on 14 March 1948, with F. W. Hindley becoming the first president, supported by Vice President W. A. Cole and Hon. Secretary/Treasurer R. E. Bright. The five affiliated clubs that played during that first season include Blantyre Sports Club, Indian Sports Club, Country Club Limbe, Mlanje and Zomba. Another league was formed in the '50s within Zomba, played in midweek consisting of five clubs.

In addition to the league being introduced, three knockout competitions were played at different intervals, starting with the Royle Cup from 1950 to 1967. This was followed by the Stanhope Trophy from 1954 to 1967, and finally the Franklin Trophy from 1962 to 1967. It is noted with some disappointment that all three knockout trophies were withdrawn in 1967 under the new association.

As they were not affiliated with any federations, the only football participation was friendly fixtures against club sides from Portuguese East Africa and Southern Rhodesia, with trophies introduced being the Oury Cup, Trataris, and Bruss.

NAFA

The NAFA organised their football playing in the Shire Highlands African Football League (SHAFL), and records indicate that it was formed in 1938. A media report shows that the second season was to commence on 10 June 1939. There were sixteen teams that were affiliated from the areas of Limbe, Blantyre, Ntenjela, and Chileka.

In addition to the SHAFL, other such associations were being formed in Limbe and Zomba, and later on a district level.

In addition to the leagues playing at the various levels, competitions introduced were King's Birthday Cup, the United Tobacco Cup between Champions of the Blantyre League against Zomba Champions, and the Abraham Shield, which was played amongst the champions of the different divisions of the SHAFL. The I. O. Adam Shield was later introduced.

In 1957, the governor introduced a tournament amongst the three provinces that later was renamed the Kamuzu Cup.

FAM

The amalgamation of the two separate bodies became effective in 1965, and apart from that, the league expanded to allow the Central Region teams to enter the southern league. Knockout trophies were introduced in 1968, with the Castle Cup being the first, followed by both the Chibuku and BAT in 1969, and several more in the '70s and onwards that we shall look at in the next book. The dream of having a national league with teams from all the three regions became a reality in 1983.

At the international level, progress was made as Malawi affiliated with both the Federation Internationale de Football Association (FIFA) and Confederation of African Football (CAF) in 1968. Until such time, all their international matches were played as friendlies against countries and club sides. Participation in organised competitions began only in 1971.

CHAPTER FIVE

THE 1930S AND THE OURY CUP

First International

The earliest record of an international fixture was recorded in 1935 when Sport Lisboa e Beira of Portuguese East Africa (now known as Mozambique) travelled to Nyasaland and defeated the host country 4–1. George Summers, who was later to be elected as the NFA president, became the first international scorer.

1937 — The first team ever to play against Sports Lisboa e Beira in the Oury Cup. Back row (l. to r.) Thomson, Forrest, Survarna, Summers. Front row (l. to r.) Roberts, Neil, Russell, Middleton, Smith, Grant, Robertson. Middleton and Grant are still in Nyasaland, while Thomson is leaving shortly.

Oury Cup

Two years after the first international fixture between Nyasaland and the Portuguese East African team from Beira, Sport Lisboa e Beira (SLB), Mr Libert Oury, who was the then chairman of Trans-Zambezi Railways, donated a trophy in 1937 for a tournament, the Oury Cup, to be played annually between the NFA National Select and their first visitors.

The first match took place at Country Club Limbe (CCL), and Nyasaland narrowly lost 1–0, with Survana of Indian Sports Club becoming the first Asian player to feature for Nyasaland. Four of the players that played in 1935—Harry Middleton, S. Robertson, George Summers, and R. Neil—retained their places.

The following year, the NFA travelled to Beira as agreed in a reverse fixture, and they retained six of the players that featured at CCL with N. Carr recalled after three years. The other players, with Harry Middleton keeping his place as a custodian, were Thomson, Forrest, Russell-Jones, R. Neil, and the lone hero scorer R. Grant. The team returned victorious with high hopes of utilising home advantage, only to crash to a heavy 6–0 defeat at Blantyre Sports Club (BSC). Four players who played in the previous game—the quartet of Forrest, Russell-Jones, R. Grant, and N. Carr—were recalled.

Friendlies

Nyasaland's first ever international match was a friendly against SLB in 1935, as mentioned above. The following year, they invited Alexandra FC from Salisbury, Southern Rhodesia. Nyasaland recorded their first ever win on the historic day of 12 July 1936, beating Alexander 3–1 at Blantyre Sports Club. George Summers scored in his second successive match, with R. Neil and Bemister as the other scorers. The following day, despite Nyasaland scoring a further 3 goals, Alexandra got their revenge by winning 5–3. R. Neil again, R. Grant, and Lionel Hayes were on target in the second match, which was also played at BSC. Two more matches were played at the same venue in 1937, but the scores are still being researched.

The team then travelled to Beira in 1938, and after winning the Oury match 1–0 through R. Grant's lone goal, they played against Beira Select XI and lost 3–1, with Russell-Jones finding the net. It became a trend that after the Oury fixture, they would play a second game the following day. In 1939, Nyasaland went on to lose 3–0 to Sport Lisboa e Beira at Zomba Gymkhana.

1935 Timeline

16 Feb 1935: Friendly: Blantyre SC: Sport Lisboa e Beira 1–4   G. Summers
Harry Middleton, J. MacDonald, S. Robertson, N. Carr, G. Francis, V. Smithyman, Lionel Hayes, George Summers, H. Fox, R. Neil, G. Longfield,

1936 Timeline

12 Jul. 1936: Friendly: Blantyre SC: Alexandra Club 3–1   R. Neil, Bemister, G. Summers
Harry Middleton, N. Carr, Thomson, Russell-Jones, Forrest, G. Francis, R. Neil, Bemister, George Summers, R. Grant, Lionel Hayes

13 Jul. 1936: Friendly: Blantyre SC: Alexandra Club 3–5   R. Neil, R. Grant, L. Hayes
Harry Middleton, N. Carr, Thomson, Russell-Jones, Forrest, Puttock, R. Neil, Bemister, George Summers, R. Grant, Lionel Hayes

1937 Timeline

Mr Libert Oury, Chairman of Trans-Zambezi Railways donated a trophy to be played annually between Nyasaland and Sport Lisboa e Beira.

10 Jul. 1937: Friendly: Blantyre SC: Alexandra Club (unknown result)
Lionel Hayes, Thomson, Russell-Jones, Hoey, Forrest, MacKinnon, Smith, R. Grant, Leach, Clarke, Irvin

11 Jul. 1937: Friendly: Blantyre SC: Alexandra Club (unknown result)
Lionel Hayes, Thomson, Russell-Jones, Campbell, Forrest, Brooking, Malcolm Phillips, R. Grant, Leach, T. Bishop, Galloway

20 Nov. 1937: Oury Cup: Limbe CC: Sport Lisboa e Beira 0–1
Harry Middleton, Thomson, Roberts, S. Robertson, Forrest, Russell-Jones, Smith, R. Grant, George Summers, R. Neil, Survana

1938 Timeline

According to a report in 1939, the Nyasaland African Football Association (NAFA) held its second annual general meeting on 10 June 1939, thus taking this year as the year it was formed and was known as Shire Highlands League (SHL).

16 Apr. 1938: Oury Cup: Beira: Sport Lisboa e Beira 1–0   R. Grant
Harry Middleton, Thomson, N. Carr, Clarke, Forrest, Russell-Jones, G. Francis, R. Grant, Hood, R. Neil, Puttock

17 Apr. 1938: Friendly: Beira: Beira Select XI 1–3   Russell-Jones
Smith, T. Carroll, N. Carr, Hoey, Forrest, Russell-Jones, G. Francis, R. Grant, Hood, R. Neil, Puttock

1939 Timeline

The second season recorded sixteen teams from Limbe, Blantyre, Ntenjela, and Chileka being affiliated to the SHL. The winners of the four different groups met for the Abraham Shield, and this championship was played between the Eastern Division Imperial Tobacco Company (ITG) and Western Division outfit Ndirande Welfare Club at CCL. The Western Division side showed no mercy, demolishing their opponents 5–0, with goals from Titus Mittoche (two), Bruce Matenje, Francis Sazuze, and David Sazuze.

8 Apr. 1939: Oury Cup: Blantyre SC: Sport Lisboa e Beira 0–6
Glass, Mackinnon, N. Carr, Clarke, Forrest, Russell-Jones, G. Francis, R. Grant, Lionel Hayes, Cameron, Puttock

9 Apr. 1939: Friendly: Zomba Gymkhana: Sport Lisboa e Beira 0–3
Van Horsten, Bingham, Campbell, Saunders, Forrest, Russell, R. Neil, R. Grant, Lionel Hayes, Cameron, Puttock

2 Sep. 1939: Abraham Shield Finals: ITC (Eastern Division) v Ndirande Welfare (Western Division) 0–5. Titus Mittoche (2), Bruce Matenje, Francis Sazuze, David Sazuze

Summary of the '30s

A total of ten games were played between 16 February 1935 and 9 April 1939, with two results against Alexandra in 1937 still being researched. Of the remaining eight games, NFA won two and lost six, of which five were friendly fixtures (one win, four defeats) and three were Oury matches (one win and two losses). NFA scored 9 goals and conceded 23. A total of thirty-seven players were selected during this period.

Opposition:	P	W	D	L	F	A	
Sport Lisboa e Beira	5	1	0	4	2	14	
Alexandra FC	4	1	0	1	6	6	(2 unknown)
Beira Select XI	1	0	0	1	1	3	

Top Five appearances
9: Forrest, R. Grant,
Russell-Jones
7: Lionel Hayes, R. Neil

Top Five Scorers (2)
2: R. Grant, R. Neil, George Summers
Clean Sheets (1)
Harry Middleton

CHAPTER SIX

THE 1940S

Oury Cup

The annual friendly between Nyasaland and Sport Lisboa e Beira was played only seven times, as World War II interrupted the series. The NFA XI managed only one win during this period, drawing twice and losing four times, scoring 10 goals and conceding 24. Their victory came in Beira once again in their second fixture, which they won 3–2 with a brace from Forrest. The next game ended in a draw at home. Research is still ongoing to determine the score and the year it was played. The games resumed after the war in 1945, and Nyasaland recorded their worst run in the series, as they lost four successive games, including their heaviest defeat of 10–0 in 1947. The last fixture of the decade at least ended a favourable 3–3 draw in Beira, where Forrest was once more on target through a penalty, with Kirby and Imlah scoring the other goals.

Friendlies

Of the four friendlies played, the details of one are unknown. They lost all three of the other games, scoring twice and conceding 11 goals. Cliff Allin is the only known scorer, with one missing. They were all played in Beira against Sport Club de Beira (1–3), De Sportivo e Beira (?), Sporting Club XI (0–3), and Beira Select XI (1–5)

Nyasaland African Football Association (NAFA)

The seeds of our Flames would have been historically planted in April 1949, when they were invited to play in Beira, but unfortunately this tour was postponed at the eleventh hour after one of the Beira players died on their way back after a football match in Umtali. Fortunately, this tour was revived, and the date of 18 June 1949 must be etched in our history, as the NAFA national team lined up against Grupo Desportivo Rebenta Fogo in Beira, then known as Portuguese East Africa. Although the game did not end favourably for Nyasaland, as they lost by 4–2, E. Thondoya made history with his goal in the second half. The following day, they played against Beira Pick Up Select XI and went down narrowly 2–1.

Formation Of Nyasaland Football Association (NFA)

The Nyasaland Football Association was created on 18 March, and Jack Royle, formerly of Stoke City, now residing in Nyasaland, donated a trophy for the NFA to organise a league. Five clubs affiliated themselves to the league, which was to be known as the Royle League. This developed into a very close affair between Blantyre SC and Mlanje.

The title was decided on the last day, when leaders Blantyre had a one-point advantage over their rivals, leaving them needing only a draw to clinch the first ever title. This they did in style when they defeated Mlanje 2–0. The two teams dominated the league again in the following season, but this time the positions were reversed.

The defending champions lost twice to eventual title winners Mlanje, who finished the season unbeaten, dropping only a point in a draw against Zomba.

1940 Timeline

23 Mar. 1940: Oury Cup: Beira: Sport Lisboa e Beira 3–2   Forrest (2), (1 unknown)
Lionel Hayes, Thomson, Forrest, S. Robertson, Russell-Jones, Woodall, Bingham, Saunders, Galloway, R. Grant, R. Neil

24 Mar. 1940: Oury Cup: Beira: Sport Club de Beira 1–3   (unknown)
Lionel Hayes, Thomson, Forrest, S. Robertson, Russell-Jones, Woodall, Bingham, Saunders, Galloway, R. Grant, R. Neil

1941 Timeline

24 May 1941: NAFA: King's Birthday Cup: Ndirande v ITC 0–0 (to be replayed)

1942 Timeline

SHAFL: Eastern Division (after 3 rounds 06 Jul)
ITC (6 pts),   Railways (3 pts),   BCA (2 pts),   Kapeni (1 pt)

1943 to 1944 Timeline

World War II

Oury Cup played at either BSC/LCC and ended as a drawn game according to reconciliation.

1945 Timeline

31 Mar. 1945: Oury Cup: Beira: Sport Lisboa e Beira 1–4   ?
Whiting, Russell-Jones, Milward, Forrest, T. Bishop, R. Grant, Malcolm Phillips, Johns, Saunders, Thomson, Cliff Allin

1 Apr. 1945: Friendly: Beira: De Sportivo e Beira (unknown result)
Whiting, Russell-Jones, Milward, Forrest, T. Bishop, R. Grant, Malcolm Phillips, Johns, Saunders, Thomson, Cliff Allin

1946 Timeline

28 Feb. 1946:   SHAFL AGM at Native Administration Chamber in Blantyre

20 Apr. 1946: Oury Cup: Blantyre SC: Sport Lisboa e Beira 2–3   C. Allin, R. Grant

Boot, S. Robertson, Hodgson, Forrest, T. Bishop, R. Grant, George Summers, Stubbs, Saunders, Longden, Cliff Allin

22 Aug. 1946: SHAFL: Abraham Shield: Abrahams v. Ntenjela

4 Nov. 1946: NAFA: United Tobacco Company Cup Final: (Champions of Blantyre v Champions of Zomba)

Zomba Athletics v Abrahams 2–1   Chisomo, Kaminjolo, T. Sazuze

Zomba Athletics: Chiwayu, Bandawa, Stephen, Chamangwana, Ndola, Chikawi, Chisomo, Ntenda, Mailawa, Kambampe, Kaminjolo (capt)

Abrahams: J. Likagwa, E. Sazuze, R. Kaliati (capt), J. Mella, S. Sazuze, E. Makwawa, K. Misomali, A. Chupa, K. Gwepe, A. Nkwazi, T. Sazuze

1947 Timeline

5 Apr. 1947: Oury Cup: Beira: Sport Lisboa e Beira 0–10
Hamment, Russell-Jones, Clarke, Fairley, Roger Royle, R. Grant, Millar, Stubbs, McIntosh, Archie Muir, George Sophos

6 Apr. 1947: Friendly: Beira: Sporting Club XI 0–3
Nash, Russell-Jones, Clarke, Fairley, Roger Royle, R. Grant, Millar, Stubbs, McIntosh, Archie Muir, George Sophos

11 Oct. 1947: Friendly: Mlanje: Sporting Club de Quelimane 1–3   M. Megraw
Mlanje: Ian Royan, Horace, Rose, Drakes, Roger Royle, Bowler, Morgan, Dickie, Micky Megraw, Mullen, Blacklaw

8 Nov. 1947: SHAFL: Abraham Shield: Kapeni v. Black Bombers

15 Nov. 1947: NAAFA: United Tobacco Company Cup Final (to meet Zomba champions African Athletics)

15 Nov. 1947: NFA: Friendly: Scotland v. England
Scotland: Ian Royan, Clark, Young, Dickie, Miller, Fairley, Malcolm Phillips, Graham, John Patterson, Archie Muir, Allison

1948 Timeline

The Nyasaland Football Association (NFA) was formed on 14 March 1948, and the following officials were elected:

- President F. W. Hindley
- Vice President W. A. Cole
- Honorary Secretary and Treasurer R. E. Bright

A league sponsored by the Royle family and to be known as the Royle League was formed. Blantyre Sports Club, Country Club Limbe, Indian Sports Club, Mlanje, and Zomba Gymkhana Club took part in this historic event.

Blantyre SC became the first Royle League champions when they defeated Mlanje 2–0 in their last fixture of the season courtesy of an own goal and a John Patterson strike. The last fixture of the season between Indian SC and Zomba Gymkhana did not take place, and no details of the failed game were mentioned. Jack Royle, ex-Stoke City player, donated the trophy on behalf of the family.

28 Mar. 1948: Oury Cup: Blantyre SC: Sport Lisboa e Beira 1–2   J. Patterson
Ian Royan, Russell-Jones, Bright, Fairley, Cliff Allin, Young, Kirby, John Patterson, White, Archie Muir, George Sophos

Final Log Table

Zomba v. Indians S.C. (not played)

Top scorer: John Patterson 26 goals (14 unknown for BSC)

No.	Teams	P	W	D	L	F	A	PTS
1	Blantyre S.C.	8	6	1	1	47	9	13
2	Mlanje	8	4	2	2	17	8	10
3	Zomba	7	2	3	2	11	18	7
4	Indian S.C.	7	3	0	4	11	29	6
5	Limbe C.C.	8	1	0	7	11	33	2

1949

D-day arrived on Saturday, 18 June 1949, in Beira when the long-awaited game that was rearranged against Grupo Desportivo Rebenta Fogo kicked off. The real seeds were sown, and soon NAFA found themselves down 3–0 at half-time. But goals from E. Thondoya and G. Jonas brought respectability to the score in a 2–4 defeat.

NAFA played their second game the following day, and a much-improved score of 1–2 was recorded in yet another loss. Mr James F. Sangala, the chairman of Ndirande Welfare Organisation, was the leader of delegation and was very instrumental in organising this tour.

The same teams participated in the second Royle League, and once again the battle was between Blantyre SC and Mlanje. But the roles were reversed this time, as the defending champions lost both their games against Mlanje, who remained unbeaten during the season. Indian SC failed to win any of their games and ended at the bottom of the log, exchanging places with the previous season's wooden spoon Limbe CC.

1949 Timeline

19 Mar. 1949: Champions v. the Rest: Champions Mlanje v. the Rest 1–1   Eggington, J. Patterson

16 Apr. 1949: Oury Cup: Beira: Sport Lisboa e Beira 3–3   Forrest (pen), Kirby, Imlah

Ian Royan, Jimmy Kongialis, Forrest, Rose, Alan Flowerdew, Young, Kirby, John Patterson, White, Archie Muir, Imlah

17 Apr. 1949: Friendly: Beira: Beira Select XI 1–5   ?
Ian Royan, Jimmy Kongialis, Forrest, Rose, Alan Flowerdew, Young, Kirby, John Patterson, White, Archie Muir, Imlah

18 Jun. 1949: Friendly: Beira: Grupo Desportivo Rebenta Fogo 2–4   E. Thondoya, G. Jonas
R. Kaliati, E. Thondoya, H. Jonga, G. Jonas, Kumkwenzu, Chikwete, K. Munthali, W. Mbekeani, Samson, Manyowa, R. Jambo

19 Jun. 1949: Friendly: Beira: Beira Pick Up 1–2   (unknown)
R. Kaliati, E. Thondoya, H. Jonga, G. Jonas, Kumkwenzu, Chikwete, K. Munthali, W. Mbekeani, Samson, Manyowa, R. Jambo

30 Oct. 1949: Friendly: Scotland v. England 2–2   Imlah (2)–Kirby, R. Grant
Scotland: Ian Royan (Mlanje), Young, D. Clarke (both LCC), Meldrum, Dickie, Fairley, Allison (all BSC), Imlah (Zomba), John Patterson, Archie Muir, G. Clark (all BSC)
England: Turvey (Zomba), Alan Flowerdew (Mlanje), White (Zomba), Lionel Hayes, Coleman (both BSC), Eager (LCC), Kirby (BSC), Roger Royle (Mlanje), Buteux (Zomba), R. Grant (LCC), Simmonds (Zomba)

13 Nov. 1949: Friendly: Mlanje (Nyasaland) v. Milanje (PEA) 7–0   Eggington (2), Muir (2), McGraw (2), Drakes

Final Log Table

John Patterson was top scorer again with 18 goals (2 unknown for BSC)

No.	Teams	P	W	D	L	F	A	PTS
1	Mlanje	8	7	1	0	32	5	15
2	Blantyre SC	8	6	0	2	28	11	12
3	Zomba	8	3	2	3	18	16	8
4	Limbe C.C.	8	2	0	6	10	33	4
5	Indian S.C.	8	0	1	7	06	29	1

Summary of the '40s

A total of eleven games were played between 23 March 1940 and 17 April 1949, with one unknown result against SLB in 1945. Of the remaining ten games, NFA won only one and lost seven with two drawn games (one unknown). Four of the matches were friendly fixtures (one unknown and three defeats) and seven Oury matches (one win, two draws, one unknown, and four losses), scoring a total of 10 goals and conceding 24. A total of forty-two players were selected during this period, of which thirteen were retained from the previous decade.

The NAFA played two international matches against Grupo Desportivo Rebenta Fogo and Beira Pick Up XI and lost fixtures, scoring three and conceding six. A total of eleven players were selected for this tour.

NFA

Opposition:	P	W	D	L	F	A	
Sport Lisboa e Beira	8	1	2	5	10	27	**(1 unknown draw score included)**
Beira Select XI	1	0	0	1	1	5	
Sporting Club XI	1	0	0	1	1	3	
De Sportivo	0	0	0	0	0	0	**(unknown result)**
	10	1	2	7	12	35	

Top Five Appearances
7: Forrest and R. Grant, Russell-Jones
5: Archie Muir, Saunders

Top Five Scorers
3: Forrest
2: Cliff Allin

Top Five Aggregate Appearances (1935 to 1949)
16: Forrest, R. Grant, Russell-Jones
10: Thomson
9: Lionel Hayes, R. Neil

Top Five Aggregate Scorers
3: Forrest, R. Grant
2: Cliff Allin, George Summers

Top Five Aggregate Clean Sheets
1: Harry Middleton

NAFA

Opposition:	F	W	D	L	F	A
Beira Pick Up XI	1	0	0	1	1	2
Grupo Desportivo Rebenta Fogo	1	0	0	1	2	4
	2	0	0	2	3	6

Most Appearances (2)
11 players, as per line-up above
Scorers (1)—1 unknown
E. Thondoya, G. Jonas

Domestic Scene—2 Trophies: 2 Royle League

Teams	Royle League (2)	
	Champions	R/Up
Blantyre	1	1
Mlanje	1	1

CHAPTER SEVEN

THE 1950S

Oury Cup

The annual Oury Cup fixtures between Nyasaland and Sport Lisboa e Beira lasted the full ten fixtures of the decade, with Nyasaland enjoying 70 per cent success. They had four successes on home soil and were unbeaten in the last three, whereas they had a 60 per cent win rate in Beira. Despite this domination, it included a repeat 10–0 drubbing in 1955, as occurred in 1947.

They started the new decade on a high note at Country Club Limbe, where scoring legend John Patterson and Don Armstrong scored a brace apiece in the 5–4 win. This was followed by their third away victory, 2–1, in Beira. The winning streak was halted at Limbe, despite John Patterson scoring again in the 2–1 loss.

This did not deter them when they travelled to Beira in 1953 as debutant Dipple scored the only goal in a historic win, as it was the first time ever they recorded back-to-back victories in Mozambaque.

The '50s success continued, and Limbe was the venue once again, this time witnessing a 5–2 thrashing of Sport Lisboa in which Ken Mansfield, donning his first national colours, scored twice, with evergreen Patterson also on the score sheet.

Unfortunately, the good run ended in a disaster at the beginning of the second half of the decade as the repeated score of 10–0 was recorded in Beira.

This must have been a wake-up call, as Nyasaland then went on to register their first ever three successive wins, starting with 5–0 at Blantyre Sport Club, where Costas Trataris, playing in his only appearance in the cup, scored a brace.

This was followed by a 4–1 win in Beira where four different players were on the scorers' list, which included Ken Mansfield, equalling Patterson's 4 goals during this decade.

Mansfield scored in his third successive game in a 3–2 win in Limbe to lead the scoring chart with 5 goals. The decade ended in defeat in Beira by 2–0.

The ten fixtures saw fifty-two players who featured in these games, with Dennis Johnston leading the chart with eight games (80 per cent), followed by Tommy Allen with seven.

The two players who completed six games were goalkeeper S. Nicholas, with two clean sheets, and top scorer Ken Mansfield, with 5 goals.

Trataris Trophy

Mr Nicholas Trataris, whose sons Costas, George, and John eventually played for the national team, donated this trophy (right) in 1954 for a tournament to be played between Nyasaland and Alexandra FC of Salisbury, Southern Rhodesia, a team that visited us in 1936 and played two fixtures, winning and losing with a total aggregate of 6 goals each.

SOCCER CUP: The Trataris Cup, which has been presented by Mr. Nicholas Trataris of Blantyre for annual competition between the Alexandra Sports Club A soccer team and a Nyasaland eleven. The first match will be played at Blantyre on October 2

In addition to this, the Rhodesian team's chairman also donated a trophy, known as the Bruss Cup, for a tournament to be played by their second team and the newly-formed Nyasaland "B" side. This brought the total to three trophies to be competed for by Nyasaland and the teams from Beira and Salisbury.

The inaugural fixture took place at Blantyre Sports Club on 2 October 1954, and Nyasaland lost 4–1, with John Patterson scoring a consolation goal.

The following year, Alexandra travelled to Malawi once again, and the venue was changed to Limbe Country Club. A hat trick by Bob Marrinan was enough to see off the visitors by 3–2.

1957 saw Nyasaland travel to Southern Rhodesia for the first time, and they were defeated 2–0 in Salisbury. The fourth fixture In Blantyre saw Nyasaland level the series at two each with a fine 4–1 win that saw Jimmy Smith score a brace.

The following year (1958), history was in the making in Salisbury as goals by Marr and John Hawthorne witnessed a 2–0 victory, but the series was brought back to level after six games when the visitors romped away with an easy 5–2 win at Blantyre Sports Club.

Thirty-three players competed in the six fixtures, with legend Dennis Johnston once more at the head of the appearances log with a 100 per cent record. Custodian Nicholas followed closely, with five games and a clean sheet. Next on the list was Brian Fox, with four games, and top scorer Bob Marrinan, with 3 goals featured in three games.

CUP WINNERS: The victorious Nyasaland soccer team which gained the Trataris Cup from the Alexandra club of Salisbury during the latter's visit here recently. The players are (l. to r.): back row: Vian, Armstrong, Taylor, Hogan, Allan, Mansfield, Marrinan. Front row: Johnston, Mr. G. Summers, President of the N.F.A., Kongialis (capt.), Armstrong, Muir, Duran.

Bruss Cup

The Nyasaland "B" group was formed in 1954 to accommodate competition for the trophy donated by the Chairman of Alexandra FC of Southern Rhodesia. The side got off to a good start as they defeated their visitors 2–1 at Blantyre Sports Club with Costas Trataris and Alan Taylor the scorers. However, it was not easy in Cholo the following year, as they were heavily defeated 4–1, with Brian Phillips scoring their consolation goal.

A goalless score was recorded in Salisbury in 1956, before Colin Findlay scored 5 goals in Zomba, becoming the first player to hit the most goals in a game, winning by 6–1. They then lost two games on the trot—5–3 in Salisbury and 5–2 in Cholo—to end the decade.

The six fixtures saw forty-four players featured in these games, and three players topped the appearances list with 50 per cent of the matches. Ken Thomson, Jimmy Smith, and Costas Trataris (he was one of three brothers that won Nyasaland caps, the others being George (goalkeeper) and John. Colin Findlay scored all 5 of his goals in one match and was the top scorer. He also played in another fixture.

Friendlies "A"

Nyasaland played thirteen friendly fixtures during the '50s against four different teams. Four of them were against Sport Lisboa e Beira when they travelled to Blantyre in 1952, 1954, 1956, and 1958. The series were evenly matched, as Zomba hosted all the games. They won the first two fixtures by 4–3 and lost the other two games by 2–1.

Whilst in Beira, they played two games against Beira Railways in 1953 and 1957, losing the first game by 1–0 and levelling the series by winning 2–1. They were undefeated against Sporting Beira, winning 2–1, and were fortunate in 1959 when 2 own goals assisted them to a 3–3 draw in which Archie Cottingham, one of the three brothers who wore the national colours, scored the tying goal.

The remaining five fixtures were played against the Southern Rhodesian club Alexandra FC, and Nyasaland succumbed to them on four different occasions 3–1, 2–1 twice, and 8–1. The only victory they achieved was in Cholo in 1955, where a hat trick by Brian Fox saw them triumph 5–2. Dennis Johnston once again led the appearance list with 11 goals, and Ken Mansfield had 4.

Friendlies "B"

The only friendly fixtures of Nyasaland Friendlies "B" were against Alexandra FC, and after five games, it was all level with two wins each and a draw, but they edged the visitors with a 9–8 tally. Nyasaland started off with a 2–0 defeat in Zomba in 1954 and won by the same score the following year at Country Club Limbe.

Costas Trataris was the hero in Salisbury, as he scored a hat trick in a 3–2 win to lead in the series that they still maintained at Blantyre Sports Club when they drew 2–2. There was no friendly in 1958, as the senior side was hosting Sport Lisboa e Beira the following week.

When the friendly games resumed the following year, Alexandra levelled the series with a 3–2 win at BSC. Forty-three players were involved in these five games, and two of the Bruss Cup appearance leaders, Ken Thomson and Costas Trataris, did it again with three games. But Trataris went one better when he also topped the scoring chart with the hat trick he scored in 1956.

Nyasaland African Football Association (Nafa)–International

Beira's Grupo Desportivo Rebenta Fogo in Beira, our first host, also became the first team to tour our land and played two fixtures at Blantyre Sports Club and Zomba Gymkhana—our two oldest clubs. Unfortunately, details of the first game are still being researched. The second game in Zomba saw the two teams deadlocked at half-time, but goals in the fifty-fifth and sixty-fifth minutes by Samson Manewa and Smart Thipa saw Nyasaland win (as details of the first game are still unknown, this is thought to be a historic first win for the future Flames). An unconfirmed report from two years later shows a visit of a Southern Rhodesian team for two games, followed by four games in Southern Rhodesia in 1957 that witnessed wins in Umtali and Gweru, and defeats in Salisbury and Bulawayo.

The year 1957 saw a squad of seventeen players depart for Johannesburg, South Africa, for two weeks on 22 October.

The squad of seventeen led by K. W. Thipa and F. G. Noah comprised captain James Kaminjolo, Shonga, Kumwenda, Smart Thipa, Sangala, Sazuze (goalkeeper), Kaunda, Matinga, Machinjili, Godfrey Kalitsiro, Thomas, Kumwembwe, Roy Maliwa, Makwelero, Kambuli, Daudi, and Salamu.

Their first game against Pick Up 1st XI ended in a 4–1 defeat. This was followed by a 2–2 draw against Litsitsili Bugs before they tasted victory in their third fixture against a Pick Up 2nd XI with a score of 3–2.

Nyasaland ended their South African tour when they went down 7–4 against a Coloured Community XI.

On their way back home, they stopped and played three fixtures in Bulawayo and Umtali.

They stopped in Bulawayo, where they met the White Army 1st XI and were heavily defeated 6–2 before drawing against their 2nd XI 2–2.

Nyasaland concluded their tour in Umtali, where a Pick Up XI won 6–2. Unconfirmed reports also show that they lost 6–0 to Yellow Peril in Salisbury in 1958.

Nyasaland Football Association (Nfa)

The league expanded by 40 per cent as the decade ended, with seven teams competing in the Royle League. Eight clubs affiliated during the decade, with five of them withdrawing after competing for between one and five seasons.

Mlanje, one of the founding members, withdrew its affiliation in 1953 and most probably joined forces with Cholo.

The most successful team during the '50s was undoubtedly Blantyre Sports Club, who grabbed 54 per cent of the total honours of the league and two knockout trophies introduced during this decade. The Royle family donated yet another trophy, known as the Royle K/O (Knockout) since 1950, and this was followed by the Stanhope Trophy in 1954.

BSC dominated the league, as they won the league and the runners-up spot four times each, and they also played in eight Royle Cup finals, winning six times. They also played in all six Stanhope finals, winning three times. Their closest rivals were Corona, who affiliated only in 1953 and were crowned champions twice in successive seasons and won three of the four finals they contested for. It took them only two years to become the first team to win the treble when they defeated BSC twice by 5–3 in both cup finals. BSC did the treble twice, in seasons 1956 and 1959, and the double once, in 1951.

Nyasaland African Football Association (Nafa)–Domestic

History was made on 8 July 1950 when a Blantyre Europeans side met the Blantyre Africans (mostly from Ndirande Welfare Club) in a friendly match organised by Archie Muir, the then BSC captain. The Europeans won 6–1, and it was noted that the Africans played barefoot.

Four years later, in Lilongwe, the Lilongwe Africans defeated the Lilongwe Europeans 4–0. At the 1952 AGM, J. Nachamba was elected chairman, and F. K. Sazuze, Hon. Secretary. The SHFL saw the number of affiliated teams increase by 25 per cent in 1952 to twenty from the inaugural sixteen teams in 1938.

The following year saw another increase of 20 per cent, bringing the total to twenty-five teams during the 1953 season. In the first known result in the Central District, Lilongwe saw Black Bombers defeat Mbabzi 2–0 in the Likuni Cup.

There were also leagues in the Central District city of Lilongwe and in the Southern District city of Zomba in 1954, and ongoing research will determine when these leagues started.

1950

The league increased to seven teams, with Athletics and Goans affiliating. Mlanje retained the Royle League title.

The Royle family introduced another trophy that was to be played for as a knockout competition. Blantyre Sports Club were the first winners; they beat Mlanje 2–1 at Country Club Limbe.

Final Log Table (Incomplete)

No.	Teams	P	W	D	L	F	A	PTS
1	Mlanje	10	8	2	0	34	14	18
2	Blantyre SC	12	5	6	1	30	16	16
3	Athletics	11	6	3	2	35	13	15

4	Zomba	10	5	2	3	33	13	12
5	Indian SC	11	3	3	5	17	27	9
6	Limbe CC	11	3	1	7	15	12	7
7	Goans	11	0	0	11	0	67	0

1950 Timeline

8 Apr. 1950: Oury Cup: Limbe CC: Sport Lisboa e Beira 5-4   D. Armstrong (2), J. Patterson (2), D. Nock
Ian Royan, Jimmy Kongialis, Forrest, Albert Hall, R. Payne, Edmonds, Kirby, John Patterson, Dennis Nock, Don Armstrong, Jimmy Smith

15 Apr. 1950: Royle Cup Final: Limbe CC: Blantyre SC v. Mlanje 2-1   Kirby, J. Patterson, Dickie
Mlanje: Ian Royan, Jimmy Kongialis, Edmonds, Alan Flowerdew, Roger Royle, Kidd, Dickie, Forrest, Eggington, Trotter (missing 1)
BSC: Williams, Cliff Allin, Archie Muir (capt.), Albert Hall, Kirby, Lionel Hayes, Smithyman, John Patterson, Dennis Nock (missing 2)

8 Jun. 1950: Blantyre: Grupo Desportivo Rebenta Fogo (Unknown Result)

10 Jun. 1950: Zomba: Grupo Desportivo Rebenta Fogo 2-0   S. Menewa, S. Thipa

8 Jul. 1950: A friendly match between the Blantyre Europeans and Blantyre Africans (mainly from Ndirande Welfare Club) ended in a 6-1 win for the Europeans. It is also mentioned that the opponents played barefoot. This match was arranged by BSC captain Archie Muir.

22 Jul. 1950: Abraham Shield to be Played at BSC (Researching Finalists)

NFA AGM (CCL):
President: F. W. Hindley   Vice President: W. A. Cole   Hon. Secretary: R. E. Bright

30 Sep. 1950: Scotland v. the Rest: BSC: Scotland v. the Rest 4-1   D. Armstrong (3), J. Patterson, Taylor
Scotland: Ian Royan (Mlanje), Jimmy Kongialis (BSC), Archie Cottingham (Limbe Wand), Kidd (Mlanje), Cliff Allin (BSC), Dickie (Zomba), Trotter (Mlanje), John Patterson (BSC—capt.), McCreadie (CCL), Don Armstrong (Zomba), Archie Muir (Zomba)
The Rest: Williams (BSC), Leslie Sequeira (ISC), Rose (Mlanje), Payne (BSC), Gough (NR), Edmonds (Mlanje), Smithyman (Zomba—capt.), Coleman (Zomba), Kirby (BSC), Roger Royle (Mlanje), Taylor (Mlanje), **Reserves:** Jarrett (NR), Dennis Nock (BSC)

1951

Three new affiliated clubs and one withdrawal saw the league increased to nine teams. Athletics lasted only one season, while Cholo, Nyasaland Railways, and Limbe Wanderers were the new teams. Blantyre Sports Club regained their title, with Zomba ending as runners-up for the first time. BSC were the first team to win the league with a 100 per cent record, scoring 102 goals and conceding only 6.

Blantyre Sports Club retained the Royle Cup and completed the first ever Double when they defeated Zomba 3-1.

Final Log Table

No.	Teams	P	W	D	L	F	A	PTS
1	Blantyre SC	16	16	0	0	102	6	32
2	Zomba	16	12	2	2	66	26	24
3	Limbe Wanderers	16	10	2	4	46	23	22
4	Indian S.C	16	8	1	7	29	22	17
5	Cholo.	16	5	3	8	18	50	13
6	Mlanje	16	5	2	9	30	28	12
7	Nyasaland Railways	16	6	0	10	20	65	12
8	Limbe C.C.	16	2	1	13	25	69	5
9	Goans	16	1	3	12	16	67	5

John Patterson was top scorer with 50 goals.

<u>1951 Timeline</u>

24 Feb. 1951: BSC v. The Rest: BSC: BSC v. The Rest 5–1   G. Sophos, J. Patterson, ?
BSC: Williams, Kirby, Jimmy Kongialis, Albert Hall, George Sophos, William Harvey, Cliff Allin, Payne, Harry Levy, Dennis Nock, John Patterson (BSC—capt.)
The Rest: Sales (Lb Wand), Dennis Johnson (Zomba) Bannerjee (ISC), Gough (CCL), Nelson (Zomba—capt.), Khuda Bux (ISC), Costas Trataris (Lb Wand), Roger Royle (Mlanje), Wilson (Lb Wand), Don Armstrong (Zomba), Pearce (CCL) **Reserves:** Leslie Sequeira (ISC), Jimmy Smith (Zomba)

24 Mar. 1951: Oury Cup: Beira: Sport Lisboa e Beira 2–1   D. Nock, G. Sophos
R. Bennett, Jimmy Kongialis, Dennis Johnston, Tommy Allen, R. Payne, Harry Levy, William Harvey, John Patterson, Dennis Nock, George Sophos, Jimmy Smith

15 Apr. 1951: Royle Cup Final: Zomba Gymkhana: Zomba v. Blantyre SC 1–3   Coleman, J. Patterson (2), W. Harvey
Zomba: Nelson, Dennis Johnston, Humphries, Cook, White, Pickard, Jimmy Smith, Don Armstrong, Coleman, Archie Muir, Lambert
BSC: Williams, Cliff Allin (capt.), Jimmy Kongialis, Albert Hall, George Sophos, Tommy Allen, John Patterson, Dennis Nock, William Harvey, R. Payne, Harry Levy

NAFA played two fixtures against Southern Rhodesia teams in Blantyre (still researching).

1952

Two withdrawals and one affiliated new club saw the league down to eight teams. Nyasaland Railways lasted only one season, as did Athletics the previous year and Goans after two seasons with only one win. Their place was taken by Sunnyside Rovers. Blantyre Sports Club retained their title, and Zomba ended as runners-up, repeating the previous year's finish.

Blantyre Sports Club, who reached their third successive Royle Cup, failed to complete the double, as they lost 1–0 to newcomers Sunnyside Rovers.

1952 Timeline

12 Jan. 1952: BSC v. The Rest: BSC: BSC v. The Rest 1–2   M. Megraw, A. Muir, J. Patterson
BSC: Bill Fourie, Thorp, Sullivan, Jimmy Kongialis, Tommy Allen, Cruickshank, Roberts, William Harvey, Micky Megraw, George Sophos, Albert Hall
The Rest: Ian Royan (Mlanje), Salvatori (Lb Wand), Sergio Nicholas (Sunnyside Rovers), Alan Flowerdew (Cholo), Khuda Bux (ISC), Houston (CCL), Costas Trataris (Sunnyside Rovers), Archie Muir (Zomba), John Patterson (Zomba), Alan Taylor (Mlanje), Pearce (CCL)

Final Log Table (Incomplete)

No.	Teams	P	W	D	L	F	A	PTS
1	Blantyre SC	14	13	0	1	61	17	26
2	Zomba	14	11	1	2	55	23	23
3	Mlanje	13	6	1	6	19	34	13
4	Sunnyside Rovers	14	5	2	7	22	36	12
5	Indian S.C	12	5	1	6	14	23	11
6	Limbe Wanderers	14	4	2	10	24	26	10
7	Limbe C.C.	14	5	0	9	25	36	10
8	Cholo	14	1	1	11	11	36	3

23 Feb 1952: Royle Cup Final: Limbe CC: Sunnyside Rovers v. Blantyre SC 1–0   Bridle
Sunnyside Rovers: Sergio Nicholas, Phocas, Jarrett (capt.), Clark, Cooper, Argente, Amorianos, Richardson, Bridle, Costas Trataris, Evans
BSC: White, Jimmy Kongialis, Sullivan, Thorp, Roberts, Albert Hall, Dennis Nock, William Harvey, Micky Megraw, George Sophos, Smith

12 Apr. 1952: Oury Cup: Limbe CC: Sport Lisboa e Beira 1–2   J. Patterson
Ian Royan, Jimmy Kongialis, Dennis Johnston, Tommy Allen, Roberts, Houston, Archie Muir, John Patterson, Dennis Nock, Micky Megraw, Jimmy Smith

13 Apr. 1952: Friendly: Zomba Gymkhana: Sport Lisboa e Beira 4–3   ?
Sergio Nicholas, Sullivan, Dennis Johnston, Tommy Allen, Khuda Bax, Cruickshank, Archie Muir, John Patterson, Dennis Nock, Alan Taylor, Jimmy Smith

14 June 1952: NAFA AGM Held in Blantyre:
Chairman J. Nachamba (Limbe), Vice Chairman A. J. Mponda (Blantyre), Secretary F. K. Sazuze, Vice Secretary C. J. W. Masambo, Treasurer J. B. Kaliati
Twenty teams registered for the 1952 season and were divided into three sections:
Eastern Section: Break Down, Gallaher, Imperial, Kapeni, Ntondwe, Railways, Urban "A", Urban "B"
Western Section: Abrahams "A", Abrahams "B", Ndirande Lions, Ndirande Tigers, Machinjili, Michiru, Police
Chileka Section: Chilangoma, Chileka, Kumanda, Matindi, Milala

29 September 1952: Lilongwe Football League Cup Final—Likuni Cup
Black Bombers v. Mbabzi, 2–0

1953

Cholo, another two-year withdrawal club, were replaced by newly affiliated Corona. After being bridesmaid for two seasons, Zomba eventually grabbed the title from their Blantyre rivals. Limbe Wanderers took the runners-up position. Blantyre Sports Club failed to reach the Royle Cup Finals for the first time in four years. A newly affiliated club, Corona, won this cup by defeating Royle League champions Zomba 3–0.

Final Log Table (Incomplete)

No.	Teams	P	W	D	L	F	A	PTS
1	Zomba	14	10	1	3	52	20	21
2	Limbe Wanderers	13	8	2	3	28	17	18
3	Corona	14	7	2	5	37	25	16
4	Sunnyside Rovers	14	6	3	5	29	30	15
5	Mlanje	12	4	3	5	19	21	11
6	Blantyre SC	13	5	1	7	30	39	11
7	Indian S.C	12	2	3	7	15	40	7
8	Limbe C.C.	12	1	3	8	18	36	5

1953 Timeline

10 Jan. 1953: Abraham Shield: African Urban (Limbe) v. Abrahams (Blantyre) at ISC

17 Jan. 1953: Kings Cup: Kapeni (Limbe) v. Abrahams (Blantyre) at ISC

7 Feb. 1953: Zomba Gymkana: Zomba v. The Rest 1–3   A. Muir, M. Megraw (2), Dipple
Zomba: Cameron, Pickard, Broome, Channell, Humphries, Dennis Johnston, Hollis, Robb, John Patterson, Archie Muir, Shutley
The Rest: Sergio Nicholas (Sunnyside Rovers), Humphries (Sunnyside Rovers), Serafin Neto (Limbe Wand), Pengelly (Sunnyside Rovers), Roberts (BSC), Morgando (Limbe Wand), Harold Wrigley (Corona), Costas Trataris (Sunnyside Rovers), Micky Megraw (Corona), Dipple (BSC), Pearce (CCL)

21 Mar. 1953: Royle Cup Final: Zomba Gymkana: Zomba v. Corona 0–3   J. Smith (2), M. Megraw
Zomba: Cameron, Pickard, Broome, Riley, Humphries, Dennis Johnston, Scott, Ounsworth, Robb, Archie Muir, Shutley
Corona: Davidson, Roger Royle, Nelson, Beardsley, Tommy Allen, Edmonds, Harold Wrigley, Morris, Micky Megraw, Taylor, Jimmy Smith

4 Apr. 1953: Oury Cup: Beira: Sport Lisboa e Beira 1–0   Dipple
Sergio Nicholas, Pengelly, Dennis Johnston, Tommy Allen, Roger Royle, Harold Wrigley, Archie Muir, Roberts, Dipple, Micky Megraw, Jimmy Smith

5 Apr. 1953: Friendly: Beira: Beira Select XI 0–1
Sergio Nicholas, Pengelly, Dennis Johnston, Tommy Allen, Roger Royle, Harold Wrigley, Archie Muir, Roberts, Dipple, Micky Megraw, Morris

16 May. 1953: UTC Cup Final: Zomba v. Blantyre 5–0

SHFL as at 27 Jun 1953

Final Log Table

Northern Section

No.	Teams	P	W	D	L	F	A	PTS
1	Matindi	5	5	0	0	9	2	10
2	Kanjeza	6	4	0	2	9	4	8
3	Chileka	6	3	1	2	6	7	7
4	Mponda	5	2	1	2	5	4	5
5	Ntenjela	6	2	1	3	2	3	5
6	Mfumba	5	2	0	3	3	6	4
7	Chilangama	6	2	0	4	2	5	4
8	Canada	5	0	1	4	2	7	1

Western Section

No.	Teams	P	W	D	L	F	A	PTS
1	Ndirande Tigers	4	4	0	0	12	4	8
2	Ndirande Lions	4	4	0	0	8	2	8
3	Abrahams "A"	4	3	0	1	10	5	6
4	Michiru	4	2	0	2	11	7	4
5	Police	4	1	0	3	4	8	2
6	Machinjili	4	0	0	4	6	12	0
7	Abrahams "B"	5	0	0	5	1	14	0

Eastern Section

No.	Teams	P	W	D	L	F	A	PTS
1	Ntondwe	6	4	1	1	12	6	9
2	Imperial TC	6	4	0	2	8	7	8
3	Kapeni	3	3	0	0	11	0	6
4	Urban	4	2	1	1	8	4	5
5	Breakdown	4	2	1	1	9	9	5
6	Gallaher	5	2	0	3	6	4	4
7	LTC	6	1	2	3	8	10	4
8	Police	4	1	1	2	3	8	3
9	Railways "A"	4	0	2	2	2	6	2
10	Railways "B"	4	0	0	4	1	14	0

1954

The club withdrawals continued with Limbe Wanderers and once Royle Champions, Mlanje, but saw Cholo return after a year's absence. Corona, who were only in the second season, won the Royle League title with Blantyre Sports Club ending as runners-up.

Blantyre Sports Club regained the Royle Cup when they defeated holders Corona by 2–1.

A second knockout competition was introduced under the banner of Stanhope. Sunnyside Rovers became the inaugural winners after defeating giants Blantyre Sports Club by 4–3 in extra time.

Nicholas Trataris presented a trophy to be played annually between Nyasaland and Alexandra Sports Club of Southern Rhodesia. The Bruss Cup was also introduced to be played by the "B" sides of Nyasaland and Alexandra SC.

<u>1954 Timeline</u>

Final Log Table

No.	Teams	P	W	D	L	F	A	PTS
1	Corona	12	1	0	1	50	14	22
2	Blantyre SC	12	9	0	3	33	17	18
3	Sunnyside Rovers	12	7	2	3	36	17	16
4	Cholo	12	4	2	6	23	27	10
5	Zomba	12	3	2	7	22	30	8
6	Indian SC	12	2	4	6	12	25	8
7	Limbe CC	12	0	2	10	11	57	2

30 Jan. 1954: BSC: Champions v. the Rest: Corona v. the Rest 3–3 (aet)   B. Marrinan (2), J. Smith, Morgado (2), C. Trataris
Corona: Brill, Entwistle, Edmonds, Don Armstrong, Tommy Allen, Alan Taylor, Bedford, Archie Muir, Bob Marrinan, Jimmy Smith, Van Arenthals
The Rest: Sergio Nicholas (BSC), Jimmy Kongialis (BSC), Humphries (S. Rovers), Khuda Bux (ISC), Ricky Robertson (S. Rovers), Serafin Neto (S. Rovers), Harold Wrigley (BSC), Costas Trataris (S. Rovers), Morgado (S. Rovers), Ken Mansfield (LCC), Shergold (S. Rovers)

13 Mar. 1954: Royle Cup Final: Blantyre SC v. Corona 2–1   J. Patterson (2), ?
Blantyre SC: Sergio Nicholas, Jimmy Kongialis, Albert Hall, Stanton, Ricky Robertson, Da Cruz, Brian Phillips, Fred Taylor, John Patterson, Ken Thomson, Micky Megraw
Corona: Davidson, Entwhistle, Coupe, Don Armstrong, Tommy Allen, Alan Taylor, Bob Marrinan, Archie Muir, T. Donaldson, Jimmy Smith, Van Arenthals

3 Apr. 1954: Stanhope Cup Final: Sunnyside Rovers v. Blantyre SC 4–3 (aet)   F. de Vito, C. Trataris, D. Robertson, Morgado, B. Phillips, M. Megraw, J. Patterson
Sunnyside Rovers: William Harvey, Stellious, Humphries, F. de Vito, Ricky Robertson, D. Robertson, Mendoza, Costas Trataris, Morgado, Serafin Neto, Andrade
Blantyre SC: Sergio Nicholas, Jimmy Kongialis, Peter Gurney, Meek, Ken Thomson, Stanton, Harold Wrigley, Brian Phillips, John Patterson, Micky Megraw, Shergold

17 Apr. 1954: Oury Cup: Limbe CC: Sport Lisboa e Beira 5–2   K. Mansfield (2), J. Patterson, B. Marrinan (o/g)

Sergio Nicholas, Jimmy Kongialis, Dennis Johnston, Tommy Allen, Ricky Robertson, Harold Wrigley, Ken Thomson, Brian Phillips, John Patterson, Ken Mansfield, Bob Marrinan

18 Apr. 1954: Friendly: Zomba Gymkhana: Sport Lisboa e Beira 4–3   B. Marrinan (2), K. Mansfield, B. Phillips
John Harvey, Jimmy Kongialis, Dennis Johnston, Tommy Allen, Ricky Robertson, Don Armstrong, Entwistle, Brian Phillips, Humphries, Ken Mansfield, Bob Marrinan

15 Jun. 1954: Friendly match between the Lilongwe Europeans and Lilongwe Africans ended in a 4–0 defeat for the Europeans

SHFL Log Table: Western Division (as of 24 July 1954)

No.	Teams	P	W	D	L	PTS
1	Clan	10	5	4	1	14
2	Ndirande "A"	8	5	2	1	12
3	Abrahams "A"	10	6	0	4	12
4	Ndirande "B"	9	4	3	2	11
5	Sparks	10	2	2	6	6
6	Abrahams "B"	9	0	1	8	1

Kings Cup Winners: Kapeni

Zomba Log Table (as of 18 September 1954)

No.	Teams	P	W	D	L	F	A	PTS
1	Athletic "A"	10	8	1	1	39	12	17
2	Print	7	5	2	0	23	5	12
3	Police	8	5	1	2	30	7	11
4	Medical	7	5	1	1	19	4	11
5	PWD	10	3	3	4	20	18	9
6	Garrison	8	3	1	3	11	15	7
7	KAR	6	3	0	3	9	10	6
8	Survey	7	2	1	4	10	17	5
9	Posts & Telecoms	7	1	0	6	2	25	2
10	Athletic "B"	8	1	0	7	13	46	2
11	Kazembe	6	0	1	5	1	18	1

2 Oct. 1954: Trataris Cup: Blantyre SC: Alexandra Club 1–4   J. Patterson
Sergio Nicholas, Jimmy Kongialis, Dennis Johnston, Tommy Allen, Ricky Robertson, Harold Wrigley, Micky Megraw, Brian Phillips, John Patterson, Ken Mansfield, Bob Marrinan

2 Oct. 1954: Friendly "B": Blantyre SC: Alexandra Club "B" 2–1   C. Trataris, A. Taylor
John Harvey, Pipes, Don Armstrong, Humphries, Peter Gurney, Ken Thomson, Fred Taylor, Costas Trataris, Jimmy Smith, Dennis Nock, Alan Taylor

3 Oct. 1954: Friendly: Zomba Gymkhana: Alexandra Club 1–3   K. Mansfield

Sergio Nicholas, Jimmy Kongialis, Dennis Johnston, Tommy Allen, Costas Trataris, Alan Taylor, Micky Megraw, Brian Phillips, John Patterson, Ken Mansfield, Bob Marrinan

3 Oct. 1954: Bruss Cup: Zomba Gymkhana: Alexandra Club "B" 0–2

John Harvey, Khuda Bax, Don Armstrong, Da Cruz, Peter Gurney, Ken Thomson, Fred Taylor, Costas Trataris, Kabul, Dennis Nock, Alan Taylor

NAFA played four fixtures against Southern Rhodesia teams, winning in Umtali and Gweru and losing in Salisbury and Bulawayo (still researching)

Zomba Midweek League Log Table (as of 8 October 1954)

No.	Teams	P	W	D	L	F	A	PTS
1	POPS	2	2	0	0	6	2	4
2	3 "P" s	2	2	0	0	6	3	4
3	Nondescripts	3	2	0	1	6	6	4
4	Asians Sports	2	0	0	2	3	6	0
5	KAR	3	0	0	3	4	8	0

Lilongwe League Log Table (as of 16 October 1954)

No.	Teams	P	W	D	L	F	A	PTS
1	Touch-me-Not	4	2	2	0	10	4	6
2	Police	2	2	0	0	5	0	4
3	Medical	5	1	2	2	4	10	4
4	Welfare	2	1	1	0	7	3	3
5	Chitedze	2	1	1	0	2	0	3
6	Spitfire	1	0	0	1	0	1	0
7	Kandodo	2	0	0	2	0	5	0
8	Mbabzi	2	0	0	2	0	5	0

1955

Blantyre Sports Club entered a second team for the Royle League to bring it back to eight teams but failed to take the trophy from their new rivals Corona, who retained the title.

Blantyre Sports Club and Corona met for the second successive year in the Royle Cup final, but this time it went to previous years' losers Corona, who triumphed 5–3.

The Stanhope Cup saw both Blantyre Sports Club and Corona in the final again, and history was created as Corona once again repeated the 5–3 score against their rivals to become the first club ever to win the Treble.

1955 Timeline

1 Jan. 1955: Scotland v. The Rest: CCL: 0–0
Scotland: Ian Royan (LCC), Jimmy Kongialis (BSC—capt.), Chick Humphries (LCC), Ross (LCC), Tommy Allen (Corona), Ricky Robertson (BSC), Trotter (Cholo), Brian Phillips (BSC), T. Donaldson (Corona), Archie Muir (Corona), Matt Hoyland (Sunnyside Rovers); Reserve: Billy Pillans (Cholo), Colin Findlay (Cholo)
The Rest: George Trataris (Sunnyside Rovers), Peter Gurney (BSC), Dennis Johnston (Zomba—captain), Peter Parker (LCC), Alan Taylor (Corona), Ken Thomson (BSC), Dennis Harris (Sunnyside Rovers), Burge (BSC), Bob Marrinan (Corona), Moreira (ISC), Les Doran (LCC); Reserve: Sergio Nicholas (BSC), Dennis Nock (LCC), Roger Royle (Cholo)

Final Log

No.	Teams	P	W	D	L	F	A	PTS
1	Corona	14	10	4	0	54	13	24
2	Blantyre SC "A"	14	11	1	2	49	13	23
3	Limbe C.C.	14	7	4	3	41	19	18
4	Sunnyside Rovers	14	6	4	4	25	17	16
5	Zomba	14	7	2	5	33	32	16
6	Cholo	14	3	1	10	26	41	7
7	Indian S.C	14	2	0	12	13	43	2
8	Blantyre SC "B"	14	2	0	12	14	77	2

6 Feb. 1955: LCC: Stanhope Cup Final: Corona v. Blantyre SC 5–3   B. Marrinan (3), J. Smith, T. Allen (p), B. Phillips, M. Megraw, J. Kongialis
Corona: Davidson, Entwhistle, Roger Royle, Alan Taylor, Tommy Allen, Don Armstrong, Bob Marrinan, Archie Muir, T. Donaldson, Jimmy Smith, Van Arenthals; Reserves: Black, Coupe
Blantyre SC: Sergio Nicholas, Jimmy Kongialis, Peter Gurney, Stanton, Ricky Robertson, Ken Thomson, Foord, Fred Taylor, Brian Phillips, Da Cruz, Micky Megraw

6 Feb. 1955: Kings Cup Semi Finals: Ndirande Lions v. Ntondwe

2 Mar. 1955: ISC: Royle Cup Final: Corona v. Blantyre SC 5–3   B. Marrinan (3), A. Taylor, A. Muir, M. Megraw (2), J. Patterson
Corona: Davidson, Entwhistle, Coupe, Don Armstrong, Tommy Allen, Alan Taylor, Bob Marrinan, Archie Muir, T. Donaldson, Jimmy Smith, Van Arenthals; Reserves: Roger Royle
Blantyre SC: Sergio Nicholas, Jimmy Kongialis, Albert Hall, Stanton, Ricky Robertson, Da Cruz, Brian Phillips, Fred Taylor, John Patterson, Ken Thomson, Micky Megraw

19 Mar. 1955: Trataris Cup: Limbe CC: Alexandra Club 3–2   B. Marrinan (3)
Ian Royan, Jimmy Kongialis, Dennis Johnston, Tommy Allen, Don Armstrong, Les Doran, Archie Muir, Van Arenthals, Alan Taylor, Ken Mansfield, Bob Marrinan

19 Mar. 1955: Bruss Cup: Limbe CC: Alexandra Club "B" 2–0   B. Phillips, D. Nock
Georges Trataris, Pipes, Brian Fox, Peter Parker (snr), Ricky Robertson, Ken Thomson, Fred Taylor, Brian Phillips, Jimmy Smith, Dennis Nock, Dennis Harris

20 Mar. 1955: Friendly: Cholo SC: Alexandra Club 5–2   B. Fox (3), K. Mansfield, A. Muir
Ian Royan, Jimmy Kongialis, Dennis Johnston, Tommy Allen, Don Armstrong, Les Doran, Archie Muir, Van Arenthals, Alan Taylor, Ken Mansfield, Brian Fox

20 Mar. 1955: Friendly: Cholo SC: Alexandra Club "B" 1–4   B. Phillips
Georges Trataris, Pipes, Entwhistle, Peter Parker (snr), Ricky Robertson, Ken Thomson, Fred Taylor, Brian Phillips, Jimmy Smith, Dennis Nock, Dennis Harris

26 Mar. 1955: BSC: Champions v. The Rest: Corona v. The Rest 2–2   B. Marrinan (2), L. Doran, K. Mansfield
Corona: Davidson, Entwhistle, Coupe, Don Armstrong, Tommy Allen, Alan Taylor, Black, Archie Muir, Bob Marrinan, Jimmy Smith, Van Arenthals; Reserves: Roger Royle
The Rest: Ian Royan (LCC), Dennis Johnston (Zomba—capt.), Brian Fox, Peter Parker (LCC), Ricky Robertson (BSC), Ken Thomson (BSC), Dennis Harris (BSC), Brian Phillips (BSC), Fred Taylor (BSC), Ken Mansfield (LCC), Les Doran (LCC)

9 Apr. 1955: Oury Cup: Beira: Sport Lisboa e Beira 0–10
Ian Royan, Jimmy Kongialis, Dennis Johnston, Tommy Allen, Don Armstrong, Les Doran, Archie Muir, Van Arenthals, Alan Taylor, Ken Mansfield, Brian Phillips

10 Apr. 1955: Friendly: Beira: Beira Sporting Club 2–1   A. Muir (2)
Ian Royan, Brian Fox, Ricky Robertson, Tommy Allen, Don Armstrong, Les Doran, Archie Muir, Van Arenthals, Alan Taylor, Ken Mansfield, Brian Phillips

16 Apr. 1955: Ndirande Lions win the Abrahams Shield

23 Apr. 1955: Kings Cup Final: Ndirande Lions v. Lime Makers 3–1 De Mobray Thipa, Sangala, Byson, Salimu

30 Apr. 1955: UTC Cup: SHFL XI v. Zomba

14 May 1955: Nyasaland Railways v. Inhaminga Railways 0–6   Ventura (5), Neca
Ken Mansfield, Roland Foy and Thomson (goalkeeper) featured for Nyasaland Railways.

1956

Blantyre Sports Club's second team was withdrawn from the Royle League, and the league went back to seven teams. After an absence of three seasons, the title went back to Blantyre Sports Club, with Sunnyside Rovers the runners-up.

Zomba qualified for their third Royle Cup final against Blantyre Sports Club but were still without the trophy at the end of the game, as they were beaten 4–1.

The Stanhope Cup final saw Blantyre Sports Club finally win the Treble as they defeated Limbe Country Club 5–1.

1956 Timeline

1 Jan. 1956: Scotland v. The Rest: CCL: 0–3   A. Taylor (2), C. Trataris
Scotland: Davidson (Corona), Archie Carver (Sunnyside Rovers), Brian Phillips (BSC), Archie Muir (Corona), Matt Hoyland (Sunnyside Rovers)
The Rest: Stockman (Cholo), Entwhistle (Corona), Peter Gurney (BSC), Alan Taylor (Corona), Costas Trataris (Sunnyside Rovers), Les Doran (LCC), Micky Megraw (LCC)

7 Jan. 1956: Indians v. Lingadzi Coloured 5–0   K. Green-Thompson, C. Hassen, A. Raman, Y. Master

14 Jan. 1956: Lilongwe v. Dedza 7–1   Losacco (3), Purkis, Robb. Ledger, Hewitt, Giles

11 Feb. 1956: BSC: Stanhope Cup Final: Blantyre SC v. Limbe CC 5–1   B. Marrinan (2), Shergold (2), F. Taylor, L. Doran
Blantyre SC: Sergio Nicholas, Micky Megraw, Ken Thomson, Peter Gurney, Ricky Robertson, Fred Taylor, Foord, Brian Phillips, Shergold, Dennis Harris, Bob Marrinan
Limbe CC: Pat Saunders, Pipes, Burgess, Monteiro, Rees, Les Doran, Alan Geldard, Chick Humphries, Don Harper, Ken Mansfield, Harding

25 Feb. 1956: CCL: Royle Cup Final: Blantyre SC v. Zomba 4–1   B. Marrinan (2), B. Phillips, Shergold, Freeman
Blantyre SC: Sergio Nicholas, Micky Megraw, Peter Gurney, Ricky Robertson, Shergold, Fred Taylor, Bob Marrinan, Dennis Harris, Brian Phillips, Cairney
Zomba: Turner, Dennis Johnston, Brooks, Chick Humphries, Freeman, Scott, Woodcock, Wilson, Smith

25 Feb. 1956: UTC Cup
Shire Highlands Football League v. Limbe League 0–3 (winners to meet Zomba League)

Cholo League v. Mlanje League 3–1 (Cholo qualified for finals)

Final (Incomplete—missing 1 game) Zomba v. ISC

No.	Teams	P	W	D	L	F	A	PTS
1	Blantyre SC "A"	12	10	2	0	55	10	22
2	Sunnyside Rovers	12	7	2	3	35	17	16
3	Limbe C.C.	12	6	2	4	33	20	14
4	Zomba	11	5	2	4	33	24	12
5	Corona	12	3	2	7	18	45	8
6	Indian SC	11	1	4	6	12	28	6
7	Cholo	12	1	2	9	14	56	4

17 Mar. 1956: BSC: Champions v. The Rest: Blantyre v. The Rest 4–3   F. Taylor (3), B. Marrinan, C. Trataris (2), F. de Vito
Blantyre: Sergio Nicholas, Shergold, Ken Thomson, Fred Taylor, Bob Marrinan
The Rest: Dennis Johnston (Zomba—capt.), Brian Fox (Sunnyside Rovers), Brooks (Zomba), Khuda Bux (ISC), Colin Findlay (Cholo), Archie Muir (Corona), Wilson (Zomba), Costas Trataris (Sunnyside Rovers), F. de Vito (Sunnyside Rovers), Ken Mansfield (LCC)

17 Mar. 1956: UTC Cup
Limbe League v. Zomba League (win for Zomba League to meet Cholo League in final)

24 Mar. 1956: Trataris Cup: Salisbury: **Alexandra Club 0–2**
Sergio Nicholas, Brian Fox, Dennis Johnston, Ricky Robertson, Micky Megraw, Les Doran, Archie Muir, Wilson, Alan Taylor, Ken Mansfield, Bob Marrinan

24 Mar. 1956: Friendly: Salisbury: **Alexandra Club "B" 0–0**
Stockman, Peter Gurney, F. De Vito, Burgess, Shergold, Ken Thomson, Don Harper, Costas Trataris, Jimmy Smith, Colin Findlay, Dennis Harris

25 Mar. 1956: Friendly: Salisbury: **Alexandra Club 1–2** **D. Harper**
Sergio Nicholas, Don Harper, Dennis Johnston, Ricky Robertson, Micky Megraw, Les Doran, Archie Muir, Wilson, Alan Taylor, Ken Mansfield, Bob Marrinan

25 Mar. 1956: Bruss Cup: Salisbury: **Alexandra Club "B" 3–1** **C. Trataris (3)**
Stockman, Peter Gurney, F. De Vito, Matt Hoyland, Shergold, Ken Thomson, Don Harper, Costas Trataris, Jimmy Smith, Colin Findlay, Dennis Harris

31 Mar. 1956: Oury Cup: Blantyre SC: **Sport Lisboa e Beira 5–0** **C. Trataris (2), A. Taylor, K. Mansfield (pen), L. Doran**
Sergio Nicholas, Don Harper, Dennis Johnston, Ricky Robertson, Micky Megraw, Les Doran, Costas Trataris, Wilson, Alan Taylor, Ken Mansfield, Brian Fox

1 Apr. 1956: Friendly: Zomba Gymkhana: **Sport Lisboa e Beira 1–2** **K. Mansfield**
Stockman, Peter Gurney, Dennis Johnston, Colin Findlay, Dennis Harris, Les Doran, Shergold, Wilson, Burgess, Ken Mansfield, Jimmy Smith

1957

The tenth Royle League Championship was played, and that's how long it took Limbe Country Club to become the fifth different winner. With Sunnyside Rovers' withdrawal, the strength of the league was reduced to six teams.

Cholo's first ever Royle Cup final saw them defeated 4–1 by Blantyre Sports Club.

The Stanhope Cup final saw a repeat of the previous year's finalists and score as Blantyre Sports Club defeated Limbe Country Club 5–1.

Another significant date occurred on Tuesday, 3 September 1957, when a meeting took place in the presence of the protectorate welfare officer, Mr H. M. Tasker, and the heads of the NFA, Mr George Summers and Mr G. Ndovi, to discuss the amalgamation of the two associations.

The following month, the NAFA were adventurous and toured South Africa and Southern Rhodesia with a squad of seventeen players and two officials. K. W. Thipa and F. G. Noah were nominated as officials on this tour.

Sir Robert Armitage presented a trophy for a tournament to be played between the Southern Region (Blantyre), Central Region (Lilongwe), and North Region (Mzimba) as a way of encouraging African football, to be known as the Governor's Trophy. (It was here that the seeds of the future Kamuzu Cup were planted.)

1957 Timeline

5 Jan. 1957: Friendly: ISC: NFA Select XI v. Asians 7–3   M. Hoyland (3), Hoatson (2), P. Kelly (2)–Santosh (2), O. Fernandes

Horlock (Zomba), Brooks (Zomba), Thomas (Blantyre), Green (Zomba), Alan Geldard (LCC), Billy Pillans (Cholo), Harold Wrigley Jnr (Cholo), Grant (LCC), Pat Kelly (LCC), J. Hoatson (BSC), Matt Hoyland (LCC)

Final Log

No.	Teams	P	W	D	L	F	A	PTS
1	Limbe C.C.	10	6	2	2	34	18	14
2	Blantyre SC "A"	10	6	1	3	28	18	13
3	Cholo	10	5	1	4	32	24	11
4	Corona	10	5	1	4	19	21	11
5	Zomba	10	3	3	4	25	23	9
6	Indian SC	10	1	4	6	12	28	6

9 Mar. 1957: ISC: Stanhope Cup Final: Blantyre SC v. Limbe CC 5–1   A. Taylor (2), B. Phillips, G. Keys (o/g), R. Ingram

Blantyre SC: Sergio Nicholas, Micky Megraw, Ken Thomson, Archie Muir, Peter Gurney, Ricky Robertson, Fred Taylor, Foord, Brian Phillips, Godfrey Keys, Dennis Harris

Limbe CC: Pat Saunders, Pipes, Pat Kelly, Burgess, Pearce, Monteiro, Rees, Alan Geldard, Chick Humphries, Roy Ingram, Ken Mansfield

Blantyre Sports Club Stanhope Winners 1957

Standing L to R: Peter Gurney, Thomas, Fred Taylor, Sergio Nicholas, Godfrey Keys, J. Hoatson, Gilchrist (Coach)
Middle row L to R: Dennis Harris, Micky Megraw, Ricky Robertson (capt), George Barley, Ken Thomson
Front row L to R: Archie Carver, Brian Phillips

Mario Antoine

30 Mar. 1957: Trataris Cup: Blantyre SC: Alexandra Club 4–1   J. Smith (2), R. Robertson, B. Phillips
Sergio Nicholas, Brian Fox, Dennis Johnston, Ricky Robertson, Micky Megraw, Tommy Allen, Costas Trataris, Brian Phillips, Pat Kelly, Godfrey Keys, Jimmy Smith

30 Mar. 1957: Bruss Cup: Blantyre SC: Alexandra Club "B" 2–2   ?
George Trataris, Billy Pillans, Brooks, Grant, Alan Geldard, Harlet, Les Doran, John Trataris, Reid, Colin Findlay, J. Hoatson

31 Mar. 1957: Friendly: Zomba Gymkhana: Alexandra Club 1–8   ?
Pat Saunders, Brian Fox, Dennis Johnston, Ricky Robertson, Ian Strachan, Tommy Allen, Costas Trataris, Brian Phillips, Pat Kelly, G. Hindhaugh, Pat Lorimer

31 Mar. 1957: Friendly: Zomba Gymkhana: Alexandra Club "B" 6–1   C. Findlay (5), A. Muir
George Trataris, Billy Pillans, Brooks, Grant, Alan Geldard, George Barley, Les Doran, Harold Wrigley (jnr), Archie Muir, Colin Findlay, Alan Taylor

6 Apr. 1957: CCL: Royle Cup Final: Blantyre SC v. Cholo 4–1   G. Barley (2), F. Taylor, G. Keys, L. Doran
Blantyre SC: Sergio Nicholas, George Burley, Ricky Robertson, Fred Taylor, Godfrey Keys, Brian Phillips (missing 5)
Cholo: Ian Royan, Tommy Allen, Archie Muir, Brian Fox, Les Doran (missing 6)

13 Apr. 1957: Champions v. The Rest: Limbe CC v. The Rest 1–4   (o/g), T. Allen (2), C. Findlay, G. Keys

21 Apr. 1957: Oury Cup: Beira: Sport Lisboa e Beira 4–1   T. Allen, B. Phillips, K. Mansfield, G. Keys
Sergio Nicholas, Alan Geldard, Dennis Johnston, Ricky Robertson, Tommy Allen, Brian Fox, Pat Kelly, Brian Phillips, Ken Mansfield, Godfrey Keys, Jimmy Smith

22 Apr. 1957: Friendly: Beira: Beira Select XI 2–1   R. Robertson (2)
Sergio Nicholas, Alan Geldard, Dennis Johnston, Ricky Robertson, Tommy Allen, Brian Fox, Colin Findlay, Brian Phillips, Ken Mansfield, Godfrey Keys, Costas Trataris

1 Aug. 1957: I.O. Adam Shield: Postals v. Ntondwe 2–1

2 Sep. 1957: Historical meeting between the Nyasaland Football Association and Nyasaland African Football Association to discuss the amalgamation of the two Associations under the chairmanship of H. M. Tasker and the two association presidents, G. Summers and G. Ndovi, in attendance, and to report back to their board

Oct. 1957: A squad of seventeen players went on tour to South Africa to play against the Johannesburg Bantu FA and, whilst in transit, to play in Southern Rhodesia for a total of seven fixtures, four in SA and three in SR. James Kaminjolo (capt.), goalkeeper Sazuze, Shonga, Kumwenda, Thipa, James Sangala, Kaunda, Matinga, Machinjili, Godfrey Kalitsiro, Thomas, Kumwembwe, Royee Maliwa, Makwelero, Kambwili, Daudi and Salamu.

Friendly: South Africa:

Pick Up 1st XI	1–4
Litsitsili Bugs	2–2
Pick Up 2nd XI	3–2
Mixed Race XI	4–7

40

Friendly: Southern Rhodesia:

White Army 1st XI	2–6
White Army 2nd XI	2–2
Pick Up XI	2–6

25 Dec. 1957: Governor's Trophy

Blantyre v. Lilongwe 9–1

Blantyre v. Mzimba 4–2

26 Dec. 1957: Lilongwe v. Mzimba 8–0

Final Log

No.	Teams	P	W	D	L	F	A	PTS
1	Blantyre	2	2	0	0	13	3	4
2	Lilongwe	2	1	0	1	9	9	2
3	Mzimba	2	0	0	2	2	12	0

1958

After an absence of five years, Zomba were crowned Royle League champions with Cholo as surprise runners-up.

Limbe Country Club's first Royle Cup final saw them defeat Cholo by 4–1.

Limbe CC and Blantyre SC met in the Stanhope Cup final for a third successive year. This time it was Limbe CC's triumph for the first time, winning 1–0.

George Summers, the first NFA scorer and president from 1954 to 1957, died late in 1957, and a memorial fundraising match took place on Saturday, 4 January 1958, between both national teams for the first time ever, creating another historic moment in our football calendar.

The Northern Province won the second Governor's Cup played in Mzuzu

The First ever mixed team played in Mwanza, with a trophy donated by Nicholas Trataris.

<u>1958 Timeline</u>

4 Jan. 1958: Fund Raising Friendly: Blantyre: NFA XI–NAFA XI   6–4
NFA: T. Allen (3), J. Hawthorne (2), G. Barley: NAFA: Nguruwe (2), S. Thipa, J. Kaminjolo
NFA XI: Sergio Nicholas, Brooks, Dennis Johnston (capt), Ricky Robertson, George Barley, Brian Fox, Jagjit Singh, Johnny Hawthorne, Tommy Allen, Ken Mansfield, Les Doran
NAFA XI: Sazuze, Msamu, Chikafa, Chinula, Chavura (capt), Kumwenda, Royee Maliwa, Godfrey Kalitsiro, James Kaminjolo, Nguruwe, Smart Thipa

Mario Antoine

8 Mar. 1958: Cholo SC: Stanhope Cup Final: Limbe CC v. Blantyre SC 1–0 A. Cottingham
Limbe CC: Pat Saunders, Jim Cottingham, Matt Hoyland, Jackie Cottingham, Jack Lowery, Archie Cottingham, Archie Muir, Dennis Pritchard, Pat Kelly, Ken Mansfield, Pat Lorimer
Blantyre SC: Sergio Nicholas, Budd, Peter Gurney, Ricky Robertson, George Burley, Ken Thomson, Marr, Godfrey Keys, Archie Carver, Brian Phillips, Harold Wrigley

Final Log

No.	Teams	P	W	D	L	F	A	PTS
1	Zomba	10	6	3	1	24	15	15
2	Cholo	10	6	1	3	28	16	13
3	Limbe C.C.	10	5	1	4	32	22	11
4	Blantyre SC "A"	10	4	2	4	20	17	10
5	Corona	10	2	2	6	15	35	6
6	Indian SC	10	2	1	7	14	28	5

Alfio Vatteroni top scorer with 14 goals

29 Mar. 1958: Trataris Cup: Salisbury: Alexandra Club 2–0   Marr, J. Hawthorne
Sergio Nicholas, Brian Fox, Dennis Johnston, Stellious, Jackie Cottingham, Tommy Allen, Marr, Johnny Hawthorne, Alfio Vatteroni, Dennis Pritchard, Les Doran

29 Mar. 1958: Bruss Cup: Salisbury: Alexandra Club "B" 3–5   A. Carver, K. Mansfield, L. Colandria
Stockman, Amilcare Cominetti, Buchan, Archie Cottingham, Jack Lowery, George Barley, Archie Carver, Brian Phillips, Lorenco Colandria, Ken Mansfield, Matt Hoyland

5 Apr. 1958: Oury Cup: Limbe CC: Sport Lisboa e Beira 3–2   Marr, K. Mansfield, L. Doran
Sergio Nicholas, Brian Fox, Dennis Johnston, Stellious, Jackie Cottingham, Tommy Allen, Marr, Johnny Hawthorne, Archie Carver, Ken Mansfield, Les Doran

6 Apr. 1958: Friendly: Zomba Gymkhana: Sport Lisboa e Beira 1–2   Marr
Sergio Nicholas, Brian Fox, Dennis Johnston, George Barley, Jackie Cottingham, Tommy Allen, Marr, Brian Phillips, Archie Carver, Ken Mansfield, Dennis Pritchard

12 Apr. 1958: BSC: Royle Cup Final: Limbe CC v. Cholo 4–1 P. Kelly (2), K. Mansfield, D. Pritchard, A. Vatteroni
Limbe CC: Pat Saunders, Alan Geldard, Pearce, Jack Lowery, Dennis Pritchard, Pat Kelly, Ken Mansfield (missing 4)
Cholo: Iaccuci, Tommy Allen, Costas Trataris, Brian Fox, Les Doran, Billy Pillans, Alfio Vatteroni (missing 4)

19 Apr. 1958: Champions v. the Rest: Zomba v. the Rest 3–0   Pagel, Webb, J. Hawthorne

8 Jun. 1958: Friendly: Mwanza: Nyasaland Select v. Zobwe 3–1
(It is not known which African players were selected, but the four Europeans were Tommy Allen, Pat Kelly, Archie Cottingham, and George Trataris)

26 Oct. 1958: 6-a-Side: Zomba GC: **16 teams participated:**

QF:	Corona "A" v. Blantyre "B" 3–1	
	Limbe "B" v. ISC 3–1	M. Hoyland, Bell, Clark, Nicol
	Limbe "A" v. Zomba 2–1	K. Mansfield (2), Evans
	Blantyre "A" v. Railways "B" 7–2	H. Wrigley (4), B. Phillips (2), A. Carver, Osborne, Valentine
SF:	Limbe "B" v. Corona "A" 4–1	Reid (2), Clarke, M. Hoyland, L. Colandria
	Limbe "A" v. Blantyre "A" 6–1	K. Mansfield (5), B. Rodgers, M. Bowery
F:	Limbe "A" v. Limbe "B" 7–2	K. Mansfield (4), B. Rodgers, A. Cottingham, Lorimer, Reid (2)

December 1958: Governor's trophy: Mzuzu:
Northern Province v. Central Province 2–1
Northern Province v. Southern Province 3–2

1959

Blantyre SC were crowned Royle League Champions for the fifth time after failing to win in the previous two seasons. Limbe CC, who were now becoming a force to be reckoned with, took second place. The strength of the league went up to seven teams again, as Nyasaland Railways affiliated after a seven-years absence.

Blantyre SC and Corona played the first drawn 2–2 Royle Cup Final, but the trophy went to Blantyre who won by 5–1.

Blantyre SC playing in their sixth successive Stanhope Cup Final, won it for the third time, defeating Cholo 3–1 to win the Treble for the second time.

The RNLSC Welfare Club from Salisbury cancelled its tour to Nyasaland to play fixtures in Limbe, Zomba, Lilongwe and Dowa due to the troubled times in the country in February as a State of Emergency was declared.

1959 Timeline

1 Jan. 1959: Scotland v. The Rest: CCL: 0–1   **K. Mansfield**
Scotland: Ian Royan, Ken Burns, Buchan, Jim Cottingham, Ricky Robertson, Archie Cottingham, Archie Carver, Brian Phillips, Colin Findlay, Archie Muir, Charlie Clarke
The Rest: Barry Horlock, John Cotton, Dennis Johnston, Fletcher, Harley, Dennis Pritchard, F. De Vito, Les Doran, Ken Mansfield, Vic Moss

29 Mar. 1959: Oury Cup: Beira: **Sport Lisboa e Beira 0–2**
Sergio Nicholas, Buchan, John Cotton, George Barley, Jackie Cottingham, Lorenco Colandria, Vic Moss, Brian Phillips, Dennis Pritchard, Ken Mansfield, Les Doran

30 Mar. 1959: Friendly: Beira: **Sporting Beira 3–3**   **A. Cottingham, (2 o/g)**
Sergio Nicholas, Jim Cottingham, John Cotton, George Barley, Jackie Cottingham, Lorenco Colandria, Vic Moss, Brian Phillips, Dennis Pritchard, Ken Mansfield, Archie Cottingham

Final Log

No.	Teams	P	W	D	L	F	A	PTS
1	Blantyre SC	12	10	2	0	48	14	**22**
2	Limbe CC	12	9	2	1	41	17	**20**
3	Corona	12	7	1	4	23	17	**15**
4	Cholo	12	6	1	5	24	19	**13**
5	Zomba	12	1	4	7	16	19	**6**
6	Indian SC	12	1	3	8	11	35	**5**
7	Nyasaland Railways	12	1	1	10	05	47	**3**

19 Apr. 1959: Stanhope Cup Final: **Blantyre v. Cholo 3–1**   **T. Donaldson (2), A. Carver, Harvey**
Blantyre: Sergio Nicholas, Ken Thomson, Dennis Johnston, Ken Burns, George Barley, Archie Muir, Archie Carver, Brian Phillips, T. Donaldson, Ricky Robertson, Godfrey Keys, M. Bowery
Cholo: Iaccuci, Stellious, Buchan, Billy Pillans, Colin Findlay, Ian Strachan, Harvey, Morris, Brian Fox, Les Doran, Grilli

25 Apr. 1959: Royle Cup Final: Blantyre v. Corona 2–2   **M. Bowery (2), Acconci, Preen**
Blantyre: Sergio Nicholas, Ricky Robertson, Dennis Johnston, Ken Burns, George Barley, Archie Muir, Archie Carver, Brian Phillips, T. Donaldson, Godfrey Keys, M. Bowery
Corona: T. Koutsadakis, Davies, Cantrell, Canham, Crawford, F De Vito, Griffiths, Lorenco Colandria, Preen, Acconci, Nicholls

2 May 1959: Royle Cup Final Replay: Blantyre v. Corona 5–1   **T. Donaldson (2), M. Bowery (2), B. Phillips, Preen**
Blantyre: Sergio Nicholas, Ken Thomson, Dennis Johnston, Ken Burns, George Barley, Archie Muir, Archie Carver, Brian Phillips, T. Donaldson, Ricky Robertson, M. Bowery
Corona: T. Koutsadakis, Davies, Cantrell or Griffiths, Canham, Crawford, F. De Vito, Todd, Lorenco Colandria, Preen, Acconci, Nicholls

10 Oct. 1959: Trataris Cup: Blantyre SC: **Alexandra Club 2–5**   **B. Phillips, D. Pritchard (pen)**
Sergio Nicholas, Brian Fox, Dennis Johnston, John Cotton, Jackie Cottingham, George Barley, Brian Phillips, Johnny Hawthorne, Preen, Dennis Pritchard, Vic Moss

10 Oct. 1959: Bruss Cup: Blantyre SC: **Alexandra Club "B" 2–3**   **?**
Cominas Yiannakis, Alan Geldard, Buchan, Costas Trataris, Jack Lowery, Archie Cottingham, Peter Lewis, Archie Carver, T. Donaldson, Acconci, M. Bowery

11 Oct. 1959: Friendly: Cholo SC: **Alexandra Club 1–2**   **?**
Sergio Nicholas, Brian Fox, Dennis Johnston, John Cotton, Jackie Cottingham, George Barley, Brian Phillips, Johnny Hawthorne, Preen, Dennis Pritchard, Vic Moss

11 Oct. 1959: Friendly: Cholo SC: **Alexandra Club "B" 2–5**   **P. Crossan (2)**
Cominas Yiannakis, Alan Geldard, Buchan, Costas Trataris, Jack Lowery, Archie Cottingham, Peter Lewis, Peter Crossan, Ken Mansfield, Acconci, M. Bowery

Summary of the '50s

A total of twenty-nine games were played between 8 April 1950 and 11 October 1959 between Nyasaland "A" and four different oppositions. Ten of these games were played for the Oury Trophy against Sport Lisboa e Beira, and six in the newly introduced Trataris Cup against Alexandra FC. In these games, Nyasaland saw ten wins and six losses. They scored 38 goals and conceded the same amount due to the 10–0 defeat suffered in Beira. However, this decade saw an improvement, as 51.7% of these matches ended in victory, compared to their previous best of 25 per cent in the '30s. Records were also registered in the scoring section, as the 2.2 goals per game was a great improvement over the 1.2 they registered previously. The 2.41 goals conceded per game was much better than the previous worst of 3.50.

Dennis Johnston was the outstanding player, as he was featured in twenty-five of the twenty-nine fixtures (82 per cent) and was one of seventy-two players selected for the first team.

Following closely was Tommy Allen, with twenty caps; keeper Sergio Nicholas, with nineteen, and Ken Mansfield, with eighteen. Mansfield was also the top scorer, with 9 goals.

Bob Marrinan became the first player to score a hat trick against Alexandra at Limbe Country Club in the Trataris Cup on 19 March 1955 in a 3–2 win. It had been a twenty-year wait for this achievement, and yet it was equalled the following day by Brian Fox against the same team in a 5–2 win in Cholo.

Great mention goes to Forrest, who made his debut in 1936 against Alexandra and played his last game (17) on 8 April 1950, spanning three decades.

The newly born second team played eleven games against Alexandra "B", of which six were for the newly introduced Bruss Cup, winning twice with one drawn game.

George Trataris and Ken Thomson were leading the appearances table with six games each, followed closely by Jimmy Smith. Thereafter, seven players followed with four games.

Colin Findlay, one of the seven players on four games, was the top scorer, with 5 goals, all scored in one game in a 6–1 win. This was the second hat trick for the second team, following one the previous year by Costas Trataris in a 3–1 victory which was in its second year, as compared to twenty years by the first team. Costas's hat trick took him to second place with 4 goals.

Fifty-three players were featured in the eleven fixtures, of which twenty-six players featured in both the first and second teams.

The NAFA played eight known international matches during the '50s, and one was against Grupo Desportivo Rebenta Fogo, whom they met in Beira in 1949. The first game played against this team is still being researched. They toured South Africa in 1957 and played four games, winning one and drawing one, and whilst in transit they played a further three games against a White Army first and second team and a select Pick Up XI, drawing one. However, scant reports show that they played fixtures in 1950 and 1952 against teams from Southern Rhodesia; this is still being researched.

Mario Antoine

1950 Stats

NFA "A" Team

Opposition:	P	W	D	L	F	A
Sport Lisboa e Beira	14	9	0	5	36	34
Alexandra FC	11	4	0	7	21	31
Beira Select XI	2	1	0	1	2	1
Sporting Club	2	1	1	0	5	4
	29	15	1	13	64	70

NFA "B" Team

Opposition:	P	W	D	L	F	A
Alexandra FC	11	4	2	5	23	24

Top Five Appearances "A" (29)

25: Dennis Johnston
20: Tommy Allen
19: Sergio Nicholas
18: Ken Mansfield
15: Brian Phillips

Top Five Scorers (64)–6 unknown

9: Ken Mansfield
6: Bob Marrinan
5: John Patterson
4: Brian Phillips
3: Brian Fox, Marr, Archie Muir, Ricky Robertson

Top Clean Sheets (5)

4: S. Nicholas
1: George Trataris

Top Five Appearances "B" (11)

6: Ken Thomson, George Trataris
5: Jimmy Smith
4: Colin Findlay, Alan Geldard, Peter Gurney, Dennis Harris, Dennis Nock, Fred Taylor, Costas Trataris

Top Five Scorers (23)–2 unknown

5: Colin Findlay
4: Costas Trataris
3: Brian Phillips
2: Peter Crossan

Top Clean Sheets (2)

1: Stockman, George Trataris

NAFA Opposition

	P	W	D	L	F	A
Grupo Desportivo Rebenta Fogo (PEA)	1	1	0	0	2	0
Litsitsili (SA)	1	0	1	0	2	2
Mixed Race (SA)	1	0	0	1	4	7
Pick Up XI SA)	1	0	0	1	1	4
Pick Up 2nd XI (SA)	1	1	0	0	3	2
Pick Up XI (SR)	1	0	0	1	2	6
White Army XI (SR)	1	0	0	1	2	6
White Army 2nd XI (SR)	1	0	1	0	2	2
	8	2	2	4	18	29

Unknown results against Grupo Desportivo Rebenta Fogo (1 game) and Southern Rhodesia (2 games at home; 4 away: 2 wins and 2 losses)

Most Appearances (2)

17 players for SA and SR tour known

Scorers (2)—16 unknown
1: Menewa, Smart Thipa

Domestic Scene—26 Trophies: 10 Royle League, 10 Royle K/O, 6 Stanhope

Teams	Royle League (10)		Royle K/O (10)		Stanhope K/O (6)		Total (26)	
	Champions	R/Up	Winners	R/Up	Winners	R/Up	Winners	R/Up
Blantyre	4	4	6	2	3	3	13	9
Corona	2		2	2	1		5	2
Limbe CC	1	1	1		1	2	3	3
Zomba	2	2		3			2	5
S. Rovers		1	1		1		2	1
Mlanje	1			1			1	1
Cholo		1		2		1		4
L. Wand		1						1

CHAPTER EIGHT

THE 1960S

Oury Cup

The historic day when the NFA and NAFA become one body on 20 October 1964 saw the end of the annual Oury Cup fixtures between Nyasaland and Sport Lisboa e Beira. Five more fixtures were held that brought the total number of games between these two sides to twenty-five, with SLB narrowly edging Nyasaland by twelve wins to eleven and two draws. The biggest win by SLB was 10–0, which occurred twice in Beira, whereas Nyasaland's 5–0 success was their best. One result in either 1941 or 1944 ended in a draw according to reconciliations, but research is still ongoing to find the score.

These last five fixtures that didn't end in a draw resulted in SLB winning thrice with 11 goals against 10. Brian Phillips became the sole Nyasaland hat trick hero in 1961 in a 4–1 victory in Beira. Dennis Pritchard was the scorer against SLB in 1964 in a 2–1 defeat. Nyasaland's top scorer during these twenty-five fixtures was John Patterson with 6 goals, followed very closely by Ken Mansfield with 5 goals.

Nyasaland failed to score in six games, whereas they had only three clean sheets, of which two were credited to Sergio Nicholas and one to Harry Middleton, the first Nyasaland goalkeeper.

Trataris Trophy

The Trataris Trophy story was short-lived, as only two further fixtures took place and the series concluded in 1961 with one win apiece and identical scores of 3–1. This brought the number of games to eight, with each side winning four games, but Alexandra edged Nyasaland by 18 goals against 16. Max Preen, who joined Bob Marrinan as the only two Nyasaland players to score a hat trick, became the top scorer with 4 goals.

Bruss Cup

The same sequence as the first team saw Nyasaland "B" play their final two fixtures against Alexandra—and what a way to conclude, as they finished it with a 9–1 thrashing of their opponents, with two hat tricks recorded. Moss, playing at his home ground in Zomba, scored 4 and was joined by Rui Bastos with 3. The two now joined Colin Findlay, who had scored 5 in 1957 on the hat trick podium, and with that had gained the title of top scorer, with 5 goals. With that great 9–1 win, they edged Alexandra by four wins to three, with one drawn game, and had a massive 26–20 aggregate score.

International

The first ever proper international fixture against another country, instead of a club or representative side, took place at Rangeley Stadium on 15 October 1960 when neighbours Southern Rhodesia were the visitors. The first match ended in a very narrow defeat of 4–3, and after five changes the following day, the heaviest ever defeat of 3–13 was recorded.

Friendlies "A"

Nyasaland repeated their thirteen friendly fixtures of the '50s, but with the difference of playing against ten different teams that included two English teams and one Scottish team.

The date of 31 May 1960 has been inscribed as a historic event, as Blackpool, who had just ended the 1959/60 English First Division in eleventh place, became the first British team to play in Nyasaland at Rangeley Stadium, in a match that ended in a 6–1 defeat after Nyasaland was trailing 2–0 at half-time. (See match report below.)

West Ham United, who ended their season in eighth place in the English Top Division, followed two years later, and this time the host held their superior visitors to a goalless half-time before going down by 4–0.

The following year, Dundee United, who finished in seventh place in the Scottish First Division, showed no mercy with a 10–2 thumping. The other crushing defeat that Nyasaland suffered during this decade came at the hands of Salisbury Callies, 9–0, in 1962.

On the bright side, the NFA team managed four 3–2 victories against a Salisbury XI, two 4–1 victories against Sport Lisboa e Beira, and a 6–1 win against Alexandra.

Blackpool give a brilliant display of soccer

By our Soccer Correspondent

GEORGE TRATARIS who, making his debut in the Nyasaland team, saved many possible goals and did well to keep the score down to six.

DENNIS JOHNSTON, the Nyasaland skipper, who played a sound game at left back, and who, at a civic reception after the match, was awarded the trophy for the Nyasaland "Footballer of the Year."

Blantyre, Thursday.

BLACKPOOL, the first ever British professional soccer team to visit Nyasaland, in a brilliant display of ball artistry and teamwork, defeated the home team, at the Rangely Stadium on Tuesday, by six goals to one, after leading 2-0 at the interval.

However Nyasaland are to be congratulated, especially the defence, for the way they fought and never gave up trying. For Blackpool, Hill, Gratrix and Perry were outstanding while for Nyasaland, the man of the match was Cottingham, ably assisted by Trataris, Fox, Johnston and the other defenders. In the forward line Phillips tried hard, while, no doubt, Prien will want to forget "the match of missed chances."

Winning the toss, Johnston the Nyasaland skipper elected to play with the sun behind, and Blackpool kicked off before a crowd of nearly 5,000 some of whom had come from as far afield as Ncheu and Fort Johnston.

In the early minutes, Blackpool were on top and Hoyland did well to stop right winger Perry had split the home team's defence. Within minutes Blackpool again came near to scoring but this time J. Cottingham brought off a timely tackle to whip the ball of the toes of Lea as he was about to shoot from inside the penalty area. Still on the attack a long pass to Hill saw his high centre cut off by goalkeeper Trataris.

LONG CLEARANCE

A long clearance from Martin found Crawford who raced through the middle to be checked by Cottingham. Crawford had to receive attention but was soon able to continue.

Keeping up the pressure Blackpool's Charnley had his centre very neatly blocked and cleared by Cottingham who was a pillar of strength in the Nyasaland defence.

The Nyasaland wing halves tried hard to get the forward line moving but tight marking and clever positional play by the Blackpool defence gave the Nyasaland forward line very little scope.

Lewis beat two Blackpool players when he went back to help his defence but his final pass across field to Doran was cut off and cleared by Jones. Then Pritchard intercepted a pass to Perry and put Phillips away. Cleverly beating Kelly Phillips drew the left back only to hit the ball too hard for Lewis to run onto.

MAKING THEM FIGHT

Nyasaland were now making Blackpool fight for the ball. Gratrix the Blackpool centre-half obtained possession and quickly slipped the ball out to Hill who from 35 yards put in a pile driver which Trataris saved brilliantly, catching the ball in mid-air. The visitors were using the long, low pass which frequently split the Nyasaland defence.

Blackpool deservedly took the lead when, in the 22nd minute,

good work by Charnley ended in Lea firing into the net from close range.' Nyasaland's hopes were again shattered when straight from the kick-off Lea intercepted a bad pass to send a long shot upfield. Hill chased the ball, brought it under control, to burst through the centre cracking home a shot which gave Trataris no chance.

Despite these two quick goals Nyasaland plugged away although Blackpool's superiority was beginning to tell.

Hill at outside right was outstanding and it was obvious

JACKIE COTTINGHAM who battled brilliantly at centre-half against superior odds.

that he had received lessons from that great maestro — Stanley Matthews.

Hoyland at left back had the unenviable task of marking this fleet-footed, nimble youngster and full credit must be given to him in that he never gave up.

After 35 minutes later a great chance was lost for Nyasaland. Lewis took a corner kick, the ball went to Doran who slipped the ball to the unmarked Prien who miskicked when well placed.

After the resumption Blackpool soon took up the attack. Gratrix found Hill who quickly brought the high ball down under control before flashing over a hard centre which was taken off the toes of Charnley by Cottingham. Nyasaland pressed and Lewis took the ball upfield where Phillips failed to stop a fast pass before going out of play.

In the 50th minute Blackpool increased their lead when, after clever work by Perry, the ball went to Martin who netted with a

terrific ground shot from 20 yards.

Straight away Nyasaland fought back and faced a corner. Lewis' corner kick was overrun by Phillips but Prien again miskicked.

Then came the miss of the match. After Doran had fired over the bar, the goalkick went straight to Prien who with an open goal blazed wide from 12 yards range. What a tonic it would have been for Nyasaland had the shot entered the net.

Then a Perry free-kick went straight to the head of Charnley who jumped head and shoulders above everyone else to steer the ball into the far corner of the net. Blackpool were now on top and more or less penned Nyasaland in their own half.

In the 60th minute Hill was fouled just outside the penalty area and the free kick resulted in a goalmouth melee ending with Trataris bringing off a great save when he dived to catch the ball at the foot of the post.

SIZZLING SHOT

It was obvious that Blackpool would increase their score as indeed they did in the 62nd minute. Lea taking advantage of a bad clearance crashed home a sizzling shot from 20 yards range.

After Trataris had saved twice from Hill, goal number six came when a Hill centre went to Crawford who pivoted to crash the ball past the goalkeeper.

Right from the kick-off Nyasaland swept into attack and Lewis passed to Prien who shot into the net with Waiters out of position. This goal was a great tonic to Nyasaland and their supporters and it was certainly great to see the home team, leg weary and tired, still battling hard.

When the final whistle blew Nyasaland were still on the attack.

Friendlies "B"

Nyasaland's second team played a further four fixtures against three different teams to conclude their journey. They started off with a 2–2 draw and followed that with an 8–0 thrashing of Alexandra in their final appearance at Rangeley Stadium. Their journey ended in 1962 when Salisbury Callies were the visitors and played two matches. The teams won and lost one each, but Callies edged the "B" team on a 3–2 aggregate score.

Nyasaland African Football Association (NAFA) and Fam–International

History would have been made on Tuesday 21 August 1962 in Dar Es Salaam, Tanganyika, as that was the proposed date for Nyasaland to play against Tanganyika following the state visit of Sékou Touré, the president of the Republic of Guinea, to that country. Unfortunately, that visit did not take place at the last minute, leading to the cancellation of the fixture.

Nyasaland would also have played two further fixtures in Tanga and Arusha. But the good news was that they did not have to wait very long, as less than two months later, the historical date was inscribed on our calendars when Ghana played against Nyasaland at Rangeley Stadium in Blantyre on 15 October 1962. The excitement was at its height, but we were taught a football lesson by Ghana's historic 12–0 defeat, which remains Nyasaland's heaviest loss ever.

The Tanganyika dream also took place during the same year, on 8 December, in Dar es Salaam, and although another defeat was on the cards, Godfrey Kalitsiro became Nyasaland's first ever scorer, followed by Smart Thipa, in a 6–2 defeat.

Nyasaland played a further twenty-three matches until the end of the decade, with the highlight being the fixtures on Independence Day, 6 July, every year from 1964, with an exception in 1965. It took Nyasaland thirteen games before they registered their first victory on 6 September 1968 in Mbabane, Swaziland, when they heavily defeated Botswana 8–1.

That record stood for nearly forty years, but another record that still stands is the two hat tricks scored in one match that belonged to Yasin "Njinga" Osman and Roy Cook. Our first hat trick hero was Solomon Mkwapatira, who managed this feat in a 4–3 loss at the hands of Basutoland, now Lesotho, during their Independence celebrations on 2 October 1966.

The next fixture in 1967 took place in Blantyre, when Rhodesia were the visitors to celebrate Malawi's affiliation to FIFA. The only time two siblings scored in the same match was realised here, as both Yasin and Allaudin Osman scored 1 apiece in a 6–3 defeat.

Fourteen matches took place between 1962 and 1968, and a massive eleven fixtures in 1969 alone were played—a high for Malawi at that time—although only one victory was recorded, at the expense of Swaziland, 3–0, during an independence game that was eventually abandoned because of power failure. A Zambian tour ended in disaster, as Nyasaland lost all three fixtures, failing to score and conceding 16 goals.

A further twelve fixtures took place against club sides that included yet another English third division side, Oldham Athletic, who visited in 1967. In a very close match, Malawi lost by 3–2, with Yasin Osman and Overton Mkandawire as scorers. Prior to that, Nyasaland travelled to Northern Rhodesia and played a full international and two fixtures against Copperbelt XI and Midlands.

Four clubs from Southern Rhodesia—Salisbury Callies, Salisbury City, Salisbury Dynamos and Wankie—also visited during the '60s, as did Sporting Club and Desportivo from Tete, Mozambique. A National Schools Team was introduced in 1967 and played against Zambia Schools.

Nyasaland Football Association (Nfa)–Domestic

Three new teams—Olympia (1960), Callies (1961), and Rovers (1963)—were affiliated to the NFA during this short decade as a result of the two different associations merging in October 1964. The significant improvement in this area now saw a real multiracial team, as players from the SHAFL and the NFA were now rubbing shoulders and showcasing their skills in this league from the 1962–63 season.

The 1950s giants Blantyre SC could not repeat their dominance on the local scene and were able to capture only four trophies (22 per cent) during these five years—one league title, two Stanhope Cups, and a Royle Cup. The honours went to the much improved Limbe Country Club and Greek newcomers Olympia, with six trophies each (33.3 per cent).

Limbe won the last three titles, the only club to have achieved that, and were denied what could have been the first quadruple when they were heavily beaten 5–2 by Railways in a Royle Cup replay after a 5–5 draw in the first game.

Meanwhile, Olympia won their six trophies in their first four years of existence and in their last year (1964) were suspended from the league. They won the Royle Cup in 1960, followed by a double the following year with the league title and Stanhope Cup. They repeated their double in 1962 with the Royle Cup and newly introduced Franklin Trophy.

Standing l to r: Royee Maliwa, Lewis Chinula, Llewellen Kishombe,
Bright Gondwe, Oliver Nakhumwa, Raleigh M'manga.
Front row: l to r: Nathan Gondwe, Smart Thipa, Richard
Banda, Godfrey Kalitsiro, James Sangala

Nyasaland African Football Association (NAFA)–Domestic

The amalgamation of both bodies was slowly occurring, as evidenced by a SHAFL Select XI versus newly formed Greek club Olympiakos on 4 September 1960—and what a game, as the two teams battled to a 5–5 draw played at Rangeley Stadium. Richard Banda, Smart Thipa, and De Mobray Thipa scored for the Select XI team. Costas Trataris, including a penalty, and Grilli scored a brace each after Max Prien opened the scoring. Two months later in Zomba, a combined Olympia and SHAFL select side played against Zomba Sports Club combined with the Zomba Africa Football Association and lost by 2–1.

Red Army (Southern Division) defeated Ndirande Welfare (Northern Division) in the Kings Cup Final played on 22 April 1961. The Governor's Cup, which had not been played since 1959, was revived and came to be known as the Kamuzu Cup. The Southern Province (South Section) defeated the Central Province 3–2, courtesy of a Godfrey Kalitsiro hat trick.

The following year, the Northern Province repeated their 1958 trick by defeating the Northern Section of the Southern Province by 2–1 before it went back to the Southern Section, as the Northern Section suffered back-to-back defeats, this time 3–1.

Malawi Football Association (MFA)–Domestic

The merger of the NFA and NAFA on 20 October 1964 saw a new title emerging as the Malawi Football Association, and the league title also changed to the City & Suburban League.

The league was still composed of seven teams despite the withdrawal of the suspended Olympia, who refused to affiliate; Rovers, a mixed-race team that lasted only two seasons; and, at the last minute, Corona, after twelve seasons in the League.

However, the 1965 season saw the birth of today's giants, Wanderers, who started off as Portuguese Wanderers (as the Wanderers club is situated at the back of the Portuguese club). Most of the Rovers players moved to this team. I am still researching to find out why "Portuguese" was deleted from "Portuguese Wanderers". Wanderers finished the season as league champions.

The other newly affiliated club was Rangers—a combination of Mpingwe Sports Club, Indian Sports Club—who were members from the onset till 1961 (fourteen seasons)—and the Goans Club, who participated in 1950 and 1951.

The Stanhope Trophy witnessed, for the first time in the history of Malawi football, a trophy shared between Portuguese Wanderers and Blantyre SC, who drew 2–2 because the association could not find a suitable date for a replay.

The remaining trophies, Franklin and Royle, were won by Railways and Blantyre SC, respectively.

The following season, the league increased to eight teams, despite Rangers withdrawing. They were replaced by a team composed of students and staff from Chichiri (who lasted only one season, as the administrator went on holiday) and Corona, who were readmitted.

The title went to Zomba, who lost only once and were rewarded with their first treble of trophies, as they also won the Franklin and Royle trophies. Blantyre SC, who retained their runners-up position, won their last ever trophy when they beat newcomers Chichiri Athletics by 2–0 in the Stanhope final.

The seeds of Bullets were sewn when some fringe Wanderers players and some from Chichiri Athletics formed Blantyre City, who ended the season in third place as Wanderers regained their title from Zomba, the runners-up.

These two rivals then shared two trophies each. Unfortunately, the three trophies played for during the NFA era were won for the last time.

The 1967–68 season saw a dramatic change. The league increased by 50 per cent, as one of the oldest clubs in the country, Michiru Castles (which had been formed in the '30s and played mostly in the SHAFL and disbanded in 1956), was revived in 1963 by the Nsewa brothers, mainly Wales.

Chichiri Athletics was also revived with the arrival of Brian Griffin, who previously played for Corona. Other new teams are Malawi Police, and Blantyre Secondary School Old Boys.

Wanderers, under the sponsorship of Stansfield Motors, changed their name to Yamaha Wanderers and retained their title, which was now known as the Blantyre and Football Districts League, against close rivals Zomba Town.

The Castle Cup was the first knockout trophy brought in under the new regime, and Chichiri Athletics, under ex–Bristol City player Brian Griffin, who lost the Stanhope Cup final in 1966 to Blantyre Sports Club, reversed the results at Limbe Country Club, as they won 3–2.

Sadly, Chichiri Athletics lost two players—Francis Nseula, a teacher, and sixteen-year-old Nazer Osman—in a road accident whilst in transit to play friendly matches in Tete in April 1968, whilst the two other passengers in the car, Prescott Magaleta and Mustafa Munshi, suffered multiple injuries. A testimonial game took place later in November 1968.

The last season of the decade saw another step towards a national league, as George Antoine, a star with Rovers and Railways, sponsored Lilongwe Dynamos through his company, Antoine's Panel Beaters.

Fernando Araujo, who starred in neighbouring Mozambique, was one of the pioneers of that team, which unfortunately had to withdraw during the season in June 1969.

BSS Old Boys lasted only one season, and both Corona and Cholo ended their affiliation with the league, and their place was taken by Malawi University and the army, who played as Red Army in the SHAFL.

Companies were now playing a role in promoting football in this region. Bata Shoe Company selected Blantyre City through a great role played by then sectreary John Gilmore, and the team changed its name to Bata Bullets, today's giants.

Two more knockout trophies were introduced during the season. One went to Malawi Police, playing in their second season, when they defeated Yamaha Wanderers by 2–1 for the BAT Trophy.

Yamaha Wanderers completed the double as they clinched the other newly introduced Chibuku Cup when Bata Bullets went down 3–2 after extra time.

It appears that the students liked the Castle Cup, as Malawi University lifted this trophy against Yamaha Wanderers, who appeared in all the three finals.

Wanderers 1965 City & Suburban League

Back row: M. Antunes (manager), Januaro de Magalhaes, Kirby Thomson, Oliver Nankhumwa, Caro, Damiano, William Green Malunga
Front row: James Mkwanda, Allaudin Osman, Joaquim Cunha, Basil Malila, Lameck Phiri

Wanderers—1965 City & Suburban League champions

1960

Newly-affiliated Olympia saw the Royle League increased to eight teams, and the team ended as runners-up, leaving Blantyre SC to retain the title.

Olympia, in their first season, defeated Blantyre SC 2–1 in the Royle Cup final.

Blantyre SC continued with their appearance in the Stanhope Cup final and retained it by defeating Cholo 2–1 in a repeat final.

History was made and another milestone was achieved after thirty-five years with the first proper international fixtures that Nyasaland ever played on 15 October against Southern Rhodesia. The visitors lost by 4–3, and 13–3 the following day.

Another historical moment was when English First Division team Blackpool became the first professional side to visit our shores on 31 May.

Visit of Mashonaland African team in December

1960 Timeline

1 Jan. 1960: Rangeley Stadium: Scotland v. The Rest
Scotland: Ian Royan, Billy Pillans, Buchan, Jackie Cottingham, Tommy Allen (capt.), Archie Cottingham, Archie Carver, Brian Phillips, Johnny Hawthorne, Peter Crossan, Archie Muir, Ian Strachan, Colin Findlay, McKenzie
The Rest: George Trataris, Dennis Johnston (capt.), Paul Yiannakis, George Barley, Brian Fox, Vic Moss, Jim Yiannakis, Dennis Pritchard, Max Prien, Ken Mansfield, Jagjit Singh, John Cotton, M. Bowery, Lorenco Colandria

Final Log

No.	Teams	P	W	D	L	F	A	PTS
1	Blantyre SC	14	12	1	1	53	14	25
2	Olympia	14	9	2	3	51	20	20
3	Nyasaland Railways	14	9	0	5	30	14	18
4	Cholo	14	8	1	5	40	29	17
5	Limbe	14	5	1	8	32	47	11
6	Corona	14	3	3	8	22	37	9
7	Indian SC	14	3	1	10	22	49	7
8	Zomba	14	2	1	11	20	59	5

Dennis Johnston is the first Footballer of the Year

26 Mar. 1960: Trataris Cup: Salisbury: Alexandra Club 1–3   M. Prien (pen)
Sergio Nicholas, Brian Fox, Dennis Johnston, John Cotton, Jackie Cottingham, J. Kopanakis, Brian Phillips, Max Prien, Peter Crossan, Dennis Pritchard, Vic Moss

26 Mar. 1960: Bruss Cup: Salisbury: Alexandra Club "B" 3–1   C. Trataris, I. Grilli, K. Mansfield
George Trataris, Jack Stuart, Crawford, Costas Trataris, George Barley, Archie Cottingham, Peter Lewis, I. Grilli, Monteiro, Ken Mansfield, M. Bowery

27 Mar. 1960: Friendly: Salisbury: Salisbury Invitation XI 3–2   B. Phillips (2), P. Crossan
Sergio Nicholas, Brian Fox, Dennis Johnston, John Cotton, Jackie Cottingham, J. Kopanakis, Brian Phillips, Max Prien, Peter Crossan, Dennis Pritchard, Vic Moss

2 Apr. 1960: Rangeley Stadium: Stanhope Cup Final: Blantyre v. Cholo 2–1   K. Thomson, T. Allen, E. Grilli
Blantyre: Sergio Nicholas, Peter Gurney, Archie Carver, Ken Thomson, Brian Phillips, Tommy Allen, Brian Phillips (missing 4)
Cholo: William Harvey, E. Grilli, Alfio Vatteroni (missing 8)

9 Apr. 1960: Royle Cup Final: Rangeley Stadium: Olympia v. Blantyre 2–1   M. Prien (2), T. Allen (p)
Olympia: M. Prien (missing 10)
Blantyre: Sergio Nicholas, George Barley, Peter Gurney, Tommy Allen, Brian Phillips, Archie Muir (missing 5)

10 Apr. 1960: Rangeley Stadium: Champions Blantyre SC v. The Rest 4–2   B. Phillips (2), Archie Muir (2), M. Prien, J. Hoatson
Blantyre: Sergio Nicholas, George Barley, Russell, Tommy Allen, Brian Phillips, Archie Muir (missing 5)
The Rest: George Trataris, J. Hoatson, M. Prien (missing 8)

16 Apr. 1960: Oury Cup: Rangeley Stadium: Sport Lisboa e Beira 0–2
Sergio Nicholas, Tommy Allen, Dennis Johnston, Brian Fox, Jackie Cottingham, Peter Crossan, Vic Moss, Brian Phillips, Dennis Pritchard, Max Prien, Les Doran

17 Apr. 1960: Friendly: Rangeley Stadium: Sport Lisboa e Beira 2–2   B. Phillips, M. Prien
Sergio Nicholas, Jack Stuart, Dennis Johnston, Brian Fox, Jackie Cottingham, Peter Lewis, Vic Moss, Brian Phillips, Dennis Pritchard, Max Prien, I. Grilli

23 Apr. 1960: Nyasaland Railways v. Zambesia Railways 5–1   Mann (3), P. Crossan, S. Singh

23 Apr. 1960: NSP Trophy QF: ITC v. Rhodesia & Nyasaland Transport 5–1
    Railways v. Stockbrokers 2–1
23 Apr. 1960:   Limbe Police v. Blantyre Police 2–0
    2nd KAR v. Coca Cola 2–1
Draw for Semi-Finals: ITC v. Limbe Police, 2nd KAR v. Railways

24 Apr. 1960: Scotland v. England 4–3   J. Hawthorne (2), P. Crossan, A. Muir–P. Lewis, L. Doran, Crawford (p)
Scotland: Ian Royan, Jack Stuart, Matt Hoyland, Jackie Cottingham, Tommy Allen, Archie Cottingham, Archie Carver, Brian Phillips, Johnny Hawthorne, Peter Crossan, Archie Muir
England: John Harvey, Fletcher, Dennis Johnston, Dennis Pritchard, Crawford, Vic Moss, Peter Lewis, Ken Thomson, Les Doran, Colley, M. Bowery

30 Apr./01 May 1960: CFM Tournament in Beira: 4 Club Tournaments: Nyasaland Railways, Clube Ferroviario de Mocambique, Sporting Club de Beira, Grupo Desportivo de Beira:
Squad: George Trataris, Fletcher (capt.), Peter Crossan, Jackie Cottingham, Mann, Badham, Acconci, McDonald, Osborne, Yiannakis, Jagjit Singh, Santokh Singh, Locke, Max Prien, Peter Lewis

Nyasaland Railways v. Clube Ferroviario de Mocambique 2–3   M. Prien (p), P. Crossan
Nyasaland Railways v. Sporting Club de Beira 2–5

1 May 1960: NSP Semi-Finals: Limbe Police v. ITC 4–1   Mtawale, Malanje, Kachale, ?
2nd KAR defeated Railways

8 May 1960: NSP Final: Limbe Police v. 2nd KAR
Limbe Police: Chimbalanga, Nyirenda, Kachapila, Nkoloma, Malanga, Banda, Mtawale, Magombo, Kachale, Chaluka, Majawa
2nd KAR: Jennings, Andrew, Charles, Gordon, Exeter, Alan, Saete, Venjaye, Wilson, Clement, Clement

14 May 1960: Friendly: Rangeley Stadium: Quelimane 4–4   M. Prien (4)
Sergio Nicholas, Jack Stuart, Dennis Johnston, Johnny Hawthorne, Jackie Cottingham, Peter Lewis, Vic Moss, Brian Phillips, Dennis Pritchard, Max Prien, Les Doran

15 May 1960: Friendly: Blantyre SC: Quelimane 2–2   Colley, M. Bowery
George Trataris, Fletcher, Matt Hoyland, Ken Burns, Costas Trataris, Ian Strachan, Archie Carver, Peter Crossan, Colley, I. Grilli, M. Bowery

31 May 1960: Friendly: Rangeley Stadium: Blackpool 1–6   M. Prien
George Trataris, Matt Hoyland, Dennis Johnston, Jackie Cottingham, Dennis Pritchard, Brian Fox, Brian Phillips, Johnny Hawthorne, Max Prien, Les Doran, Peter Lewis

4 Sep. 1960: Olympia v. SHAFL Select XI 5–5   Grilli (2), C. Trataris (2–1p), Prien, R. Banda (2), S. Thipa (2), D. Thipa
Olympia: Cominas Yiannakis, Poriazis, T. Nakos, G. Koutsadakis, Costas Trataris, Johnnie Ruprecht, Jim Yiannakis, Paul Yiannakis, Max Prien, J. Hoatson, Amorianos, Grilli
SHAFL XI: Sazuze, Msamu, Mdoka, Gondwe, Mkalyainga, Wales Nsewa, James Sangala, Smart Thipa, Richard Banda, DeMobray Thipa, Ronald

15 Oct. 1960: Friendly: Rangeley Stadium: Southern Rhodesia 3–4   B. Phillips, P. Crossan, (o/g)
George Trataris, Matt Hoyland, Harold Davies, Jackie Cottingham, Dennis Pritchard, Brian Fox, Brian Phillips, Godfrey Keys, Bob Rodgers, Peter Crossan, Peter Parker (jnr)

16 Oct. 1960: Friendly: Cholo SC: Southern Rhodesia 3–13   B. Phillips, P. Parker (jnr), B. Rodgers
Cominas Yiannakis, Jack Stuart, Alan Geldard, Jackie Cottingham, Dennis Pritchard, Brian Fox, Brian Phillips, Max Prien, Bob Rodgers, Les Doran, Peter Parker (jnr)

23/24 Oct. 1960: Olympia Preseason Tournament:

SF:	Zomba v. Lilongwe	5–0	Callies v. ISC	1–0
F:	Zomba v. Callies	2–0	Dendi (o/g)	

17 Nov. 1960: Discussions to have a multiracial professional national league from the countries of Nyasaland (one team), Southern Rhodesia (seven teams), and Northern Rhodesia (six teams) got underway in Salisbury. A total of fourteen teams would compete with the Copperbelt, featuring four teams, with Bulawayo and Salisbury contributing two teams each. The remaining teams would come from Umtali, Gatooma, Gwelo, Ndola, Lusaka, and Blantyre, the rule being that not more than eight players of any race were to feature in any team.

30 Nov. 1960: Rangeley Stadium: Multiracial friendly
Zomba Sport Club/Zomba African Football Association v. Olympia/SHAFL 2–1   Daudi, Botha, Mwatinamba
ZSC/ZAFA: Sergio Nicholas, Jack Stuart, Wizard, Vic Moss, Botha, Ian Strachan, Daudi, Kidman, Burge (missing 2)
Oly/SHAFL: Cominas Yiannakis, Costas Trataris, Johnnie Ruprecht, Gondwe, Mwatinamba, Rui Bastos

4 Dec. 1960: Rangeley Stadium: SHAFL v. Lilongwe Football Association 3–1 R. Banda (2), Kunyenje

10 Dec. 1960: Rangeley Stadium: NAFA v. Mashonaland African

1961

Callies became the latest team to join the Royle League, now bringing the total to nine teams. Olympia, who joined only the previous season, were that years' champions.

Blantyre SC avenged their previous year's defeat against Olympia by defeating them 4–1 in the Royle Cup final. It was the first time in eight seasons that Blantyre SC failed to reach the Stanhope Cup final, leaving Olympia achieving the Double by beating newcomers Callies 8–1.

Nyasa United was formed to participate in Rhodesia and Nyasaland Professional Football League.

1961 Timeline

1 Jan. 1961: CCL: Scotland v. The Rest 1–0   P. Crossan
Scotland: Ian Royan (LCC), Jack Stuart (Zomba), Matt Hoyland (LCC), Jackie Cottingham (Callies), Tommy Allen (Callies—capt.), Buchan (Cholo), Archie Carver (BSC), Brian Phillips (BSC), Johnny Hawthorne (Callies), Peter Crossan (N. Rail), Littlejohn (LCC) **Reserves:** Logan (Corona), Ian Strachan (Zomba), Billy Pillans (Cholo), McIntosh (Callies), Pat Kelly (Callies)
The Rest: George Trataris (N. Rail), Alan Geldard (LCC), Fletcher (N. Rail), Dennis Pritchard (LCC—capt.), Costas Trataris (Oly), Brian Fox (LCC), Vic Moss (Zomba), Rui Bastos (Oly), Max Prien (Oly), Les Doran (Cholo), Frank Rogers (Cholo),
Reserves: Nakos (Oly), J. Hoatson (Oly), Ken Mansfield (N. Rail), Todd (Corona), Alfio Vatteroni (Cholo

2 and 16 Feb. 1961: Letter from Teddy Gordon to Dr. Banda Relating to Proposed Professional Football and Reply

TEDDY GORDON WRITES AN OPEN LETTER TO DR. BANDA

'Give professional soccer a chance"

Blantyre, Thursday.

DEAR Dr. Banda,—With professional soccer kicking off on Easter Monday, April 3, Nyasaland will have to get a hustle on if it is to have a team ready in time. To get things moving a meeting of all interested is to be held at 5.30 p.m. at the Corona Club on February 6, and it is emphasised by the Nyasaland Football Association that in the Rhodesia and Nyasaland Football League the accent is on multi-racial soccer.

In fact the regulations are explicit—there must be at least three non-Europeans in each team fielded and although great enthusiasm was at first shown by African players here, their ardour was soon damped by political intimidation—even to the extent of friendly multi-racial matches having to be called off.

It is a downright disgrace if the rights of the individual are to be dictated to that extent and I appeal to you, here and now, if you have any sense of sportsmanship at all, to tell your followers to give the green light to those players who wish to sign professional forms and participate in the league.

WELL-KNOWN

Your hatred of Federation is well known but the Rhodesia and Nyasaland Football League is simply what it says — it is merely a league formed in order that teams from each individual country can compete against each other on the football field.

It is completely non-political and is being treated as such by all who have anything to do with it.

What have the Malawi Congress Party got against it? It will do it no harm. It can, in fact, do a lot of good.

The maximum wage for a part-time player is set at £10 a game. The minimum weekly payment will be £2 during the season, plus £1 a game, with bonuses of £1 for a draw and £2 for a win.

Players will continue with their ordinary jobs but will have to attend training sessions when told. A chartered aircraft will take them to away matches on Sunday mornings and bring them back in time for work on Monday mornings.

EVERYTHING TO GAIN

They have absolutely nothing to lose and everything to gain while, in addition, with the keen competition that will develop for places on the 26-player staff of the professional club, the standard of soccer, generally, and of Africans, in particular will improve by leaps and bounds.

Finally, as a doctor, you do not need me to tell you that all work and no play is bad for Africans and Europeans alike, so tell your followers to snap out of it and give your blessing to the new venture.

TEDDY GORDON.

DR. BANDA REPLIES TO TEDDY GORDON

Blantyre, Thursday.

DR. HASTINGS BANDA, leader of the Malawi Congress Party, in a reply to Teddy Gordon's open letter to him on the subject of multi-racial professional soccer, points out that the African people of this country are at war just now. "They are fighting imperialism and colonialism from 6,000 miles away."

"Teddy Gordon and his colleagues should wait until after the elections" the Doctor adds. "After the elections the African people will be willing to join professional football. But it will not be multi-racial soccer then. It will be just 'soccer'."

A leader article in today's Malawi News, says that the Doctor knows as well as Teddy Gordon and his friends do that "all work and no play is bad for Africans and Europeans alike. But we would like to remind you that the African people of this country are at war just now.

They are fighting imperialism and colonialism from 6,000 — miles distant London and Federation from nearer home Salisbury. Their efforts are concentrated on this battle. They have refused in the past and will still refuse in future to allow themselves to be deviated from their goal of freedom and independence by things which they will be able to do when they are free.

"Our people are no fools. They are interested in soccer. But they are not interested in multi-racial soccer. There is no multi-racial soccer in Britain. There is soccer and that is all. The British people play together with other people from India, Africa and the West Indies. They do not call it multi-racial soccer. They call it soccer. Why should people in Central Africa be speaking about multi-racial soccer?

"Teddy Gordon writes about multi-racial soccer because the soccer he is speaking about has bad motives behind it. Like the so-called University College of Rhodesia and Nyasaland in Salisbury which is also described as "a multi-racial institution," the Rhodesia and Nyasaland Football league is purported to boost up Federation.

NOT INTERESTED

"It is aimed at proving that there is partnership between the races in Central Africa. We are not interested in partnership.

"People are people, whatever colour or race they may be. They are human beings. The question of multi-racts only obtain in artificial societies such as the ones we have in Central Africa.

One thing that is obvious from Teddy Gordon's letter, is ... that the writer has the ... of the United Federal ... which believes in the ... that does not exist ...

Who has intimidated the footballers? It is very presumptious for people to think that the African footballers in Nyasaland have no minds of their own and some people do the thinking for them and they do only what they are told to do. Africans in this country, including footballers are wide awake. They are very much unlike Africans in other parts of Central Africa. They realise that they are in a battle just now. They are fighting for their freedom. And they know that their victory in this formidable battle depends on the amount of concentration they give to the battle.

"Teddy Gordon and his colleagues should wait until after the elections. After the elections the African people will be willing to join professional football. But it will not be multi-racial soccer then. It will just be 'soccer'."

2 Feb 1961: The birth of Professional Football at the Corona Club in the presence of NFA president Eric Orton and the organising manager of the league, George Yeatman. The Blantyre team would be known as Nyasa United. So far, nine Europeans and one Asian had committed themselves: Jackie Cottingham (Callies), Dennis Pritchard (LCC), Dennis Johnston (BSC), Costas Trataris (Oly), Max Prien (Oly), George Trataris (N. Rail), Alfio Vatteroni (Cholo), Brian Todd (Corona), Matt Hoyland (LCC) and Ikram Sheriff (ISC). However, the African nationalists were preventing some Africans who showed some interest from coming forward. The result would be known as the Rhodesia and Nyasaland Football League. However, they withdrew after only two matches because of financial problems.

25 Mar. 1961: Trataris Cup: Rangeley Stadium: Alexandra Club 3–1   M. Prien (3)
Sergio Nicholas, Brian Fox, Dennis Johnston, Mann, Jackie Cottingham, French, Brian Phillips, Max Prien, Godfrey Keys, Dennis Pritchard, Peter Parker (jnr)

25 Mar. 1961: Friendly: Rangeley Stadium: Alexandra Club "B" 8–0   ?
George Trataris, Alan Geldard, Matt Hoyland, J. Hoatson, Corb, Bob Power, Peter Lewis, Rosenast, Rui Bastos, Vic Moss, Bob Rodgers

Mario Antoine

26 Mar. 1961: Friendly: Zomba Gymkhana: Alexandra Club 6–1   M. Prien (3), ?
Sergio Nicholas, Brian Fox, Dennis Johnston, Mann, Jackie Cottingham, French, Brian Phillips, Max Prien, Godfrey Keys, Dennis Pritchard, Peter Parker (jnr)

26 Mar. 1961: Bruss Cup: Zomba Gymkhana: Alexandra Club "B" 9–1   V. Moss (4), R. Bastos (3), B. Rodgers (2)
George Trataris, Alan Geldard, Matt Hoyland, J. Hoatson, Corb, Bob Power, Peter Lewis, Rosenast, Rui Bastos, Vic Moss, Bob Rodgers

1–2 Apr. 1961: South African Olympiad—6 Greek teams from Pretoria, Johannesburg, Cape Town, and Nyasaland
Travelling Squad: A. Gafforio, Cominas, Paul, Jim and A. Yiannakis, Costas Trataris, Max Prien, G. Koutsadakis, J. Hoatson, C. Nakos, Rui Bastos, Wimberger, Ruprecht, Stellious

	Hellenic Club Pretoria 4–1	M. Prien (2), R. Bastos (2)
SF:	Corinthians Johannesburg 5–4 aet	R. Bastos (3), M. Prien, Wimberger
F:	Hellenic Club Cape Town 0–1	

2 Apr. 1961: Oury Cup: Beira: Sport Lisboa e Beira 4–1   B. Phillips (3), P. Lewis
Sergio Nicholas, Matt Hoyland, Dennis Johnston, Brian Fox, Jackie Cottingham, Archie Carver, Vic Moss, Brian Phillips, Peter Lewis, Bob Power, Peter Parker (jnr)

3 Apr. 1961: Friendly: Beira: Sporting Beira 0–3
Sergio Nicholas, Matt Hoyland (sub: Mann), Dennis Johnston, Brian Fox, Jackie Cottingham, Archie Carver, Vic Moss (sub: MacDonald), Brian Phillips, Peter Lewis, Bob Power, Peter Parker (jnr) (sub: Ken Mansfield)

9 Apr. 1961: RNPFL: Salisbury: Salisbury City/United v. Nyasa United 3–1   D. Pritchard
George Trataris, Vic Moss, Mann, Matt Hoyland, Sergio Nicholas, Vic Rodkin, Hassam, Davis, Jackie Cottingham (capt.), Dennis Pritchard, Ikram Sheriff

22 Apr. 1961: SHAFL: Kings Cup Final: Red Army (S. Div) v. Ndirande Welfare Club (N. Div) 2–1   J. Sangala, G. Sembereka, M. Chikoko

23 Apr. 1961: RNPFL: Rangeley Stadium: Nyasa United v. Lusaka City 1–2   M. Prien
George Trataris, Mann, Matt Hoyland, Hassam, Peter Parker, Jackie Cottingham (capt.), Malikula, Max Prien, Costas Trataris, Brian Phillips, Malikula

Final Log

No.	Teams	P	W	D	L	F	A	PTS
1	Olympia	16	10	2	4	60	24	22
2	Callies	16	8	3	5	50	39	19
3	Zomba	16	8	2	6	35	30	18
4	Limbe CC	16	7	3	6	20	20	17
5	Cholo	16	6	3	7	40	40	15
6	Blantyre SC	16	5	4	7	33	36	14
7	Nyasaland Railways	16	5	4	7	32	42	14
8	Corona	16	5	4	7	26	49	14
9	Indian SC	16	5	1	10	28	44	11

62

29 Apr., 1961: Stanhope Cup Final: BSC: Olympia v. Callies 8–1 R. Bastos (4–1p), M. Prien (3), Wimberger, (o/g)
Olympia: A. Gafforio, Stellious, C. Nakos, Jim Yiannakis, Paul Yiannakis, J. Hoatson, Max Prien, Costas Trataris, Rui Bastos, Johnnie Ruprecht, Wimberger
Callies: Seabrook, McLean, Watt, Tommy Allen, Pat Kelly, Jackie Cottingham, Peter Parker (missing 4 players)

Footballer of the Year: Jackie Cottingham

Apr. 1961:   SHAFL AGM presented by President Ernest Kalimah
Coronation Cup: Limbe beat Cholo
Ernest Kalimah Inter Divisional Championship: Southern Division League: Ndirande Welfare Club
Season 1961 to start on 13 May 1961

7 May, 1961: Royle Cup Final: Cholo: Blantyre SC v. Olympia 4–1   Hamilton (2), B. Power, G. Keys (p), Stellious
Blantyre: Warren, Woodward, Lee, Godfrey Keys, Dennis Johnston, Bob Power, Archie Carver, Brian Phillips, Klopper, Colley, Hamilton
Olympia: Cominas Yiannakis, Stellious, C. Nakos, Jim Yiannakis, Paul Yiannakis, J. Hoatson, Max Prien, Costas Trataris, Rui Bastos, Johnnie Ruprecht, Wimberger

12 May 1961:   Nyasa United withdraw from Professional League

13–14 May 1961: Nyasaland Railways Football Trophy (Four Teams, Including Beira Champions Clube Ferroviario de Beira [CFB])
Blantyre SC: Warren, Lee, Woodward, Godfrey Keys, Dennis Johnston, Bob Power, Archie Carver, Brian Phillips, Klopper, Colley, Hamilton, Russell, Smith, Martin, Matt Hoyland, Pat Kelly
Olympia: Cominas Yiannakis, Stellious, C. Nakos, Mann, Paul Yiannakis, Costas Trataris, Johnnie Ruprecht, Jim Yiannakis, Rui Bastos, Max Prien, J. Hoatson, Wimberger, Dennis Pritchard, G. Koutsadakis, I. Grilli
Nyasaland Railways: George Trataris, Walters, French, F. De Vito, Monteiro, Reis, Mann, Paul Crossan, Jagjit Singh, Santokh Singh, Michel Melotte, Suleman, Ken Mansfield, Osborne
          Olympia v. Blantyre   5–2   M. Prien (4), I. Grilli, Colley, B. Power
          CFB v. Nyasaland Railways 6–0
3–4 PO: Blantyre v. Nyasaland Railways 3–0   M. Hoyland, Colley, P. Kelly
Final: CFB v. Olympia   3–2   D. Pritchard (2)

2 Jun. 1961: Ken Furphy, ex-Everton Player, arrives in the Country to Assist in Coaching

22 Jun. 1961: Ken Furphy Trial Match: NFA XI v. Southern Province African XI 3–0   M. Prien (2–1p), B. Fox
NFA XI: George Trataris, Mann, Matt Hoyland, Corb, Peter Lewis, Brian Fox (missing 5)
SPA XI: Graham, Ken Furphy, Roy Maliwa, Chinula, Raleigh M'manga, Katchemwa, Godfrey Kalitsiro (missing 4)

24 Jul. 1961: Ken Furphy Returns Home

30 Sep. 1961: Friendly: Corona Club: Callies v. Raylton (SR) 3–1   McDonald (2), P. Parker, H. Paton
Callies: George Trataris, John Cotton, McLean, Dennis Pritchard, Jackie Cottingham, Sfendilis, Peter Parker, Johnny Hawthorne, McDonald, Archie Cottingham, French

1 Oct. 1961: Friendly: Corona Club: NFA President XI v. Callies/Raylton XI 4–0   Cravetti, R. Leo, V. Rodkin, McDonald

NFA President XI: Iaccuci, Mann, Matt Hoyland, Dennis Johnson, Buchan, Littlejohn, Hassam, Max Prien, Ken Mansfield, Peter Crossan, Jagjit Singh
Callies/Raylton: Henny Grobbelaar, Vic Haupt, Alec Blair, Dennis Pritchard, Blair Esson, Jackie Cottingham, Cravetti, Rex Leo, McDonald, Vic Rodkin, Peter Parker
I.O. Adam Shield: Winners Red Bombers

1962

Indian Sports Club, who were one of the pioneers of the league, became the latest team to withdraw from the Royle League, reducing it to eight teams. Limbe Country Club, who won their only title in 1957, had four more points and took the lead over Blantyre SC at this time.

Previous years' beaten finalist, Olympia regained this trophy when they beat Callies by 5–2 in the Royle Cup final.

Blantyre SC captured the Stanhope Cup for the fifth time when Callies lost their second successive final 2–1, improving from their disastrous show the previous year.

A third knockout trophy, the Franklin Cup, was introduced, with Olympia grabbing their second cup of the season, beating Blantyre SC 2–1.

The historical date of 15 October saw the inaugural full international against Ghana.

The governor's cup was revived after three years' absence.

Twelve players were involved in the first two international fixtures. Ten players who played in both fixtures are Llewellen Kishombe, Bright Gondwe, Lewis Chinula, Oliver Nakhumwa, Royee Maliwa, Raleigh M'manga, Smart Thipa, Richard Banda, Godfrey Kalitsiro, and James Sangala, and De Mobray Thipa and Nathan Gondwe played in one each. It is possible that three players—James Sangala, Godfrey Kalitsiro, and Royee Maliwa—were in the 1957 tour of South Africa and Southern Rhodesia. This is in need of confirmation, as their last names appear in the squad list, their first names excluded.

1962 Timeline

1 Jan. 1962: BSC: Scotland v. The Rest 5–5   J. Allan (4), Watt, R. Bastos (3), D. Pritchard, French
Scotland: Warren, McLean, Buchan, Archie Muir, Jackie Cottingham, Matt Hoyland, J. Allan, Bain, Tommy Allen, Littlejohn, Archie Cottingham, Watt
The Rest: George Trataris, John Cotton, Dennis Johnston, Dennis Pritchard, Costas Trataris, Brian Fox, Jim Yiannakis, Rui Bastos, Max Prien, French, Bob Rodgers **Reserves:** Dettmar, Ken Mansfield, Ronnie King, Michel Melotte

13 Jan. 1962: Cholo: Franklin Cup Final: Olympia v. Blantyre 2–1   McIntosh, L. Colandria, B. Rodgers
Olympia: A. Gafforio, McIntosh, C. Nakos, Paul Yiannakis, Costas Trataris, Johnnie Ruprecht, Jim Yiannakis, Rui Bastos, Max Prien, Lourenco Colandria, Joaquim Cunha
Blantyre SC: Sergio Nicholas, Ken Thomson, Woodward, Bob Power, Dennis Johnston, Lee, Harold Wrigley (jnr), Archie Muir, Archie Carver, Bob Rodgers, Colley, M. Bowery

14 Jan. 1962:   **Vic Rodkin 6-a-Side Shield:**   **Olympia v. Zomba 4–1**   **M. Prien (3)**

Final Log

No.	Teams	P	W	D	L	F	A	PTS
1	Limbe CC	14	11	2	1	41	16	24
2	Blantyre SC	14	9	2	3	40	20	20
3	Callies	14	9	1	4	36	19	19
4	Olympia	14	6	2	6	42	21	14
5	Nyasaland Railways	14	6	1	7	31	24	13
6	Cholo	14	3	3	8	34	49	9
7	Corona	14	2	5	7	18	46	9
8	Zomba	14	1	2	11	17	64	4

Footballer of the Year: Godfrey Keys

24 Mar. 1962: Stanhope Cup Final: Blantyre SC v. Callies 2–1 aet   **B. Power (p), A. Carver, T. Allen**
Blantyre: Sergio Nicholas, Woodward, Ken Thomson, Dennis Johnston, M. Bowery, Lee, Bob Power, Archie Carver, Brian Phillips (missing 2)
Callies: George Trataris, John Cotton, McLean, Costas Trataris, Jackie Cottingham, Tommy Allen, Johnny Hawthorne, Stellious, Archie Cottingham, McDonald (missing 1)

31 Mar. 1962: Royle Cup Final: Limbe CC: Olympia v. Callies 5–2   **R. Bastos (3), M. Prien, J. Cunha, J. Hawthorne, McDonald**
Olympia: A. Gafforio, Ronnie King, F. De Vito, Jim Yiannakis, Max Prien, Rui Bastos, Joaquim Cunha, Lorenco Colandria, Paul Yiannakis, Johnnie Ruprecht (missing 1)
Callies: George Trataris, Webster, John Cotton, Costas Trataris, Jackie Cottingham, Tommy Allen, Johnny Hawthorne, Archie Cottingham, McDonald (missing 2)

14–15 Apr. 1962: NFA 4-Team Tournament Due to Cancellation of Alexandra Tour
Olympia v. Blantyre SC 5–1   ;   **Callies v. Limbe 1–0**
3rd/4th PO   **Blantyre SC v. Limbe CC 2–2**   Colley (2), K. Mansfield, J. Lowery
Final: **Olympia v. Callies 5–2**   M. Prien (3), R. Bastos (p), McIntosh, King, A. Cottingham

21 Apr. 1962: Oury Cup: Rangeley Stadium: **Sport Lisboa e Beira 2–1**   **B. Fox, D. Pritchard**
Sergio Nicholas, John Cotton, Dennis Johnston, Brian Fox, Jackie Cottingham, Bill Keddie, Mann, Brian Phillips, Dennis Pritchard, Bob Power, Peter West

22 Apr. 1962: Friendly: Limbe CC: **Sport Lisboa e Beira 4–1**   **B. Fox (2), T. Mills (2)**
A. Gafforio, John Cotton, Dennis Johnston, Brian Fox, Ken Mansfield, Bill Keddie, Terry Mills, Brian Phillips, Dennis Pritchard, Michel Melotte, Peter West

1 May 1962: LCC: Champions (Limbe CC) v. The Rest   **2–1**   **J. Pieterse, Mann, T. Mills**
Limbe CC: Cominas Yiannakis, Alan Geldard, Bill Keddie, J. Pieterse, Dennis Pritchard, Matt Hoyland, Jack Lowery, Brian Fox, Brian Phillips, Mann, Reid
The Rest: Sergio Nicholas, Grilli, Dettmar, Bob Power, Jackie Cottingham, Terry Mills, Peter West, Dennis Harris, Don Meintzies, Santokh Singh, Ken Mansfield

26 May 1962: Friendly: Rangeley Stadium: Salisbury Callies 1–1   R. Bastos
Sergio Nicholas, I. Grilli, Dennis Johnston, Brian Fox, Rui Bastos, Bill Keddie, Max Prien, Brian Phillips, Dennis Pritchard, Joaquim Cunha, Peter West

26 May 1962: Friendly: Rangeley Stadium: Salisbury Callies "B" 1–3   ?
B. McArdle, John Cotton, Jim Yiannakis, Bob Power, Michel Melotte, Jackie Cottingham, Terry Mills, Lorenco Colandria, Dettmar, Ken Mansfield, Don Mientjies,

27 May 1962: Friendly: Cholo SC: Salisbury Callies 0–9
Sergio Nicholas, I. Grilli, Dennis Johnston, Brian Fox, Rui Bastos, Bill Keddie, Max Prien, Brian Phillips, Dennis Pritchard, Joaquim Cunha, Peter West

27 May 1962: Friendly: Cholo SC: Salisbury Callies "B" 1–0   M. Hoyland
A. Gafforio, Mann, Jim Yiannakis, Matt Hoyland, Michel Melotte, Jackie Cottingham, Terry Mills, Lorenco Colandria, Dettmar, Ken Mansfield, Don Mientjies

6 Jun. 1962: Friendly: Rangeley Stadium: West Ham United 0–4
Sergio Nicholas, Tommy Prentice, Dennis Johnston, Brian Fox, Rui Bastos, Jackie Cottingham, Max Prien, Brian Phillips, Dennis Pritchard, Terry Mills, Tommy Ballantyne

Graham Edwards Sponsored by British Council to Coach in the Three Provinces from 04 July to 17 August; SP 4 to 15 July and 02 to 17 August, CP 25 July to 01 August, NP 16 to 24 July (thereafter the NAFA National Team)

16 Jun. 1962: Friendly: Tete: Clube de Tete   3–3
Cominas Yiannakis (Limbe CC), Januaro D'Magalhaes—capt. (Rovers), Johnnie Ruprecht (Olympia), Michel Melotte (Nyasaland Railways), S. Damalakis (Callies), J. Pieterse (Limbe CC), Joaquim Cunha (Olympia), Lorenco Colandria (Olympia), Haroon Karim (Rovers), Allaudin Osman (Rovers), Don Meintjies (Rovers)

17 Jun. 1962: Friendly: Tete: Desportivo de Tete   3–1   S. Nicholas, J. Cunha, J. Ruprecht
Cominas Yiannakis (Limbe CC), Januaro D'Magalhaes (Rovers), Ronnie King (Callies), Lorenco Colandria (Olympia), S. Damalakis (Callies), Johnnie Ruprecht-capt (Olympia), Michel Melotte (Nyasaland Railways), (sub J. Pieterse (Limbe CC), Joaquim Cunha (Olympia), Sergio Nicholas (Blantyre SC) (sub Haroon Karim [Rovers]), Allaudin Osman (Rovers), Don Meintjies (Rovers)

24 Jun. 1962: Inter Districts Football Final: London & Blantyre Cup: (Rangeley Stadium)
Blantyre v. Dowa 7–0   W. Sangala (3–1p), R. Banda (2), S. Thipa, J. Sangala

1 Jul. 1962: Southern Province African Football Association Chilembwe Cup: (Rangeley Stadium)
SHAFL v. Limbe African Football League (LAFL) 2–1   J. Sangala, S. Thipa, C. Msiya
SHAFL: Gondwe, B. Phombeya, Richard Banda, Smart Thipa (capt.), De Mobray Thipa
LAFL: Joseph Leno Chauluka (goalkeeper), Crighton Msiya

14 Jul. 1962: Governor's Trophy: Zomba
SP (Southern Section) v. SP (Northern Section) 2–2 Central Province v. Northern Province 1–0

15 Jul. 1962: Rangeley Stadium   SP "B" v. NP   3–0   Macemva, W. Sangala (o/g)
                                            SP "A" v. CP   3–2 aet   G. Kalitsiro (3)–F. Chitenje, Zimba

4 Aug. 1962: Coronation Cup Final: (Rangeley Stadium)   SHAFL v. LAFL 9–1   R. Banda (6–1p), W. Sangala (2), J. Sangala, Karoh
SHAFL: Sazuze (gk), Chinula, B. Phombeya, Bright Gondwe, Wesley Sangala, Richard Banda, Smart Thipa, James Sangala

10 Aug. 1962: Brief Report from Graham Edwards: Astounded by the Ignorance of the Elementary Rules of the Game in the Central and Northern Regions and Surprised about the Two Separate Leagues

02 Sep. 1962: Rangeley Stadium: NFA Invitation XI v. SHAFL 2–2   M. Prien, Dettmar, R. Banda (2)
NFA XI: George Trataris, John Cotton, Dennis Johnston, Matt Hoyland, Jackie Cottingham, Brian Fox, Terry Mills, Brian Phillips, Max Prien, John Brown, Dettmar
SHAFL: Sazuze, Chinula, Msamu, B. Phombeya, Mkalyainga Sitoro, Bright Gondwe, Wesley Sangala, Smart Thipa, Richard Banda, De Mobray Thipa, James Sangala

30 Sep. 1962: Rangeley Stadium: NFA Champions Limbe CC v. SHAFL 7–0   J. Pieterse (3), Chalmers (2), B. Keddie, J. Brown
Limbe CC: A. Gafforio, Alan Geldard, Matt Hoyland, Dennis Pritchard, Bill Keddie, Brian Fox, J. Pieterse, Brian Phillips, Chalmers, John Brown, Osborne
SHAFL: Sazuze, Chinula, Raleigh M'manga, B. Phombeya, Mkalyainga Sitoro, Bright Gondwe, Wesley Sangala, Smart Thipa, Richard Banda, De Mobray Thipa, James Sangala

15 Oct. 1962: Friendly: Rangeley Stadium: Ghana   0–12
Llewellen Kishombe, Bright Gondwe, Lewis Chinula, Oliver Nakhumwa, Royee Maliwa, Raleigh M'manga, Nathan Gondwe, Smart Thipa, Richard Banda, Godfrey Kalitsiro, James Sangala   **Coach:**   Dennis Johnston

8 Dec. 1962: Friendly: Dar es Salaam: Tanganyika   2–6   G. Kalitsiro, S. Thipa
Llewellen Kishombe, Bright Gondwe, Lewis Chinula, Oliver Nakhumwa, Royee Maliwa, Raleigh M'manga, De Mobray Thipa, Smart Thipa, Richard Banda, Godfrey Kalitsiro, James Sangala   **Coach:**   Dennis Johnston

SHAFL: Coca-Cola Winners: Ndirande Welfare

I.O. Adam Shield: Winners Red Bombers

Local teams humble Malawi Stars

By LEVSON LIFIKILO

Blantyre, Thursday.

THE Shire Highlands African Football League beat the visiting Malawi Stars soccer team from Salisbury by the odd goal in five in a friendly match played at the Rangeley Stadium on Saturday.

S.H.A.F.L. took the lead when, in the 20th minute, J. Sangala made no mistake to bang home from a corner kick.

After five minutes S.H.A.F.L. scored their second goal which James Sangala engineered when he collected the ball from the middle-field and, after working well, passed to skipper Smart Thipa who wasted no time to centre the ball near the goal mouth where unmarked R. Banda (Shoeshine) found it easy to head home.

In the 40th minute the visiting Malawi Stars were awarded a penalty kick for hand ball and Julieta scored to reduce the deficit to 2-1.

Five minutes later S.H.A.F.L. put the issue beyond doubt when a systematic inter-pass movement found J. Sangala passing to S. Thipa who crossed the ball near the goal mouth to R. Banda (Shoeshine) who, with the Malawi Stars goalkeeper coming towards him, sent a rocket-like shot into the empty net.

In the 50th minute the Malawi Stars reduced the lead further with a well taken goal and the final whistle found the home team winning 3-2.

At Zomba on Sunday the Malawi Stars lost to Zomba United 6-4.

1963

There was another withdrawal from the Royle League as Callies, after two seasons, called it a day, but their replacement was Rovers, a mixed-race team. Country Club Limbe retained their title, with Olympia taking the runners-up position.

Railways reached their first ever cup final and narrowly lost to League Champions Limbe CC, 4–3.

This was the second successive cup final for Railways, who were first-time winners against Cholo, 2–1, in the Franklin Cup.

Cholo were once more losing finalists against Olympia in the 6–3 Stanhope final.

1963 Timeline

1 Jan. 1963:   Scotland v. The Rest 3–3   **A. Muir (2), P. Crossan, M. Prien (2), C. Trataris**

07 Feb. 1963:   Mzuzu Football League AGM
Chairman K. Nyasulu, Vice Chairman B. Lungu, Secretary A. Ndovi, Vice Secretary J. Msowoya, Treasurer M. Nyirenda, Vice Treasurer: M. Hara

NAFA's first proper tour of Northern Rhodesia saw a squad of fifteen players travel, and they played their third international fixture as well as two other matches against Copperbelt and Midlands. Eight new players were introduced: Noel Nthala, F. Tembo, Stanley Bweya, Emmanuel Gondwe, Lameck Phiri, L. Mhango, Mkalanyinga Sitoro, and Joseph Leno Chauluka. The seven retained players were Royee Maliwa, De Mobray Thipa, Oliver Nakhumwa, Raleigh M'manga, James Sangala, Smart Thipa, and Richard Banda

16 Mar. 1963: Franklin Cup Final: Cholo: Railways v. Cholo 2–1   S. Singh, M. Melotte, Dettmar
Railways: Ishmail Khamisa, John Cotton, French, Jagjit Singh, F. De Vito, Peter Crossan, Ken Mansfield, Ikram Sheriff, Michel Melotte, Santokh Singh, George Antoine
Cholo: George Trataris, McLean, Toyne, H. Tait, G. Florini, Dettmar, Terry Mills, Frank Rodgers, L. Ferguson, Johnny Hawthorne, Walter Nicholls

Final Log

No.	Teams	P	W	D	L	F	A	PTS
1	Limbe CC	14	10	1	3	47	21	21
2	Olympia	14	10	0	4	53	22	20
3	Blantyre SC	14	8	1	5	45	31	17
4	Nyasaland Railways	14	7	2	5	38	29	16
5	Rovers	14	7	2	5	55	46	16
6	Cholo	14	7	0	7	46	39	14
7	Corona	14	2	1	11	16	72	5
8	Zomba	14	1	1	12	15	55	3

Footballer of the Year: Jackie Cottingham

6 Apr. 1963: Stanhope Cup Final: CCL: Olympia v. Cholo 6–3   O. Kalitsiro (3), M. Prien (2), C. Trataris, Dettmar (2)   T. Mills
Olympia: Cominas Yiannakis, B. Phombeya, Costas Trataris, Jackie Cottingham, G. Koutsadakis, Sangala, Godfrey Kalitsiro, Max Prien, Paul Yiannakis, Oresti Yiannakis (missing 1)
Cholo: George Trataris, Lewis Chinula, McLean, H. Tait, I. Grilli, L. Ferguson, Frank Rodgers, Dettmar, Terry Mills, G. Florini, Walter Nicholl

7 Apr. 1963: Coca Cola Final: Ndirande Welfare v. Abrahams 5–1   D. Thipa (2), W. Sangala (2), J. Sangala (p), R. Banda

7 Apr. 1963: Vic Rodkin 6-a-Side: BSC: Entry of 12 teams, 3 in each group
SF: Blantyre SC v. Railways   4–2;   Olympia v. Rovers 4–0
Final: Olympia v. Blantyre SC   3–1   M. Prien (2), G. Kalitsiro, T. Mills

13 Apr. 1963: Friendly: Rangeley Stadium: SHFL XI v. Malawi Stars (SR)   3–2 R. Banda (2), J. Sangala
R. Kapote, Royee Maliwa, Mobray de Thipa, B. Phombeya, Mkalanyinga Sitoro, Lewis Chinula, Smart Thipa, Richard Banda, James Sangala, Wesley Sangala, Godfrey Kalitsiro   Reserves: Albert Nsewa, Mdoka, Berson, Ndulilo, James Kunyenge

13 Apr. 1963: Oury Cup: Beira: Sport Lisboa e Beira 1–2   B. Rodgers
George Trataris, John Cotton, Dennis Johnston, Brian Fox, Jackie Cottingham, Hugh Smith, Michel Melotte, Peter Crossan, Dennis Pritchard, L. Ferguson, Bob Rodgers

13 Apr. 1963: Friendly: Corona Invitation XI "B" v. Mabelreign Rovers "B" 8–1
Ishmail Khamisa, Ibrahim Mojoo, H. Tait, J. Petersie, Ken Thomson, Don Meintzies, Patrick De Silva, A. Lawrence, Allaudin Osman, Ikram Sheriff, Mike Bowery

13 Apr. 1963: Friendly: Corona Invitation XI "A" v. Mabelreign Rovers "A" 1–1   J. Lowery
T. Koutsadakis, Watt, Matt Hoyland, Canham, Harold Davies, French, Walter Nicholls, Lee, Johnny Hawthorne, Brian Phillips, Peter West

14 Apr. 1963: Friendly: Zomba Gymkhana: Zomba United v. Malawi Stars (SR)   6–4 O. Mkandawire (2), F. Chitenje, Mdala (unknown 2 scorers)
Michel, Mdala, Elijah Joshua, Kamlaza, Jere, Raleigh, Kuyere, Frazer Chitenje, Overton Mkandawire, Daudi, Chimwaza

14 Apr. 1963: Friendly: Beira: Beira Railways 2–2   L. Ferguson, D. Pritchard
George Trataris, John Cotton, Dennis Johnston, Bob Power, Jackie Cottingham, Franco Bregger, Michel Melotte, Brian Phillips, Dennis Pritchard, L. Ferguson, Bob Rodgers

14 Apr. 1963: Friendly: Corona Invitation XI "B" v. Mabelreign Rovers "B" 1–4
Ishmail Khamisa, Januaro de Magalhaes, Ramsker, J. Petersie, Ken Thomson, F. De Vito, Patrick De Silva, Jagjit Singh, S. Munian, Ikram Sheriff, M. Bowery

14 Apr. 1963: Friendly: Corona Invitation XI "A" v. Mabelreign Rovers "A" 4–1   A. Osman (3), B. Phillips
Sergio Nicholas, Davies, Matt Hoyland, Johnny Hawthorne, Dennis Johnston, Don Meintzies, Jack Lowery, Lee, Brian Phillips, Allaudin Osman, Peter West

20 Apr. 1963: Royle Cup Final: Limbe CC v. Railways 4–3   Chalmers, D. Pritchard, B. Phillips, J. Lowery, I. Sheriff (2), S. Singh
Limbe: Ian Royan, Bill Keddie, Hugh Smith, J. Petersie, Dennis Pritchard, Brian Fox, Jack Lowery, Brian Phillips, Chalmers, Bukoke, D. Gibbs
Railways: Ishmail Khamisa, John Cotton, F. de Vito, Jagjit Singh, French, Michel Melotte, Peter Crossan, Santokh Singh, Ken Mansfield, Ikram Sheriff, George Antoine

27 Apr. 1963: CCL: Champions Limbe CC v. The Rest 1–1   J. Petersie, F. Rodgers
Limbe CC: Ian Royan, Hugh Smith, Bill Keddie, J. Petersie, Jack Lowery, Bukoke, Brian Phillips, Brian Fox, Dennis Pritchard, Chalmers, D. Gibbs
The Rest: John Johnson, John Cotton, Januaro de Magalhaes, John Brown, Costas Trataris, Frank Rodgers, Peter Crossan, Jackie Cottingham, L. Ferguson, Ken Mansfield, Michel Melotte

18 May 1963: Friendly: Portuguese Association Select v. De Sportivo Clube de Tete 4–0 A. Osman (2), D. Pritchard (p), J. Petersie
Cominas Yiannakis, Januaro de Magalhaes, Dennis Pritchard, Allaudin Osman, Don Meintzies, Jackie Cottingham, J. Petersie, Joaquim Cunha, Lorenco Colandria, Michel Melotte, John Cotton

19 May 1963: Friendly: NFA Select v. De Sportivo Clube de Tete 0–1
Cominas Yiannakis, Januaro Magalhaes, Bob Rodgers, John Brown, Dennis Johnston, John Cotton, Brian Fox, Joaquim Cunha, Lorenco Colandria, Michel Melotte, Allaudin Osman

25 May 1963: Rangeley Stadium: Southern Region Inter District Junior Final: Limbe AFL v. Mlanje 6-2
Limbe: John, Nkhani, Phumbi, Phwalambwa, Bright Banda, Waya, Steven, Guga, Libalo, Malinki, Kasungwi

Mzuzu v. Lilongwe 4-0

25 May 1963: Rangeley Stadium: Southern Region Inter District Final: Limbe AFL v. Cholo 5-0
Limbe: Joseph Leno Chauluka, Wanje, Joseph, Malenga, Roman Bwanali, Walamwa, D. Njema, Dama, Nyirenda, Crighton Msiya, Cullen Mwase

Lilongwe v. Mzuzu 9-0

2 Jun. 1963: Rangeley Stadium: National Inter Districts Junior Finals: Limbe AFL v. Mzuzu
2 Jun. 1963: Rangeley Stadium: National Inter Districts Finals: Limbe AFL v. Lilongwe

19 Jun. 1963: Friendly: Rangeley Stadium: Dundee United 2-10   D. Meintjies, A. Osman
George Trataris, John Cotton (sub Jackie Cottingham), Dennis Johnston, Allaudin Osman, Bill Keddie, Brian Fox, Michel Melotte (sub Costas Trataris), Brian Phillips, Dennis Pritchard, Don Meintjies, John Brown

29 Jun. 1963: Kamuzu Cup: Rangeley Stadium
Southern Region (Northern Section) v. Central Region 2-1
Northern Region v. Southern Region (Southern Section) 3-2

30 Jun. 1963: Kamuzu Cup Final: Rangeley Stadium
Northern Region v. Southern Region (Northern Section) 2-1   S. Gondwe (2), R. Banda

27 Jul. 1963: SHAFL Reaches Halfway Stage and Partial Log Table as Follows:
Northern Division: Ndirande Welfare 14 points, Michiru Castles 12 points
Southern Division: NESCOM United 11 points, Red Army "A" 10 points, Abrahams 9 points (Red Army "A" and Abrahams a game in hand)

29 September 1963: SHAFL Log Tables (incomplete)

Northern Division

No.	Teams	P	W	D	L	F	A	PTS
1	Ndirande Welfare	14	12	2	0	26	06	26
2	Michiru Castles	14	11	1	2	34	09	23
3	Coca Cola	12	6	1	5	24	21	13
4	Highlanders	11	5	1	5	18	14	11
5	Republic	10	3	2	5	13	12	8
6	Wenela Red Stars	10	1	4	5	08	24	6
7	Young Tigers	11	0	3	8	07	20	3
8	B.A.T.	10	0	2	8	03	27	2

Southern Division

No.	Teams	P	W	D	L	F	A	PTS
1	N.E.S.C.O.M. Utd	14	12	1	1	32	09	25
2	Red Army "A"	14	8	3	3	37	15	19
3	Zingwangwa Nationals	11	8	0	3	21	15	16
4	Abrahams	14	7	2	5	12	18	16
5	Zingwangwa Voters	13	6	2	5	16	23	14
6	Red Army "B"	12	4	2	6	13	22	10
7	Laing & Roberts Giants	12	2	0	10	07	35	4
8	Police	14	0	0	14	00	01	0

4 Oct. 1963: I. O. Adam Shield QF: Red Bombers holders for last two seasons
FMB v. ITC "B"   Postals v. Kandjeza

5 Oct. 1963: I. O. Adam Shield QF: NTC v. Police   Red Bombers v. ITC "A"

11 Oct. 1963: Friendly: Luanshya: Copperbelt XI 4–5   E. Gondwe (2), J. Sangala, ?
Joseph Leno Chauluka, Royee Maliwa, Mkalanyinga Sitoro, Mobray de Thipa, Oliver Nakhumwa, Raleigh M'manga, Stanley Bweya, James Sangala, Richard Banda, Emmanuel Gondwe, Smart Thipa   **Officials: K. Thipa, S. Chikafa, P. Muwamba**

13 Oct. 1963: Friendly: Ndola: Northern Rhodesia 1–5   S. Bweya
Noel Nthala, Royee Maliwa, F. Tembo, Mobray de Thipa, Oliver Nakhumwa, Raleigh M'manga, Stanley Bweya, James Sangala, Richard Banda, Emmanuel Gondwe, Lameck Phiri   **Officials: K. Thipa, S. Chikafa, P. Muwamba**

15 Oct. 1963: Friendly: Lusaka: Midlands 2–8   M. De Thipa, R. Banda
Noel Nthala, Royee Maliwa, F. Tembo, Mobray de Thipa, Oliver Nakhumwa, Raleigh M'manga, Stanley Bweya, James Sangala, Richard Banda, Emmanuel Gondwe, Lameck Phiri   **Officials: K. Thipa, S. Chikafa, P. Muwamba**

18 Oct. 1963: Football Association Northern Region Formed
President M. Nyasulu, Secretary A. Ndovi, Treasurer: H. Chilongo

1964

The last season under the administration of the NFA saw Limbe CC became the first team to win the Royle League for three consecutive seasons. Olympia were suspended from the league and withdrew after five seasons.

It seemed to be Country Club Limbe's year, as they beat Blantyre Sports Club in the Royle Cup Final by 4–3.

It was a treble season for Limbe CC as Blantyre SC were thrashed 5–2 after extra time in the Stanhope Cup final.

Rovers, in only their second season, prevented Limbe CC being the first ever team to win all four trophies in the same season as they won 4–2.

A historic moment in Malawi football took place at the Nyasaland Football Association Annual General Meeting held at Blantyre Sports Club on Thursday, 24 September 1964, when the association was dissolved to be replaced by a new body. Proposed names such as Inter Club Football League and Southern Region League were to be sent to the director of sports, Mr Augustine Chavura. The name "City and Suburban League" was eventually approved on 20 October 1964, a historic day.

Malawi played three internationals during the year and introduced eleven new players, with James Kaminjolo, the 1957 captain of the South Africa and Southern Rhodesia tour, being recalled after his return from overseas study.

Kaminjolo also made history as he became the first indigenous Malawian player to have represented both national teams, NFA and NAFA.

The newcomers were George Linzie, D. Njema, Robert Kalembo, Simon Kapalamula, Hastings Nsewa, Charles Nyirongo, Sheke, Wales Juma, Fraser Chitenje, Overton Mkandawire, and Roman Bwanali.

Although ten players had been in the squad before, only three of them—Oliver Nakhumwa, Royee Maliwa, and Raleigh M'manga—were there from the onset.

1964 Timeline

1 Jan. 1964: Scotland v. The Rest   2–5   P. Crossan, L. Ferguson, S. Singh (2), P. Isham, B. Fox, ?
Scotland: Ian Royan, McCreadie, Bill Keddie, Jackie Cottingham, P. Crossan, L. Ferguson (missing 5)
The Rest: Cominas Yiannakis, Costas Trataris, Rosenast, Joaquim Cunha, Paul Yiannakis, Paul Isham, Santokh Singh, Brian Fox, Dennis Pritchard (missing 2)

11 Jan. 1964: King's Cup Final: N.E.S.C.O.M. Utd v. Red Army "A"   3–1   R. Kapote, J. Zefa, Dave (p), ?

1 Feb. 1964: Franklin Cup Final: Rovers v. Limbe CC 4–2   A. Osman (3), J. Kaminjolo, J. Petersie (2)
Rovers: E. Pheruwa, Januaro Magalhaes, Ernie Stuart, Sharpe, Kirby Thomson, Royee Maliwa, Basil Malila, James Kaminjolo, Allaudin Osman, Lameck Phiri, Crighton Msiya
Limbe CC: Ian Royan, Chalmers, Hugh Smith, Bill Keddie, Paul Isham, Brian Fox, Adam McKinley, Brian Phillips, J. Petersie, Dennis Pritchard, Robin Imray

1 Mar. 1964: Inter-Regional Tournament to Select National Team
Southern Region (Southern Section—SS) v. Northern Region 3–2   W. Juma (2–1p), H. Nsewa, Chipasula (2–1p)
Southern Region (SS B) v. Northern Region B   2–1   Kagwa (2), Mtumuka

7–8 Mar. 1964: Inter-Regional Tournament to Select National Team

Southern Region (SS) v. Central Region 7–2   G. Kalitsiro (4), W. Juma, D. Njema, H. Nsewa, Bota, S. Bweya
Southern Region (SS B) v. Central Region B 2–0   Tsonga, Tyangatyanga
Southern Region (NS) v. Northern Region 6–4   O. Mkandawire (4), S. Kapalamula, Chimwaza, E. Gondwe, Mhango, Nyirongo, Shake
Southern Region (NS B) v. Northern Region B 6–3

Final Log

No.	Teams	P	W	D	L	F	A	PTS
1	Limbe CC	11	8	2	1	53	19	18
2	Corona	11	6	3	2	33	19	15
3	Blantyre SC	10	6	0	4	36	23	12
4	Nyasaland Railways	11	5	1	5	39	26	11
5	Rovers	11	4	0	7	27	39	8
6	Zomba	11	3	2	6	25	47	8
7	Cholo	11	2	0	9	16	56	4

Olympia were suspended from the league as a result of a disciplinary action taken against them after their fixture against Limbe CC was abandoned when Smart Thipa refused to leave the field after being sent off. At that time, they had played eleven games and their record was W6 D1 L4 F34 A15, and all their results were declared null and void.

23 Mar. 1964: Vic Rodkin 6-a-Side Shield

SF: Corona "A" v. Corona "B" 5–2   M. Prien (4), H. Nsewa, G. Antoine (2)
    Railways "B" v. Blantyre SC "A" 5–0
F: Corona "A" v. Railways "B" 8–1   H. Nsewa (5–1p), M. Prien (2), J. Cottingham, J. Cunha

CORONA 'A' who won the six-a-side soccer tournament on Sunday (l. to r. V. Rodkin, M. Prien, O. Yiannakis, H. Nsewa, A. Nsewa, J. Cottingham.

27 Mar. 1964: Oury Cup: Limbe CC: Sport Lisboa e Beira 1–2   D. Pritchard
George Trataris, Chalmers, Hugh Smith, Joaquim Cunha, Jackie Cottingham, Bill Keddie, Philip Bradley, James Kaminjolo, Dennis Pritchard, Ikram Sheriff, John Brown

28 Mar. 1964: Friendly: Blantyre SC: Sport Lisboa e Beira 4–1   I. Sheriff, S. Singh, J. de Magalaes, B. Keddie
Cominas Yiannakis, Chalmers, Hugh Smith, Santokh Singh, Jackie Cottingham, Bill Keddie, Januaro de Magalaes, James Kaminjolo, Dennis Pritchard, Ikram Sheriff, Paul Yiannakis

28 Mar. 1964:   Footballer of the Year: Bill Keddie

4 Apr. 1964:   Stanhope Cup Final: BSC: Limbe CC v. Blantyre SC 5–2 aet   D. Pritchard (3), B. Phillips (2), T. Mills, P. Bradley
Limbe CC: Ian Royan, Hugh Smith, Chalmers, Paul Isham, Bill Keddie, Brian Fox, Bob Rodgers, Dennis Pritchard, J. Petersie, Brian Phillips, Robin Imray
Blantyre SC: Bolo, Carham, Costas Trataris, John Brown, Graham, Harold Wrigley (jnr), Terry Mills, Phillip Bradley, Ken Thomson, Fraser, Wood

5 Apr. 1964:   Amazon Cup Final: SHAFL v. Limbe AFL 4–2 aet   W. Juma (3), Kagwa, C. Msiya, Dama

11 Apr. 1964: Royle Cup Final: CCL: Limbe CC v. Blantyre SC 4–3   D. Pritchard, P. Isham, B. Rodgers, (o/g), P. Bradley (2), J. Brown (p)
Limbe CC: Ian Royan, Hugh Smith, Chalmers, Paul Isham, Bill Keddie, Brian Fox, Bob Rodgers, Dennis Pritchard, J. Petersie, Brian Phillips, Robin Imray
Blantyre SC: Bolo, Carham, Costas Trataris, John Brown, Graham, Harold Wrigley (jnr), Terry Mills, Phillip Bradley, Ken Thomson, Fraser, Wood

11 Apr. 1964:   Red Army FC AGM

Chairman F. Mphepo   Vice Chairman Gongolo
Secretary D. Chiyongo   Vice Secretary J. Kapalamula
Treasurer P. Kupilingu   Vice Treasurer Jali
"A" captain: Kagwa   "A" vice captain: E. Mtawali
"B" captain: Kachokola   "B" vice captain: Takomana
Organising Secretary: L. Kunyenge
Committee members: Shoe, E. Zingwangwa, Dave, William

25 Apr. 1964: Champions v. The Rest: Limbe CC v. The Rest 2–2   D. Pritchard, Chalmers–P. Bradley, H. Karim
Limbe CC: Ian Royan, Hugh Smith, Chalmers, Paul Isham, Bill Keddie, Brian Fox (capt.), Matt Hoyland, Dennis Pritchard, J. Petersie, Brian Phillips, Robin Imray
The Rest: Cominas Yiannakis (Corona), Dennis Johnston (Zomba—capt.), Januaro Magalhaes (Rovers), Ken Mansfield (Railways), Costas Trataris (BSC), Dettmar (Cholo), Haroon Karim (Railways), James Kaminjolo (Rovers), Phillip Bradley (BSC), Ikram Sheriff (Railways), Joaquim Cunha (Railways)

2 May 1964: Stoffel Trophy: Beira: Clube Ferroviario de Beira v. Nyasaland Railways 1–3 I. Sheriff (2), H. Karim

3 May 1964:   Friendly: Beira: Sports Lisboa e Beira v. Nyasaland Railways   4–1

29 May 1964: **Limbe African Football League AGM**

President M. Kachisi   Vice President J. Mwasinga
Secretary A. Kagasu   Vice Secretary B. Chirwa
Treasurer K. Taumbe   Vice Treasurer L. Bwanali

5 Jun. 1964: Change of Stadium Name from Rangeley to Central

20 Jun. 1964: Friendly: Central Stadium: Southern Rhodesia 1–3   W. Juma
Llewellen Kishombe, George Linzie, D. Njema, Mkalanyinga Sitoro, Robert Kalembo, Simon Kapalamula, Henry Nsewa, Charles Nyirongo, James Sangala, Shake, Wales Juma   **Official:**   **Augustine Chavura**

21 Jun. 1964: Friendly: Central Stadium: Southern Rhodesia 2–2   E. Gondwe, R. M'manga
Noel Nthala, Royee Maliwa, Roman Bwanali, Frazer Chitenje, Oliver Nakhumwa, Raleigh M'manga, Stanley Bweya, James Kaminjolo, Overton Mkandawire, Emmanuel Gondwe, Godfrey Kalitsiro   **Official:**   **Augustine Chavura**

27 Jun. 1964: Coca Cola Final: Red Army "A" v. Ndirande Welfare 1–1 aet   E. Mtawali, J. Sangala
Ndirande Welfare: Juwa, James Kaminjolo, Raleigh M'manga, De Mobray Thipa, Max Prien, Wales Juma, James Sangala (missing 4)
Red Army "A": James Kuyenge, George, E. Mtawali

4 Jul. 1964: Friendly: Rangeley Stadium: Northern Rhodesia 0–5
Noel Nthala, Royee Maliwa, Roman Bwanali, Frazer Chitenje, Oliver Nakhumwa, Raleigh M'manga, Stanley Bweya, James Kaminjolo, Overton Mkandawire, Emmanuel Gondwe, Godfrey Kalitsiro   **Official:**   **Augustine Chavura**

24 Sep. 1964
City & Suburban League Board officials as follows:
Chairman Jack Brookfield
Secretary/Treasurer Tom Russell
Committee members Alan Flowerdew, Phil Turvey, Khuda Bakhsh

1 Nov. 1964: Kamuzu Cup Final: Rangeley Stadium
Southern Region (Southern Section) v. Southern Region (Northern Section) 3–1   G. Kalitsiro (2), A. Osman, S. Kapalamula

Clubs That Participated in the NFA Era

There were fifteen clubs that were affiliated to the association, and the most that the league had in one season were nine clubs in 1950–51 and 1960–61. Blantyre Sports Club were the only affiliate to have two clubs competing in the same league, in the 1955–56 season. Below is a brief history of the clubs involved. Six different clubs had their names inscribed on the league trophy: BSC (seven), CCL (four), Mlanje and Zomba (two each), and Corona and Olympia (one each).

Athletics

Athletics completed in only one season, 1949–50, and were placed second on the table log with two games to complete. They were two points ahead of BSC so could have ended as either runners-up or in third place. It is not known why they did not participate the following season. Later they changed their name to Limbe Wanderers.

Blantyre Sports Club

Established in 1896 and known to be the second-oldest club in the country, Blantyre participated in all seventeen league seasons (1947–48 to 1963–64) and folded in 1970. They were the giants of that era, as they won the title seven times beginning in the inaugural 1947–48 season and then in 1950–51, 1951–52, 1953–54, 1955–56, 1958–59, and 1959–60. Furthermore, they won the Royle K/O seven times and five Stanhope Cups, making a grand total of nineteen trophies. One trophy that eluded them was the Franklin Cup, which was introduced in 1962 for six seasons, as they failed to even reach the finals. They were also league runners four times and losing finalists nine times.

They completed the Treble in 1955–56 and 1958–59, when they won the League, Royle, and Stanhope trophies. They won the Double on three different occasions, winning the league and the Royle Cup in 1950–51 and 1953–54, and the league and the Stanhope Cup in 1959–60. Although they did not achieve a league win in 1956–57, they managed to win both the Royle and Stanhope Cups.

Blantyre Sports Club Football team 1967.
Back row: M. Prien, G. Trataris, H. Nsewa, C. Trataris, J. Cottingham, R. Wooley.
Front row: V. Rodkin, T. McAuley, P. Bishop, H. Wrigley, J. Henderson, J. Mackie.

Callies

Callies joined the league only in the 1960–61 season and lasted one more season, in which they finished in a credible third place behind Champions Country Club Limbe and Blantyre Sports

Mario Antoine

Club. They appeared in three cup finals, losing all of them—twice to Olympia in their maiden season in the Royle and Stanhope Cups, and the following year to BSC in the Stanhope Cup.

Cholo

Cholo entered the league in the 1950–51 season and lasted one season. The good news was that they rejoined in 1953–54 and went through to the end. They were runners-up twice in 1957–58 and 1960–61 and appeared in six cup finals, losing them all, between 1957 and 1963—three times in the Stanhope Cup, twice in the Royle, and once in the Franklin Cup.

CHOLO
Standing from l to r: K. Thompson, G. Tassi, M. Grilli, J. Johnson, M. Leotta, H. Tait (capt).
Front row l to r: W. Buckles, R. Nicholl, G. Florini, L. Ferguson, I. Baglion
Entered the League in season 1950/51 and lasted one season. The good fortune was that they re-joined it in 1953/54 and went through to the end. They were runners-up twice in seasons 1957/58 and 1960/61 and appeared in six Cup Finals losing them all between 1957 and 1963, three times in the Stanhope Cup, twice in the Royle and once in the Franklin Cup.

Corona

Corona joined in the 1952–53 season and were ever present till the end, winning the league in successive seasons in 1953–54 and 1954–55. They were the first team ever to win the Treble, in 1955, by defeating BSC twice in the finals of Royle and Stanhope, 5–3 on both occasions. They had also previously won the Royle Cup in 1953 against Zomba 3–0.

Country Club Limbe

Country Club Limbe (CCL) was one of the oldest colonial clubs in Nyasaland, established in 1923. Their best season was in 1964 as they achieved the Treble of becoming league champions, and winning the Royle and Stanhope Cups. They were additionally the losing finalist in the Franklin Cup. Previously they had also won the league in 1956–57, 1961–62, and 1962–63, and they were the first and only club to win it in three successive years. They were also victorious in claiming the Royle and Stanhope Trophies in 1958.

COUNTRY CLUB LIMBE
Standing from l to r: Paul Isham, J. Petersie, Bill Keddie, Ian Royan, Hugh Smith, Brian Fox (capt)
 Front row l to r: Robin Imray, Brian Phillips, Dennis Pritchard, Adam McKinley, D. Gibbs
One of the oldest Colonial club in Nyasaland as Country Club Limbe was established in 1923 had their best season in 1964 as they achieved the treble of League Champions, winners of the Royle and Stanhope Cup and losing Finalist in the Franklin Cup. Previously they had also won the League in seasons 1956/57, 1961/62 and 1962/63 and were the first and only club to win it in three successive years. They were also victorious in the Royle and Stanhope trophies in 1958.

Goans

Goans participated twice in the league during 1949–50 and 1950–51 and finished as wooden spoons on both occasions. Their inaugural season was a disaster, as they had lost all their fixtures and shipped a total of 67 goals. The following season at least saw them win one game and draw in three; they occupied the last place only because of an inferior goal difference against CCL.

Indian Sports Club

The oldest Asian club in the country, formed in 1920, competed in the first fourteen seasons but was never a threat to the other clubs. They were hardly out of the final bottom two places but enjoyed two good seasons when they ended in fourth place in 1950–51 and 1951–52. They never appeared in any cup finals.

Limbe Wanderers

The Limbe Wanderers are no relation to the Malawi-era team; they participated in the league for only three seasons, from 1950–51 to 1952–53. They played one season as Athletics in 1949–50. At least they had a better performance compared to some teams that played for a few seasons, as they ended as runners-up in their last campaign in 1952–53. They also finished in third place in their opening season.

Mlanje

Founding members of the league, Mlanje lasted only six seasons, but at least they had the honour of being champions twice in seasons 1948–49 and 1949–50 after ending as runners-up in their first year. They also appeared in the first Royle Cup final, played on 15 April 1950, in which they lost 2–1 to Blantyre Sports Club.

Standing L to R: J. Dunn, J. Morrison, D. Dall, A. Lorentz, J. Laing, G. Hadlow, J. Pelic
Middle row: L to R: C. White, C. Snell, Jack Royle, R. Campbell-Miles
Front row: R. Stevens (with mascot Mary Stevens), G. Anderson, A. Stark

Nyasaland Railways

Nyasaland Railways entered the league in 1950–51 and then disappeared for seven seasons before making an appearance in the 1958–59 season. They then remained until the NFA era. Once Malawi became independent, "Nyasaland" was removed from the name. Their best final placing was achieved in 1959–60, when they took third place.

Olympia

The Greek community wanted their identity represented on the pitch and formed Olympia to join the league in the 1959–60 season and played till the end. They had a very great side, as they were runners-up twice, in their inaugural season of 1959–60 and in 1962–63, and were champions in only their second year, in 1960–61. However, they did not complete the 1963–64 season, as they were suspended from the league and withdrew their affiliation. They are the only club to have won all three knockout cups. They began with the Royle Cup, appearing in three successive finals, winning in 1960 and in 1962. They won the Stanhope Trophy in 1961 and the Franklin Cup in its maiden season.

Standing from L to R: Franco Bregger, Max Prien (capt), T. Nakos, G. Koutsadakis, Paul Yiannakis, B. Phombeya
Kneeling from L to R: Smart Thipa, Lorenco Colandria, Cominas Yiannakis, Oresti Yiannakis, DeMobray Thipa

Rovers

Rovers was one of the first mixed-race teams. It was formed in the 1962–63 season and was the pioneer of future clubs such as Chichiri Athletics, Wanderers, and Bata Bullets. Although they ended in mid-table during their two years' existence under this name, they won the Franklin Cup when they defeated Country Club Limbe 4–2 in the finals.

The four NFA national players that featured for this team were skipper Don Meintjies, Allaudin Osman (one of four brothers involved in local football), Januaro Magalaes, and Jack Stuart. Lameck Phiri was selected for the NAFA tour of Northern Rhodesia in 1964.

Ibrahim Mojoo, who was a founder member of Chichiri Athletics Football Club (a school team) was later elected as secretary general of the Football Association of Malawi.

ROVERS
Standing from L to R: Ibrahim Mojoo, Jack Stuart, A. Lawrence, Januaro de Magalaes, Roy Maliwa, S. Munian Front row from L to R: Allaudin Osman, Don Meintjies (capt), Paul Khamisa, Basil Malila, Lameck Phiri This club was one of the first mixed raced

team that was formed in season 1962/63 and was the pioneer of the future clubs such as Chichiri Athletics, Wanderers and Bata Bullets. Although they ended in mid-table during their two years' existence under this name, they won the Franklin Cup when they defeated Country Club Limbe by 4-2 in the Finals.

Sunnyside Rovers

Formed in 1951–52, Sunnyside Rovers competed for five seasons in the league, and their highest final placing came in their last season, where they ended as runners-up.

They enjoyed cup victories in the Royle Cup in 1952 when Blantyre Sports Club narrowly lost by 1–0 and the Stanhope final in 1954, where BSC was once more their victim, this time by a 4–3 score.

Zomba

One of only three clubs to compete every year from the beginning in 1947–48, Zomba were league champions twice in the 1952–53 and 1957–58 seasons and ended as runners-up twice. They were losing finalists in the Royle Cup on three separate occasions, twice to Blantyre Sport Club and once to Corona, in 1951, 1953, and 1956.

The 1966 City and Suburban League champions and winners of the Royle Cup, Zomba. Standing, left to right: Bundy, Mwabile, Sullivan, Kumwembe, Chitenje, Joshua. Front: Laughran, West, Gallagher, Mkandawire, Kapalamula.

1965

The new season under the new administration, now known as the City and Suburban League (CSL), saw the withdrawals of Olympia (suspended the previous season) and Corona, and Nyasaland Railways changed their name to Railways.

Two new clubs were accepted to join the CSL, and the seeds of the current Wanderers team were sown as Portuguese Wanderers (as evidenced by the Wanderers clubhouse being at the rear of the Portuguese club).

They were crowned champions in their inaugural season, and the second affiliated club was Rangers (joint clubs of Mpingwe SC, Goans, and Indian Sports Club).

This was a second successive season in which Limbe Country Club and Blantyre Sports Club met in the Royle Cup final, with Blantyre winning it by 2–1 this time.

The Stanhope Cup Trophy was shared between Portuguese Wanderers and Blantyre SC after they drew 2–2, as an alternate date could not be found in a very crowded season.

At long last, a trophy was won by Railways, as they defeated Limbe CC 5–2 in a replay after a high-scoring draw of 5–5.

Central Region won the Kamuzu Cup; the result and opponent are still being researched.

Mario Antoine

In the Southern Region Xmas Tournament, Limbe beat Blantyre 5–1 while Chiradzulu beat Port Herald 2–1. Zomba were 6–3 winners over Mlanje in the preliminary round.

In semi-finals, Limbe beat Kasupe 5–1 (Smile scored 4 goals while James scored the other goal for Limbe). In the other semi-final, Zomba beat Chiradzulu 5–1.

Limbe won the championship after Zomba failed to turn up for the final.

1965 Timeline

1 Jan. 1965: Scotland v. The Rest 5–3   P. Crossan (3), B. Keddie (p), J. Gallacher, P. Bradley (2), M. Prien
Scotland: L. Ferguson (Cholo), Fraser (BSC), Hugh Smith (BSC), John Brown (BSC), Bill Keddie (Limbe CC), Jackie Cottingham (BSC), Brian Phillips (Limbe CC), Joe Gallacher (Zomba), Johnny Hawthorne (BSC), Paul Crossan (Railways), McLeod (Cholo); Reserves: Littlejohn (BSC), Charlie Clarke (Zomba)
The Rest: Cominas Yiannakis (Limbe CC), Chalmers (Limbe CC), Jack Stuart (Rangers), Paul Isham (Limbe CC), Oliver Nankhumwa (Wanderers), Jagjit Singh (Railways), Wood (BSC), Santokh Singh (Railways), Phillip Bradley (BSC), Max Prien (Limbe CC), Joaquim Cunha (Wanderers)

30 Jan. 1965: Franklin Cup Final: Cholo: Railways v. Limbe CC 5–5   I. Sheriff (2), G. Antoine, P. Crossan, K. Mansfield, M. Prien (2), P. Yiannakis (2), P. Isham
Railways: Ishmail Khamisa, George Antoine, Bashir Tarmahomed, Jagjit Singh, Roman Bwanali, Edmund Fernandes, Haroon Karim, Peter Crossan, Ikram Sheriff, Santokh Singh, Ken Mansfield
Limbe CC: Cominas Yiannakis, Chalmers, Paul Isham, Bill Keddie, Don Quennell, M. Yiannakis, Brian Phillips, Max Prien, Paul Yiannakis, Oresti Yiannakis, Matt Hoyland; Reserves: Aidan Humphries, Dave Brookfield

27–28 Mar. 1965:   Inter-Regional Tournament
Southern Region Southern Section: Ishmail Khamisa, George Linzie, Albert Nsewa, Roman Bwanali (capt.), Oliver Nankhumwa, Raleigh M'manga, Lameck Phiri, De Mobray Thipa, Simplex Bedi, James Chisasa, Crosby Chisasa; Reserves: Royee Maliwa, Green Malunga
Southern Region Northern Section: Henry Kapalamula, Elijah Joshua, Mwabile, Jere, Frazer Chitenje (capt.), Daudi, Kuyere, Samuel Kapalamula, Overton Mkandawire, Lipenga, E. Banda; Reserves: F. Kaminjolo
Central Region: Tiger, Bulla, Mkandawire, Julio Kamlaza, Bedford, Mkalanyinga Sitolo, Beric, Chingoli, Robert Kalembo (capt.), M'dumuka, Stanley Bweya; Reserves: Galatoni Njoka, Kaunda, B. Phombeya, Smile
Northern Region: Noel Nthala, Mwemba, Kunyoli, Gondwe, Mhango, Fanta, Charles Nyirongo, Colby, Shake, Godfrey Kalitsiro, Stephen Gondwe

Southern Region (Southern Section) v. Southern Region (Northern Section)   2–1 A. Nsewa, C. Chisasa (o/g)

Central Region v. Northern Region   3–3 Kalembo (2), S. Bweya, Shake, ?

Select 1ˢᵗ XI v. Select 2ⁿᵈ XI   5–5

There were not many activities during the year despite a national team being selected by the new director of sports and culture, Mr S. Thipa, in March. The twenty-three players selected were selected from the three regions.

- SR: Elijah Joshua, Lipenga, Overton Mkandawire, Samuel Kapalamula, Smile Kampeza, Crosby Chisasa, James Chisasa, Frazer Chitenje, Jere, George Linzie (10)

- CR: Tiger, B. Phombeya, Bula, Smile, Stanley Bweya, Bedford, Gwemba, Julio Kamlaza (8)
- NR: Godfrey Kalitsiro, Shake, Charles Nyirongo, Noel Nthala (4)

Final Log

No.	Teams	P	W	D	L	F	A	PTS
1	Portuguese Wanderers	12	9	2	1	37	16	20
2	Blantyre SC	12	8	2	2	52	22	18
3	Railways	12	6	2	4	45	26	14
4	Limbe CC	12	6	2	4	45	28	14
5	Zomba	12	3	1	8	27	53	7
6	Rangers	12	3	1	8	11	40	7
7	Cholo	12	1	2	9	26	58	4

**3 Apr. 1965: Stanhope Cup Final: Wanderers v. Blantyre SC 2–2   L. Phiri, H. Nsewa, Rosenast (2)
Trophy shared, as no alternative grounds and dates available**
Wanderers: Green Malunga, Kirby Thomson, Oliver Nankhumwa, Wales Nsewa, Henry Nsewa, Lameck Phiri, Allaudin Osman, Joaquim Cunha, James Mkwanda, Smile Chibambo, Basil Malila
Blantyre SC: George Trataris, John Brown, Vic Rodkin, Dennis Johnston, Costas Trataris, Hugh Smith, Jackie Cottingham, Phillip Bradley, Rosenhast, Wood, Harold Wrigley (jnr)

4 Apr. 1965: Franklin Cup Final Replay: Railways v. Limbe CC 5–2 I. Sheriff (3), S. Singh (2)–M. Prien, P. Isham
Railways: Ishmail Khamisa, Roman Bwanali, George Antoine, Bashir Tarmahomed, Peter Crossan, Jagjit Singh, Ken Mansfield, Santokh Singh, Haroon Karim, Ikram Sheriff, French
Limbe: Cominas Yiannakis, Jerry Burns, Bill Keddie, Paul Isham, Chalmers, Matt Hoyland, Robin Imray, Max Prien, Oresti Yiannakis, Paul Yiannakis, Brian Phillips

10 Apr. 1965: Royle Cup Final: Blantyre SC v. Limbe CC   2–1   H. Wrigley, Wood, B. Phillips
Blantyre: George Trataris, John Brown, Hugh Smith, Vic Rodkin, Dennis Johnston, Jackie Cottingham, Costas Trataris, Phillip Bradley, Harold Wrigley (jnr), Wood, Rosenhast
Limbe CC: Cominas Trataris, Bill Keddie, Jerry Burns, Chalmers, Brian Phillips, Robin Imray, Paul Isham, Max Prien, Matt Hoyland, Oresti Yiannakis, Paul Yiannakis

Rovers Tour of Southern Rhodesia v. Salisbury Dazzlers and Combined sSde
17 Apr. 1965:   Salisbury Dazzlers/Spurs 2–2   A. Osman, P. de Silva
18 Apr. 1965:   Salisbury Dazzlers/Spurs 5–5   I. Sheriff (3), A. Osman (2)

Wanderers Tour of Tete for the Launch of the Governor Craveiro Lopes Stadium (Four Teams from Tete, One Each from Villa Perry and Malawi)
17 Apr. 1965:   Villa Perry 1–1 (lost 5–4 on pens)   O. Mkandawire
18 Apr. 1965:   Moatize 3–5   J. Cunha, O. Mkandawire, Y. Osman

24 Apr. 1965:   Champions Wanderers v. The Rest   3–1   A. Osman (2), J. Cunha, P. Bradley
Wanderers: Green Malunga, Januaro Magalhaes, Damiano, Kirby Thomson, Oliver Nankhumwa, Raleigh M'manga, Henry Nsewa, Joaquim Cunha, Allaudin Osman, James Mkwanda, Lameck Phiri
The Rest: Ishmail Khamisa, Chalmers, Jerry Burns, Don Quennell, Joe Gallacher, Peter Crossan, Roman Bwanali, Ikram Sheriff, Ken Mansfield, Phillip Bradley, Wood

Mario Antoine

Vic Rodkin 6-a-Side Shield: Corona: **Blantyre v. Railways 3–1**

7 May 1965: Stoffle Cup: Railways v. Clube Ferroviario de Mozambique (CFM) 1–1 **I. Sheriff**

10 May 1965: City & Suburban XI v. CFM 1–5 **P. Bradley**
City & Suburban XI: Cliff Wintle, Januaro de Magalhaes, Costas Trataris, John Brown, Jackie Cottingham, Jerry Burns, Harold Wrigley (jnr), Allaudin Osman, Phillip Bradley, Joaquim Cunha, Woods

23 May 1965: Portuguese Consul Pembeira de Souza Trophy
Wanderers v. Clube Desportivo de Tete 3–2 **H. Nsewa (2p), J. Cunha**
Wanderers: Green Malunga, Januaro de Magalhaes, Damiano, Cullen Mwase, Wales Nsewa, Kirby Thomson, Oliver Nankhumwa, Raleigh M'manga, Lameck Phiri, Henry Nsewa, James Mkwanda, Allaudin Osman, Yasin Osman, Joaquim Cunha, Smile Kampeza

Blantyre/Limbe Xi v. Blantyre SC **4–3 aet** **R. Bwanali, C. Chisasa, W. Juma, D. Thipa, Wood, P. Bradley, M. Prien**
Blantyre/Limbe XI: Joseph Leno Chauluka, George Linzie, James Kunyenge, De Mobray Thipa, Roman Bwanali, Royee Maliwa, Kafaniya, Crosby Chisasa, Wales Juma, Henry, Peter Chisasa; Reserves: F. Cholo, M. Tyangatyanga, Ishmail Khamisa

24 May 1965: Martins and Noronha Trophy
Wanderers v. Blantyre/Limbe XI **4–1** **A. Osman, H. Nsewa, Y. Osman, J. Cunha, R. Bwanali**

Clube Desportivo de Tete v. Blantyre SC 3–1

Kamuzu Cup: **Central Region are the Winners (Research Ongoing)**

1966

Rangers lasted only one season and withdrew from the league, and they were replaced by Corona, who made a comeback after an absence of one season, and a group of schoolboys and staff from Chichiri playing as Chichiri Athletics. At that time, ex-Huddersfield Town goalkeeper Bob Hesford, who played in the 1938 cup final, losing to a last-minute extra-time goal against Preston North End, was the headmaster at Chichiri Secondary School. Zomba Town won only their third championship title; they had last won in 1957–58.

It was another first for Zomba Town when they defeated Railways, appearing in their second Royle Cup final, 2–1.

It was Blantyre Sports Club's sixth and last Stanhope Cup Trophy after they beat schoolboys Chichiri Athletics by 2–0.

A Zomba Town treble was achieved when youthful Chichiri Athletics were crushed 4–0 in the Franklin Cup Final.

Central Region won the Kamuzu Cup against Southern Region Northern Section 2–1.

On the international scene, after a year's absence, Malawi for the first time participated in four friendlies, unfortunately losing all of them. They used nineteen players, of which fourteen were introduced. Allaudin Osman and John Brown followed James Kaminjolo by becoming players to have featured in both NFA and NAFA teams. Allaudin's younger sibling Yasin, still only seventeen years old, and eleven other players—Henry Kapalamula, Paul Morin, Joe Gallagher, Peter Chisasa, Crosby Chisasa, Cullen Mwase, Albert Nsewa, S. Bulla, Elijah Joshua, Solomon Mkwapatira, and Prince Nyirenda—were called up. Out of the four players retained, only Royee Maliwa and Oliver Nakhumwa were the original survivors from the 1962 squad, with Overton Mkandawire and Noel Nthala retaining their places and a recall for De Mobray Thipa.

Solomon Mkwapatira created another piece of history by becoming the first player to register a hat trick in their 4–3 defeat in Maseru against Basutoland (Lesotho), celebrating their independence.

In August, an emergency meeting was held in Lilongwe to discuss the formation of the National Football Association of Malawi (NFAM). Officials elected as were as follows: President Ken Mansfield, Vice President Sydney Chikafa, Secretary F. Munthali, and Treasurer J. Chisi.

The new body was to be known as the National Football Association (NFA), and once approved by HE Kamuzu Banda, the name of Malawi would then be added (NFAM). Other main discussions related to the formation of regional associations, in addition to the only existing one from the South (SRFA). Future selections were to start at districts, followed by regional selections and finally NFA selections. Application to join FIFA was also discussed. The six members elected, two from each region, were (Centre Region) K. Mjojo, P. Kaunda (North Region) G. Nhelma, W. Chibambo, and (South Region) Mkunuley, A. Kagaso.

1966 Timeline

Final Log

No.	Teams	P	W	D	L	F	A	PTS	Remarks
1	Zomba Town	14	13	0	1	54	18	24	deducted 2 pts
2	Blantyre SC	14	8	2	4	39	24	18	
3	Wanderers	14	6	3	5	43	22	15	
4	Railways	14	6	2	6	32	30	14	
5	Cholo	14	5	0	9	36	55	14	awarded 4 pts
6	Limbe CC	14	5	2	7	27	32	12	
7	Chichiri Athletics	14	3	2	9	19	43	8	
8	Corona	14	4	1	9	27	53	7	deducted 2 pts

Franklin Cup Final:	**Zomba Town v. Chichiri Athletics**	**4–0**	
Stanhope Cup Final:	**Blantyre SC v. Chichiri Athletics**	**2–0**	

9/10 Apr 1966: **Inter-Regional Tournament (to Select National team)**

Southern Region Greens: Terry Sullivan, Frazer Chitenje, Royee Maliwa, Jere, Oliver Nankhumwa, Paul Morin, Kuyere, Santokh Singh, Yasin Osman, Paul Chisasa, Choipa Kapalamula

Southern Region Black/Reds: Henry Kapalamula, Toyne, George Linzie, De Mobray Thipa, Jackie Cottingham, James Kuyenge, Smile Kampeza, Basil Malila, Overton Mkandawire, Crosby Chisasa, Allaudin Osman

Central Region: Tiger, Bulla, Gwemba, Galatoni Njoka, Julio Kamlaza, Sinumba, Stanley Bweya, Salima, Emmanuel Gondwe, Prince Nyirenda, Saka

Northern Region: Godfrey Kalitsiro, Shake, Charles Nyirongo, Stephen Gondwe, M. Gondwe, E. Tembo, Mhango, Mkandawire, Noel Nthala

Southern Region Black/Reds v. Northern Region 6–4 **O. Mkandawire (3), C. Chisasa (2), A. Osman, N. Nthala (3), Shake**

Southern Region Greens v. Central Region 4–0 **Y. Osman (2), S. Singh, C. Kapalamula**

Reds v. Blacks 4–2

Probables v. Possibles 9–1 **O. Mkandawire (3–1p), N. Nthala (3), C. Kapalamula (2), P. Chisasa, C. Chisasa**

Probables: Henry Kapalamula, Bulla, Oliver Nankhumwa, Frazer Chitenje, Jackie Cottingham, Allaudin Osman, Noel Nthala, Choipa Kapalamula, Overton Mkandawire, Peter Chisasa, Simon Kapalamula

Possibles: Tiger (sub Terry Sullivan), Bulla, Royee Maliwa, Charles Nyirongo, De Mobray Thipa, Paul Morin, Crosby Chisasa, Smile Chirambo, Owen Kalitsiro, Yasin Osman, Santokh Singh

Eighteen Players Selected for National Training: Henry Kapalamula, Choipa Kapalamula, Overton Mkandawire, Frazer Chitenje, Terry Sullivan (Zomba Town), Yasin Osman (Chichiri Athletics), Jackie Cottingham (Blantyre SC), Paul Morin (Railways), Peter Chisasa, Allaudin Osman, Oliver Nankhumwa (Wanderers), De Mobray Thipa (Bookers), Crosby Chisasa (Kapeni), Royee Maliwa (Ndirande Lions), Bulla (CR), Prince Nyirenda, Smile Chirambo, Noel Nthara (NR)

16 Apr 1966: Royle Cup Final: **Zomba Town v. Railways 2–1** **P. West, O. Mkandawire, P. Crossan**

Zomba: Terry Sullivan, Joe Gallagher, Frazer Chitenje, Mwabile, Colin Bundy, Elijah Joshua, Kumwembe, Jim Laughran, Peter West, Overton Mkandawire, Choipa Kapalamula

Railways: Ishmail Khamisa, Nicholls, Jagjit Singh, Paul Morin, George Linzie, Balraj Bouri, Joe Fernandes, Santokh Singh, Paul Crossan, Ikram Sheriff, Ken Mansfield

The 1966 City and Suburban League champions and winners of the Royle Cup, Zomba. Standing, left to right: Bundy, Mwabile, Sullivan, Kumwembe, Chitenje, Joshua. Front: Laughran, West, Gallagher, Mkandawire, Kapalamula.

30 Apr 1966: Stoffle Cup: Beira: Clube Ferroviario de Mozambique v. Railways 3-3   O. Mkandawire (2), I. Sheriff
Railways: Ishmail Khamisa, George Linzie, Joe Fernandes, Jagjit Singh, Jackie Cottingham, Paul Morin, Peter Crossan, Ikram Sheriff, Overton Mkandawire, Joe Gallagher, Ken Mansfield

1 Jun. 1966:   Ron Meades Arrives in the Country to Coach the National Team.

6 Jul. 1966: Friendly: Central Stadium: Zambia 0-6
Henry Kapalamula, Royee Maliwa, John Brown, Paul Morin, Oliver Nakhumwa, Mobray de Thipa, Joe Gallagher, Allaudin Osman, Overton Mkandawire, Yasin Osman, Peter Chisasa   **Coach:**   Ron Meades

7 Jul. 1966: Friendly: Central Stadium: Madagascar 1-6   O. Mkandawire
Henry Kapalamula, Royee Maliwa, John Brown, Paul Morin, Oliver Nakhumwa, Mobray de Thipa, Joe Gallagher, Allaudin Osman, Overton Mkandawire, Yasin Osman, Peter Chisasa   **Coach:**   Ron Meades

8 Jul. 1966: Friendly: Central Stadium: Zambia 1-5   P. Chisasa
Noel Nthala, Royee Maliwa, John Brown, Cullen Mwase, Oliver Nakhumwa, Mobray de Thipa, Albert Nsewa, Allaudin Osman, Overton Mkandawire, Yasin Osman, Peter Chisasa   **Coach:**   Ron Meades

23 Jul. 1966: Portuguese Consul Pembeira de Souza Trophy: Tete:
Desportivo Clube de Tete v. Wanderers   4-3   A. Osman (3)

24 Jul. 1966: Friendly: Tete: Tete Select XI v. Wanderers 4-3   Y. Osman (3)

13-14 Aug 1966: Emergency meeting held in Lilongwe to discuss formation of National Football Association of Malawi (NFAM). Officials elected as follows:

30 Aug. 1966: 23 Players Called Up for National Team
Henry Kapalamula, Choipa Kapalamula, Peter Chisasa, Crosby Chisasa, Overton Mkandawire, Yasin Osman, Allaudin Osman, Bulla, Charles Nyirongo, Royee Maliwa, Oliver Nankhumwa, Paul Morin, De Mobray Thipa, Solomon Mkwapatira, Sheke, Prince Nyirenda, Chilambe, Elijah Joshua, Frazer Chitenje, Gwemba, Roman Bwanali, Mtawali, Cullen Mwase

1 Sep. 1966: Ron Meades Returns to England after Training National Team; Malawi Invited to Play Basutoland during Their Independence Celebrations in October

10 Sep. 1966: 18 Players Selected for National Training to Play Basutoland, of Which 13 Would Travel; Jackie Cottingham to Train the Side
Henry Kapalamula, Choipa Kapalamula, Peter Chisasa, Crosby Chisasa, Overton Mkandawire, Yasin Osman, Allaudin Osman, Bulla, Royee Maliwa, Oliver Nankhumwa, Paul Morin, De Mobray Thipa, Solomon Mkwapatira, Prince Nyirenda, Elijah Joshua, Frazer Chitenje, Roman Bwanali, Gwiramwendo

27 Sep. 1966: Ken Mansfield resigns as President of National Football Association of Malawi, Sydney Chikafa the New President, and P. Kaunda as Vice President

02 Oct. 1966: Friendly: Maseru: Basutoland 3-4   S. Mkwapatira (3)
Henry Kapalamula, S. Bulla, Elijah Joshua, Paul Morin, Oliver Nakhumwa, Frazer Chitenje, Solomon Mkwapatira, Allaudin Osman, Overton Mkandawire, Yasin Osman, Samuel Kapalamula; **Subs:** Prince Nyirenda, Crosby Chisasa, Roman Bwanali   **Coach:** Jackie Cottingham

18 Dec. 1966: Kamuzu Cup Final: Central Region v. Southern Region (Northern Section) 2–1   R. Kalembo (2), O. Mkandawire

1967

The year 1967 was another one-season wonder in which the boys from Chichiri withdrew from the league owing to their administration person going on leave, leaving no one to run the team. In their place came Blantyre City (the pioneers of today's Bullets). Wanderers were champions for the second time in three years.

Zomba Town retained the Royle Cup as newcomers Blantyre City were thrashed 5–2. This was the last time that this trophy was played for.

Zomba Town won the Stanhope Trophy for the first time in its last season that it was played for, as Wanderers were on the receiving end of a 6–1 defeat.

It was now the turn of Wanderers to defeat Zomba Town 3–1 in a revenge fixture for the Franklin Trophy, denying them a treble of knockout trophies.

Malawi played another four internationals during the year and at last registered a win on the fourteenth attempt on 12 November 1967 when they defeated Rhodesia 1–0, with Overton Mkandawire scoring the goal. Twenty-seven players were called, with fourteen being introduced and with veteran Jackie Cottingham becoming the fourth player to have represented both national teams.

The others called up were James Kunyenge, Kirby Thomson, Joe Fernandes, Balraj Bouri, Brian Griffin, Losacco, Gordon Brighton, Wales Nsewa, George Manda, James Mkwanda, Ray Wooley, John Raisbeck and Owen Kalitsiro. Of the thirteen that were there before, evergreen Oliver Nakhumwa was the last man standing from our debut year of 1962.

Allaudin Osman created two pieces of history on 25 March 1967 against Rhodesia when he scored a goal in the 6–3 defeat. He became the first player to have scored in the two different national teams, and in the same match, he also became the first of two brothers to score in the same game, as Yasin Osman later scored as well.

Malawi also featured in seven more fixtures against club sides that included the visit of the English Third Division side Oldham Athletic, who ended their season in tenth place. Eleven new players were introduced at this level: Mustafa Munshi, Hamid Nazim, C. Kamlaza, Katete, Maluwa, Zimba, Green Malunga, Power, Prescott Magaleta, Ntaba and S. Kampeza. Malawi won three and lost two with Overton Mkandawire netting 7 of the 15 goals.

The National Schools side was introduced during the year and played two fixtures against their Zambian counterparts. Under the captainship of Mustafa Munshi, they won and lost a game each. Of the first squad selected, six of them went on to win full caps. The full squad was as follows: Mustafa Munshi, Prescott Magaleta, Nasser Osman (Chichiri SS), Samson Chibambo, Hadhyri, Ntaba (BSS), James Mkwanda, Banda (HHI), Magalasi (St. Patricks), Kanjedza Kamwendo, Sparrow Maliro, Robert Kutengule, M. Kumilonde (Zomba)

1967 Timeline

10 Feb. 1967: NFAM Was to Apply for FIFA Membership in Two Weeks' Time

12 Mar. 1967: I.O. Adam Shield: FMB v. Kandjeza Rios 3–1 A. Mpinganjira (2), Kalulu, S. Kamwendo

25 Mar. 1967: Malawi Celebrating FIFA Membership and Brian Griffin Player Coach
Friendly: Central Stadium: Rhodesia 3–6 O. Mkandawire, Y. Osman, A. Osman
Henry Kapalamula, James Kuyenge, Roman Bwanali, Paul Morin, Kirby Thomson, Frazer Chitenje, Elijah Joshua, Allaudin Osman, Overton Mkandawire, Yasin Osman, Samuel Kapalamula **Player Coach:** Brian Griffin

26 Mar. 1967: Friendly SR XI: Blantyre SC: Rhodesia 2–5 O. Mkandawire, B. Griffin
Henry Kapalamula, Joe Fernandes, John Brown, Paul Morin, Jackie Cottingham, Frazer Chitenje, Balraj Bouri, Brian Griffin, Overton Mkandawire, Yasin Osman, Losacco **Player Coach:** Brian Griffin

30 Apr. 1967: Friendly: Central Stadium: Sporting Club de Tete 4–1 O. Mkandawire (2), B. Griffin (2–1 pen)
Henry Kapalamula, Wales Nsewa, Elijah Joshua, S. Bulla, Oliver Nakhumwa, Frazer Chitenje, Henry Nsewa, Brian Griffin, Overton Mkandawire, Allaudin Osman, Samuel Kapalamula **Player Coach:** Brian Griffin

3/04 Jun. 1967: Kamuzu Cup
Southern Region "A": Henry Kapalamula, Henderson, Bulla, Fraser Chitenje, Oliver Nakhumwa, Albert Nsewa, Allaudin Osman, Brian Griffin, Overton Mkandawire, Yasin Osman, Jana
Southern Region "B": Ishmail Khamisa, Nagoli, Hamid Nazim, Wales Nsewa, Ray Wooley, Elijah Joshua, Henry Nsewa, James Kalitsiro, Samuel Kapalamula, Smile Chibambo, S. Gondwe; Reserves: Crighton Msiya, Cullen Mwase, Green Malunga, George Linzie, Antoine Madinga, Jafari Zefa
Central Region: Mulla, Induna, Mlera, Gwilamwendo, Uteka, Julio Kamlaza, Galatoni Njoka, Magwaya, Robert Kalembo, Solomon Mkwapatira, Darwin, Mwiza: Reserves: Stanley Bweya, Mwanondo, Flawo
Northern Region: Chirambo, Charles Nyirongo, M. Ngosi, Prince Nyirenda, Chuhga, Mhango, Banda, Chimaliro, Gwiliza, Chibambo, Stephen Gondwe, Mikochi, Fletcher, Nyirongo

3 Jun 1967: Southern Region "B" v. Northern Region 8–1 O. Kalitsiro (3), S. Kapalamula (3), J. Mkwanda (2), Chirambo
Central Region v. Southern Region "A" 2–1 R. Kalembo (2), A. Osman

4 Jun. 1967: Central Region v. Southern Region "B" 2–1
Limbe League: 10 teams: Bata Stars, Farmers Marketing Board (FMB), Imperial Tobacco Company (ITC), Kanjedza Rios, Police, Postals, Red Bombers, Sunlight Rovers, Vagabonds, Yiannakis

11 Jun. 1967: Friendly: Central Stadium: Desportivo Club de Tete 4–1 O. Mkandawire (3), A. Osman
Henry Kapalamula, Wales Nsewa, Hamid Nazim, Ray Wooley, Oliver Nakhumwa, Frazer Chitenje, Yasin Osman, Brian Griffin, Overton Mkandawire, Allaudin Osman, James Mkwanda Player Coach: Brian Griffin

Limbe League after Three Rounds

No.	Teams	P	W	D	L	F	A	PTS
1	Kanjedza Rios	3	3	0	0	12	3	6
2	Vagabonds	3	2	0	1	5	6	4
3	ITC	3	2	0	1	3	4	4

No.	Teams	P	W	D	L	F	A	PTS
4	Sunlight Rovers	3	1	1	1	4	2	3
5	Postals	3	1	1	1	6	6	3
6	FMB	3	1	1	1	1	1	3
7	Bata Stars	3	1	1	1	3	4	3
8	Yiannakis	3	1	0	2	5	5	2
9	Red Bombers	3	1	0	2	1	6	2
10	Police	3	0	0	3	1	4	0

6 Jul. 1967: Friendly: Central Stadium: Oldham Athletic 2–3   O. Mkandawire, Y. Osman
Henry Kapalamula, Julio Kamlaza, Hamid Nazim, Ray Wooley, Oliver Nakhumwa, Frazer Chitenje, Yasin Osman, Brian Griffin, Overton Mkandawire, Allaudin Osman, James Mkwanda   **Player Coach:** Brian Griffin

8 Jul. 1967: Friendly: BSC: BSC Invitation XI v. Oldham Athletic 2–6   S. Chibambo, B. Malila
Henry Kapalamula, James Kunyenge, Bob Power, Henderson, Vic Rodkin, Ray Wooley,

9 Jul. 1967: Friendly: Wanderers v. Southern Suburbs (Rhodesia) 5–0   J. Mkwanda, Smile C., A. Osman, B. Van Gelder (p), C. Mwase

Final Log

No.	Teams	P	W	D	L	F	A	PTS
1	Wanderers	14	11	1	2	47	21	23
2	Zomba Town	13	7	4	2	53	22	18
3	Blantyre City	13	8	1	4	35	31	17
4	Railways	14	5	4	5	21	40	14
5	Limbe CC	14	4	5	5	30	31	13
6	Blantyre SC	14	4	3	7	36	44	11
7	Cholo	14	3	1	10	33	40	7
8	Corona	14	3	1	10	39	65	7

Franklin Cup Final: Wanderers v Zomba Town   2–1
Stanhope Cup Final: Zomba Town v Wanderers   6–1
Royle Cup Final: Zomba Town v. Blantyre City   5–2

14 Jul. 1967: Ray Batchelor, ex Kenya Coach and West Ham United Player Appointed Director of Sports and Malawi Football Coach

15 Jul. 1967: Friendly: Central Stadium: Salisbury City 3–0   S. Kapalamula (2), B. Griffin
Henry Kapalamula, Hamid Nazim, Ray Wooley, Frazer Chitenje, Oliver Nakhumwa, Allaudin Osman, Brian Griffin, Prince Nyirenda, Overton Mkandawire, Yasin Osman, Samuel Kapalamula   **Player Coach:** Brian Griffin

16 Jul. 1967: Friendly "B": Central Stadium: Salisbury City 0–0
Green Malunga, S. Bulla, Wales Nsewa, Albert Nsewa, Katete, Maluwa, Peter Chisasa, Prince Nyirenda, Henry Nsewa, Crosby Chisasa, James Mkwanda   **Player Coach:** Brian Griffin

16 Aug. 1967:   Malawi Applies for African Football Confederation (CAF) Membership

26 Aug. 1967: **Shire Highlands Football League 1967/68 to Start on 26 August 1967 with 2 Divisions**
Division One: 8 teams: Aces, Blantyre Police, ESCOM, Gold Leaf Players, Kapeni, Medicals, Michiru Castles, Ndirande Lions
Division Two: 9 teams: Associated Bakeries, Chichiri Police, Coca Cola, Mandala Zephyrs, Ministry of Works, Misfits (American Peace Corps), Red Army, The Times, United Transport Malawi (UTM)

26 Aug. 1967: Zambia Schools Tour of Malawi to Play Four Fixtures, Two against Malawi Schools—Wanderers and Zomba Town
Squad: Mustafa Munshi (capt.), Robert Kutengule, Sparrow Maliro, Nazar Osman, Prescott Magaleta, Magalasi, Kondwani Hadhyri, Kanjedza Kamwendo, James Mkwanda, R. Kumilonde, Ntaba, Stephen Chibambo, Banda, Mhango

26 Aug. 1967: **Malawi Schools v. Zambia Schools** **1–7** **N. Osman**
Mhango, Mustafa Munshi (capt.), George Manda, Robert Kutengule, James Mkwanda, Sparrow Maliro, Peter Chisasa, Prescott Magaleta, Kanjedza Kamwendo, Nazar Osman, M. Kumilonde Substitutes: K. Hadhyri

27 Aug. 1967: **Wanderers v. Zambia Schools** **1–2** **Y. Osman (p)**

2 Sep. 1967: **Malawi Schools v. Zambia Schools** **1–0** **S. Chibambo**
Mhango, Mustafa Munshi (capt.), George Manda, Robert Kutengule, James Mkwanda, Samson Chibambo, Peter Chisasa, Prescott Magaleta, Kanjedza Kamwendo, Nazar Osman, K. Hadhyri Substitutes: S. Maliro, M. Kumilonde

2 Sep. 1967: **Zomba Town v. Zambia Schools** **3–2** **O. Mkandawire (2), (o/g)**

6 Sep. 1967: **B.A.T.** **0–12**

10 Sep. 1967: Limbe League: Gallagher Final: **Kanjedza Rios Beat Imperial Tobacco Company**

25 Sep. 1967: National Football League (NFL) formed to run the Southern Football.
Chairman: Clive Fox Vice Chairman: Vic Brighton
Secretary: Harold Humphreys Treasurer: Brian Griffin
Committee members: John Emebel, F. Nseula, Ian Royan, J. Toyne

6 Oct. 1967: **SHFL and Limbe League Disband; Teams to Join NFL**

21 Oct. 1967: Friendly: Central Stadium: Salisbury Callies **0–0**
Henry Kapalamula, Wales Nsewa, Ray Wooley, Frazer Chitenje, Oliver Nakhumwa, Mustafa Munshi, Owen Kalitsiro, Prince Nyirenda, Overton Mkandawire, Yasin Osman, Zimba **Coach:** Ray Batchelor

22 Oct. 1967: Friendly NFL XI: Central Stadium: Salisbury Callies 2–3 **O. Mkandawire, S. Chibambo**
Green Malunga, George Linzie, Hamid Nazim, Bob Power, Prescott Magaleta, Roman Bwanali, Owen Kalitsiro, Ntaba, Samson Chibambo, Overton Mkandawire, James Mkwanda **Coach:** Ray Batchelor

7 Nov. 1967: Squad of 16 players in Ray Batchelor's First Games in Charge against Rhodesia:
Henry Kapalamula, Gordon Brighton, Wales Nsewa, Hamid Nazim, George Manda, Oliver Nakhumwa, Fraser Chitenje, Mustafa Munshi, Ray Wooley, James Mkwanda, Overton Mkandawire, Owen Kalitsiro, Samson Chibambo, Yasin Osman, Brian Griffin, Prince Nyirenda

9 Nov. 1967: Squad Increased to 18 players; 2 players (Mustafa Munshi and Samson Chibambo) Withdraw for Exams and Are Replaced by Balraj Bouri and John Raisbeck; Late Additions to the Squad Are George Linzie and Crighton Msiya

11 Nov. 1967: Friendly: Salisbury: Rhodesia 1–1   B. Bouri
Gordon Brighton, Wales Nsewa, George Linzie, George Manda, Oliver Nakhumwa, Fraser Chitenje, Balraj Bouri, James Mkwanda, Overton Mkandawire, Owen Kalitsiro, Crighton Msiya; (sub Yasin Osman)   **Coach:** Ray Batchelor

12 Nov. 1967: Friendly: Salisbury: Rhodesia 1–0   O. Mkandawire
Henry Kapalamula, John Raisbeck, George Linzie, Ray Wooley, Oliver Nakhumwa, Fraser Chitenje, Brian Griffin, James Mkwanda, Overton Mkandawire, Yasin Osman, Prince Nyirenda   **Coach:** Ray Batchelor

1968

Under the newly introduced National Football League, which now included the SHFL and Limbe League, the league expanded to twelve teams, the highest so far. The eight teams were joined by one of the oldest clubs in Malawi, Michiru Castles, who were regular members of the SHAFL. Although they had disbanded in the '50s, the Nsewa brothers revived the club.

Chichiri Athletics, under the guidance of one of their teachers, Brian Griffin, an ex-Bristol City player who arrived in the country the previous year and played for Corona, reaffiliated after a year's absence.

The remaining two clubs that affiliated were Malawi Police and Blantyre Secondary School Old Boys. Stansfield Motors, agents for Peugeot vehicles, and Yamaha Motorcycles and Outboard Marine Engines became the first companies to sponsor a football team, and the lucky club were Wanderers, who were now called Yamaha Wanderers; they retained their league title.

With the three knockout trophies that were played during the NFA days withdrawn, the NFA were blessed with a new one, as the Castle Cup was introduced, and Chichiri Athletics became the first winners when they defeated Blantyre Sports Club by 3–2 after extra time at Limbe Country Club.

Northern Region won the Kamuzu Cup, defeating Southern Region "A" 3–0, their first win since 1963.

Malawi played three internationals during the year against three new countries and registered a win, a draw, and a loss, scoring 10 goals against 6 conceded, with newly capped Roy Cook as the top scorer with 4 goals.

Both Cook and Yasin Osman created another piece of history as they became the first two players to have scored a hat trick each in a same match against Botswana in an 8–1 record win.

Eighteen players were called, with seven of them being capped for the first time: William Green Malunga, Hamid "Jack" Nazim, Samuel Chirwa, Samson Chibambo, Roy Cook, Damiano Malefula (who was still in primary school), and Chirambo.

Royee Maliwa was recalled after an absence of two years, and Joseph Leno Chauluka, who travelled with the team to Northern Rhodesia in 1964 as a goalkeeper and was yet to win his first cap, was now playing as a forward.

Half of the players were retained, and Oliver Nakhumwa was now in his sixth year in the team and had now won fourteen caps.

Malawi also featured in three other fixtures against Rhodesian club sides Wankie and Salisbury Dynamos, winning two games 3–1.

Sixteen players were called for these matches, of whom Roy Cook was the only one elevated to the first team.

Richard Banda, who returned from overseas studies, was recalled, while Ikram Sheriff became the fifth and last player to have been involved in both national teams.

The other thirteen players were Cullen Mwase, Z. Mphande, Henry Moyo, James Thembulembu, Alex Mpinganjira (popularly known as Poison), and Ben Phoya (known as the Wizard because of his dribbling power), Chidzero, Samuel Chirwa, David Chirwa, Damiano Malefula, Samson Chibambo, Prescott Magaleta, and Tito Kelly.

The schools team toured Zambia and played five games, of which three were against the Zambian Schools and two against the Western and Southern Provinces, and they lost all.

Of the sixteen players in the squad, only four were retained: Prescott Magaleta, Robert Kutengule, M. Kumilonde, and Kanjedza Kamwendo.

The new faces in the squad were Chris Kassia, James Tembulembu (HHI), Precious Kumbatira, Hunter Chikhadzula (Chichiri SS), Winston Zintambila, Harry Mapondo, Tom Kazembe (BSS), Henry Moyo (Likuni), A. Itimu (Malosa), B. Jimusole, E. Bulli (St. Patricks), and Damiano Malefula (Zomba Primary).

1968 Timeline

Lilongwe League Log Table as at 20 January 1968

No.	Teams	P	W	D	L	PTS
1	Flashers	20	14	1	5	29
2	Police	19	13	0	6	26
3	Medicals	20	11	3	6	25
4	UTM	19	9	5	5	23
5	Young Fellows	19	9	3	7	21
6	Bookers	20	6	5	9	17
7	Dodgers	20	7	2	11	16
8	Rangers	20	5	3	12	13
9	Prisons	20	5	2	13	12
10	Wenela	21	1	1	19	3

17–18 Feb. 1968: Football Association of Malawi to hold their Annual General Meeting at Kwacha Centre
Officials elected: Chairman Sydney Chikafa, Vice Chairman C. Kaunda, Secretary Harold Humphreys, Treasurer G. Gondwe

2 Mar. 1968: Friendly: Malawi U23: Kamuzu Stadium: Wankie   1–3   (o/g)
Chidzero, Samuel Chirwa, Hamid Nazim, Paul Morin, George Manda, Mustafa Munshi, David Chirwa, Damiano Malefula, Samson Chibambo, Titto Kelly, Prescott Magaleta   **Coach:**   Ray Batchelor

4 Mar. 1968: Friendly Lilongwe XI: Lilongwe: Wankie 4–6   E. Gondwe (2), S. Mkwapatira, Katanga
Chiwanda, Uteka, Ngwangwa, Julio Kamlaza, Galatoni Njoka, R. Pilato, Antoine Madinga (sub Katanga), Emmanuel Gondwe, Solomon Mkwapatira, Kaipsya, (sub Fernando Araujo), Stanley Bweya

6 Mar. 1968: Friendly Zomba XI: Zomba Gymkana: Wankie   2–1   D. Malefula, S. Kapalamula
Henry Kapalamula, Nagoli, Mwabile, Namwali, Carmichael, Fraser Chitenje, Kuyere, Damiano Malefula, Elijah Joshua, Overton Mkandawire, Samuel Kapalamula

8 Mar. 1968: Friendly Chikwawa XI: Chikwawa: Wankie 1–2   Mhango
Mheya, Kumanje, Masambera, Chadza, B. Mkandawire, Chasweka, Joza, Mhango, F. Mkwanda, Shawa, A. Kalitsiro, Hunter Chikadzula

10 Mar. 1968: Friendly FAM XI: Kamuzu Stadium: Wankie 3–1   O. Mkandawire (2), R. Cook
Henry Kapalamula, Prince Nyirenda, Ray Wooley, Oliver Nakhumwa, Cullen Mwase, Fraser Chitenje, James Mkwanda, Eric Watts, Richard Banda, Overton Mkandawire, Roy Cook   Coach: Ray Batchelor

12 Apr. 1968: This was a sad day for the Malawi football fraternity, as two Chichiri Athletics players—Nazer Osman, a student, and Francis Nseula, a teacher at Chichiri Secondary School—died in a car accident about five miles from their Tete destination to play two friendly fixtures against Desportivo and Sporting Club. Two other players, Mustafa Munshi and Prescott Magaleta, also pupils, suffered multiple injuries.

13 Apr. 1968: Friendly: Salisbury: Arcadia United v. Wanderers 5–1   N. Nthala

14 Apr. 1968: Friendly: Salisbury: Salisbury Dynamos v. Wanderers 2–0

No.	Teams	P	W	D	L	F	A	PTS
1	Yamaha Wanderers	20	14	2	4	69	14	30
2	Zomba Town	19	15	0	4	75	30	30
3	Railways	21	14	2	5	80	45	30
4	Chichiri Athletics	20	11	3	6	48	42	25
5	Michiru Castles	18	10	3	5	45	24	23
6	Blantyre City	19	9	2	8	48	39	20
7	Corona	20	9	1	10	43	52	19
8	Malawi Police	19	7	4	8	43	45	18
9	Limbe CC	21	7	1	13	40	69	15
10	BSS Old Boys	20	6	0	14	31	73	12
11	Blantyre SC	21	4	3	14	37	61	11
12	Cholo	20	2	1	17	36	93	5

04 May 1968: Castle Cup Final: LCC: Chichiri Athletics v. Blantyre SC 3–2   B. Griffin (2), I. Sheriff, D. Douglas, Macauley

Chichiri Athletics: Precious Kumbatira, Hunter Chikadzula, Wilfred Chitwanga, Alan Leech, Royee Maliwa, Prescott Magaleta, Sparrow Malilo, Mario Capela, Ikram Sheriff, Brian Griffin, Ben Phoya

Blantyre SC: George Trataris, Goode, Ray Wooley, Harold Wrigley, Jack Cottingham, Peter Reece, MacDonald, Ray Batchelor, Thorn Buglass (sub Charlie Clarke), Derek Douglas, Macauley

Duarte Silver Cup: Beira: **Clube Ferroviario de Mozambique v. Malawi Railways 7–1**

19 Jun. 1968:   **Blantyre City Annual General Meeting: Chairman Allan Stuart, Secretary John Gilmore, Treasurer Dave Lulker**

6 Jul. 1968: Friendly: Kamuzu Stadium: **Kenya 2–2**   **S. Chibambo, R. Cook**

Henry Kapalamula, Royee Maliwa, George Manda, Oliver Nakhumwa, Hamid Nazim, Fraser Chitenje, Prince Nyirenda, Samson Chibambo, Owen Kalitsiro (sub Damiano Malefula), Yasin Osman, Roy Cook   **Coach:**   Ray Batchelor

26 Jul. 1968:   **Kamuzu Cup Southern Region Selection:**

Northern Section: Henry Kapalamula, Fraser Chitenje, Damiano Malefula, (Zomba Town), George Linzie, Paul Morin, Alex Mpinganjira (Railways), Chavura (Malawi Police), Royee Maliwa, Brian Griffin, Prescott Magaleta (Chichiri Athletics), Samson Chibambo (BSS Old Boys); Reserves: Tambala, Punch, Robert Kalembo, Kaliati

Southern Section: William Green, George Manda, Hamid Nazim, Prince Nyirenda, Oliver Nakhumwa, James Mkwanda, Yasin Osman, Oven Kalitsiro, Roy Cook (Yamaha Wanderers), Blackley (Corona), Joseph Leno Chauluka (ITC); Reserves: Ishmail Khamisa, Wales Nsewa (Michiru Castles), Titto Kelly (Blantyre City), Maliano (Cholo)

Northern Region: D. Nkhosi, Sinkhonde, Charles Nyirongo, I. Pendor (Mzimba North), Malilo (Mzimba South), I. Kishombe, Kadenje, Chance Munde, Shoeshine Ndovie, Zorro Msiska (Karonga), Mboma (Nkhata Bay); Reserves: Joseph Chunga, Moses (Mzimba North)

Central Region: Holders: Mullah (Young Fellows), Henry Moyo, Tony Mulela, (Likuni), Ngwangwa, N. Gondwe (Works), Lunguzi (Police), Chikhasu (UTM), Darwin (Posts), Galatoni Njoka (Flashers), Emmanuel Gondwe, Mwiza (Dodgers); Reserves: Jimmy(Wenela), Pilato, Fernando Araujo, Chiwanda (UTM), Chikafa (Rangers), Tawelu, Tonmy (Dodgers)

2 Aug. 1968:   **Northern Region v. Central Region (win for Northern Region)**   **Chance Munde**

Southern Region: Southern Section v. Northern Section   win for Southern Section

3 Aug. 1968: Finals: **Northern Region v. Southern Region (SS) 3–0**   **C. Munde, C. Nyirongo, ?**

9 Aug. 1968:   **Squad of 30 Players Selected for Swaziland Trip:** Green Malunga, Bopelho, George Manda, Hamid Nazim, Prince Nyirenda, Oliver Nakhumwa, Roy Cook, Yasin Osman, Noel Nthara (Yahama Wanderers), Henry Kapalamula, Overton Mkandawire, Fraser Chitenje (Zomba Town), Precious Kumbatira, Prescott Magaleta, Royee Maliwa, Mustafa Munshi (Chichiri Athletics), Sinkhonde, Joseph Chunga, Charles Nyirongo (Mzimba North), Malilo (Mzimba South), Kadenje, Zorro Msiska, Shoeshine Ndovie (Karonga), Smile Chirambo (NR), Samuel Chirwa (Blantyre City), Paul Morin (Railways), Joseph Leno Chauluka (ITC), Samson Chibambo (BSS OB), Emanuel Gondwe (Dodgers)

28 Aug. 1968:   **Malawi Schools Travels to Zambia to Play Five Games**

Friendly: Livingstone: Southern Province 1–4   **K. Kamwendo**

Chris Kassia, Hunter Chikadzula, Harry Mapondo, Robert Kutengule, Henry Moyo, Damiano Malefula, James Thembulembu, Prescott Magaleta, Kanjedza Kamwendo, Tom Kazembe, B. Jimusole   Substitutes: E. Bulli, M. Kumilonde   **Coach:** Brian Griffin

30 Aug. 1968:   Squad Trimmed to 12 Players for Swaziland Tour
Green Malunga, Hamid Nazim, Prince Nyirenda, Oliver Nakhumwa, Roy Cook, Yasin Osman (Yahama Wanderers), Henry Kapalamula, Fraser Chitenje (Zomba Town), Royee Maliwa, (Chichiri Athletics), Sinkhonde, Smile Chirambo (NR), Samuel Chirwa (Blantyre City), Joseph Leno Chauluka (ITC), Samson Chibambo (BSS OB)

2 Sep. 1968:   BAT Trophy: Ndola: Zambia Schools 0–7
Precious Kumbatira, E. Bulli, Harry Mapondo, M. Kumilonde, Henry Moyo, Damiano Malefula, James Thembulembu, Prescott Magaleta, Kanjedza Kamwendo, Tom Kazembe, B. Jimusole, Substitutes: Hunter Chikadzula, A. Itimu   **Coach:** Brian Griffin

3 Sep. 1968:   Fraser Chitenje Dropped from Squad and Replaced by Paul Morin, James Mkwanda Also Included

5 Sep. 1968:   BAT Trophy: Kitwe: Zambia Schools 1–2   D. Malefula
Chris Kassia, Hunter Chikadzula, Harry Mapondo, Robert Kutengule, Henry Moyo, Damiano Malefula, James Thembulembu, Prescott Magaleta, Kanjedza Kamwendo, Tom Kazembe, M. Kumilonde   Substitutes: B. Jimusole, A. Itimu   **Coach:** Brian Griffin

6 Sep. 1968: Friendly: Mbabane: Botswana 8–1   Y. Osman (3). R. Cook (3), S. Chibambo, J. Chauluka
Green Malunga, Royee Maliwa, Paul Morin, Oliver Nakhumwa, Hamid Nazim, James Mkwanda, Prince Nyirenda, Smile Kampeza, Joseph Leno Chauluka, Yasin Osman, Roy Cook   **Coach:** Ray Batchelor

7 Sep. 1968: Friendly: Mbabane: Swaziland 0–2
Henry Kapalamula, Royee Maliwa, Paul Morin, Oliver Nakhumwa, Hamid Nazim, Samuel Chirwa, Prince Nyirenda, Samson Chibambo, Joseph Leno Chauluka (sub Smile Kampeza), Yasin Osman, Roy Cook   **Coach:** Ray Batchelor

8 Sep. 1968:   Bat Trophy: Lusaka: Zambia Schools 0–6
Precious Kumbatira, Wilson Zimtambila, Harry Mapondo, Robert Kutengule, Henry Moyo, Damiano Malefula, James Thembulembu, Prescott Magaleta, Kanjedza Kamwendo, Tom Kazembe, B. Jimusole Substitutes: Hunter Chikadzula, E. Bulli   **Coach:** Brian Griffin

9 Sep. 1968:   Friendly: Luanshya: Western Province   0–3
Precious Kumbatira, Hunter Chikadzula, Harry Mapondo, Robert Kutengule, Henry Moyo, Damiano Malefula, James Thembulembu, Prescott Magaleta, Kanjedza Kamwendo, Tom Kazembe, M. Kumilonde   Substitutes: B. Jimusole, Wilson Zimtambila   **Coach:** Brian Griffin

16 Sep. 1968:   Lilongwe Dynamos and Lilongwe United, two teams from Lilongwe, were invited and accepted to participate in the league run by the revised name of Malawi Football League. Corona, who ended in eightth place the previous season with 20 points from 22 games, withdrew, citing that officials had left the country.

1 Nov. 1968: Cholo Becomes the Second Team to Withdraw from the Malawi Football League

2 Nov. 1968: Charity Match in Honour of the Two Chichiri Athletics Players Who Died in Transit to Play in Tete   Chichiri Athletic v. Desportivo Tete   4–4   V. Tarmahomed, I. Sheriff, S. Maliro, B. Griffin

Chidzero, Prescott Magaleta, Alan Leech, Royee Maliwa, Brian Griffin, Vali Tarmahomed, Ikram Sheriff, Sparrow Maliro, James Thembulembu, Winfred Mphande, Hunter Chikadzula

4 Nov. 1968:   The Yamaha Wanderers put Yasin Osman on the transfer list valued at £500, and he joined newly-sponsored Blantyre City, who were now called Bata Bullets, for £100, a record transfer fee.

5 Nov. 1968:   Blantyre Secondary School Old Boys became the third team from the previous season to withdraw from the league. However, the league, with the inclusion of the two Lilongwe teams and with Malawi University and Malawi Army affiliating, brought the total to thirteen teams. The First Division had twelve teams and eight in the city league, bringing the total to thirty-three clubs in the Southern Region. The league started during the weekend of 9–10 November

25 Nov. 1968: Squads Selected to Play Salisbury Dynamos:
Malawi: Henry Kapalamula, Yasin Osman (Bata Bullets), George Linzie, Paul Morin, Alex (Poison) Mpinganjira (Railways), Brian Griffin (capt.), Ben Phoya (Chichiri Athletics), Ray Wooley (Blantyre SC), Robert Kutengule, Henry Moyo, Kanjedza Kamwendo (Malawi Schools);
Reserves: Precious Kumbatira, James Thembulembu (Malawi Schools), Mahewa (Michiru Castles), Ikram sheriff (Chichiri Athletics)
Wanderers: Green Malunga, George Trataris, Cullen Mwase, Hamid Nazim, Prince Nyirenda, James Mkwanda, Owen Kalitsiro, Samson Chibambo, Allaudin Osman, George Manda, Roy Cook, Smile Kampeza, Joseph Luka Chauluka, Kirby Thomson, B. Jimusole
Cholo Select XI: Paul Khamisa, Chikanda, Thipa, Kachokola, Chikanda (jnr), Dodoma, Akara, Malata, Danger, Mboga, Chisambi; Reserves: John Bonzo, Try Sameta
Zomba Town: Naming'ona, Mwabile, Nagoli, Namwali, Carmichael, Raleigh M'manga, Kuyere, Mang'anda or Fletcher, Chirwa, Elijah Joshua, Chanasa; Reserves: Ronald Gondwe

26 Nov. 1968: Friendly Cholo XI: Cholo: **Salisbury Dynamos 2–6**   **Mboga, B. Malila**
Giovanni Leotta, Chikanda, Kachokola, Chikanda (jnr), Akara, Malata, Danger, Mboga, Mashe (sub Basil Malila), Chisambi, Franco Bregger

28 Nov. 1968: Friendly Zomba XI: Zomba Gymkana: Salisbury Dynamos 2–7   **Chirwa (2)**
H. Naming'ona, Nagoli, Ronald Gondwe, Raleigh M'manga, Smart, Carmichael, Fletcher, Chirwa, Namwali, Elijah Joshua, Chanasa

30 Nov. 1968: Friendly Wanderers: Kamuzu Stadium: Salisbury Dynamos 3–4   **S. Chibambo (2), A. Osman**
Wanderers: Bothelho, James Kunyenge, Hamid Nazim, Prince Nyirenda, Oliver Nakhumwa, James Mkwanda, Bulli, Samson Chibambo, Allaudin Osman, Roy Cook, B. Jimusole

1 Dec. 1968: Friendly FAM XI: Kamuzu Stadium: Salisbury Dynamos 3–1 B. Griffin, A. Mpinganjira, Y. Osman
Henry Kapalamula, George Linzie, Paul Morin, Ray Wooley, Henry Moyo, Brian Griffin, James Thembulembu, Alex Mpinganjira, Ikram Sheriff, Yasin Osman, Ben Phoya   **Coach:**   Ray Batchelor

13 Dec. 1968:   **Malawi Fail to Participate in the All Africa Cup Championship Owing to Financial Difficulties**

1969

In its second season, the Malawi Football League saw some reshuffles in their association as history was made when two clubs from Lilongwe, UTM and Dynamos, made up the composition of the league, although UTM withdrew on the first match day, citing transport problems.

In addition to that, Blantyre Secondary School Old Boys lasted only one season and also saw two of the NFA clubs disappear from the sporting scene. Cholo Sports Club, who first affiliated in 1951, pulled out after only two seasons, but since they were reaffiliated in 1954, it was a continuous fourteen seasons.

The other club, Corona, who were twice NFA Champions, had in fact replaced Cholo the season they were missing in 1953, and they were part of the league apart from one season in 1965.

That now left only three teams from the previous NFA League: Blantyre Sports Club, Limbe Country Club, and Railways (who were then called Nyasaland Railways).

The newly affiliated clubs were University from Zomba and Malawi Army, leaving the number of clubs at twelve.

Bata Shoe Company became the second company to sponsor a club, as Blantyre City changed its name to Bata Bullets, and little was it suspected at that time that this club was going to create havoc in the football history of Malawi by becoming a real giant with many trophies won.

John Gilmore, then secretary, played a great part in transforming this club with that season showing new faces in the team, such as (£100) Yasin Osman, Mustafa Munshi, Henry Kapalamula, and Basil Malila, just to mention a few.

The knockout trophies were restored back to three as Chibuku Products sponsored the richest cash prize of £500 at that time, with BAT also adding another trophy, together with the ongoing Castle Cup, which made history the previous year with the introduction of the £100 sponsorship.

Another historic event is that these knockout competitions were to be played for by all three regions.

The Kamuzu Cup was still being played at the regional level, and research is still ongoing to find details for this season.

Malawi surpassed the previous most games of four during a calendar year by trebling it to twelve internationals, although only four countries were their opponents, with neighbours Rhodesia (six) and Zambia (three), accounting for 75 per cent of these matches. The other two countries were Swaziland and Madagascar.

Despite these many games, only one win was registered, when revenge against Swaziland was the order of the day, but even this was not completed, as a power failure interrupted the match after fifty-five minutes when Malawi were in control, leading 3–0.

Of the games against Rhodesia, 50 per cent ended in draws, and a disastrous tour of Zambia was recorded with a 16–0 aggregate score.

Samson Chibambo was the scoring hero, as he notched four out of the 8 goals, with the previous year's top scorer Roy Cook with 2.

Twenty-three new players were capped during this busy calendar, and fourteen retained their places, with Allaudin Osman being recalled after an absence of two years.

Oliver Nakhumwa, the sole survivor of 1962, was still in action, bringing his total to twenty-two caps.

Malawi featured only once against visiting West Ham United Youth side, losing this one as well, 1–0.

The Zambia Schools returned to Malawi and defeated the Schools in all three games played.

It was another winless year, as West Ham Youth also beat the Schools by 4–1. Eleven players were retained from the previous year, and eleven new faces were introduced to the squad.

1969 Timeline

1 Jan. 1969:   **Scotland v. England 4–2**   **B. Phillips, McDonald, McKenzie, C. Campbell, D. Quennell, D. Douglas**
Scotland: Steel, Tom Russell, Fraser, Wood, Jackie Cottingham, Charlie Clarke, McDonald, Brian Phillips, Matt Hoyland, McKenzie, Colin Campbell
England: S. Hesford, Eric Buckley, Harold Davies, Harold Wrigley (jnr), Davies (jnr), Parker, Aidan Humphries, Ray Batchelor, Derek Douglas, Don Quennell, Ray Wooley

6 Jan. 1969: Squad of Thirty Players Chosen for Matches against Rhodesia:
Precious Kumbatira, James Thembulembu, Brian Griffin, Ben Phoya, Kanjedza Kamwendo (Chichiri Athletics), Henry Kapalamula, Samuel Chirwa, David Chirwa, Charles Kagwa, Yasin Osman (Bata Bullets), Giovanni Leotta, Paul Morin, George Linzie, Roman Bwanali, Alex Mpinganjira (Railways), Robert Kutengule, Nagoli, M. Kumilonde (Zomba Town), Henry Moyo, Stephen Gondwe, Antoine Madinga (Lilongwe Dynamos), Ray Wooley (Blantyre SC), Oliver Nakhumwa, Prince Nyirenda, Hamid Nazim, Samson Chibambo, Roy Cook (Yamaha Wanderers), Damiano (Limbe CC), Hanjahanja, Winfred Mphande, Zoom (University)

31 Jan. 1969: Kamuzu Stadium: Malawi v. Rhodesia 0–0
Giovanni Leotta (sub Precious Kumbatira), Charles Kagwa, James Thembulembu, George Linzie, Henry Moyo, Robert Kutengule, Roman Bwanali, David Chirwa, Robert Kalembo, Stephen Gondwe, Ben Phoya   **Coach:**   Ray Batchelor

1 Feb. 1969: Lilongwe Community: Malawi v. Rhodesia 2–2   **R. Cook (o/g)**
Henry Kapalamula, Hamid Nazim, Samuel Chirwa (sub Charles Kagwa), Prince Nyirenda (sub Henry Moyo), Oliver Nakhumwa, Brian Griffin, Paul Morin, Samson Chibambo, Yasin Osman, Alex Mpinganjira. Roy Cook   **Coach:**   Ray Batchelor

2 Feb. 1969: Kamuzu Stadium: Malawi v. Rhodesia 0–1
Henry Kapalamula (sub Giovanni Leotta), Charles Kagwa, Robert Kutengule, George Linzie, Henry Moyo, Paul Morin, Alex Mpinganjira, Yasin Osman (sub Kanjedza Kamwendo), Samson Chibambo, Brian Griffin, Roy Cook   **Coach:**   Ray Batchelor

3 Feb. 1969: George Manda of Yamaha Wanderers Banned for the Rest of the Season

8 Feb. 1969: Salisbury: Rhodesia v. Malawi 4–0   Coach: Ray Batchelor
Giovanni Leotta, Charles Kagwa, Robert Kutengule, George Linzie (sub Sparrow Malilo, sub Roman Bwanali), Henry Moyo, Brian Griffin, Paul Morin, Kandjeza Kamwendo, Yasin Osman, Alex Mpinganjira, Roy Cook

9 Feb. 1969: Salisbury: Rhodesia v. Malawi 1–1   Y. Osman (pen)
Precious Kumbatira, Charles Kagwa, Robert Kutengule, Roman Bwanali, Henry Moyo, Royee Maliwa, Allaudin Osman (sub Robert Kalembo), Brian Griffin, Yasin Osman (sub Samuel Chirwa), Roy Cook, Ben Phoya   **Coach:**   Ray Batchelor

10 Feb. 1969:   Harold Humphreys, Football Association of Malawi General Secretary, Suspended; Egbert Mzandu to Act as the General Secretary, and a Meeting to Take Place on 16 February

13 Feb. 1969:   Damiano Malefula Signed for Bata Bullets from Zomba Town

16 Feb. 1969:   The suspension of Harold Humphreys and appointment of Egbert Mzandu as acting secretary was approved at a meeting, and both Chairman of the Football Association of Malawi Sydney Chikafa and Chairman of the Football League of Malawi Clive Fox refuted allegations of racism within the two boards. McDonald Mkunuley was appointed as acting treasurer.

17 Feb. 1969:   Basil Malila, captain of Bata Bullets, suspended for three weeks

17 Mar. 1969:   Jim Pinto, Yamaha Wanderers team manager, was banned for one year following disciplinary action during the Limbe v. Yamaha Wanderers match played in January that ended in a 1–1 draw. Two spectators, Mr Mendes, and Miss M. Milward, were also banned from attending any games.

15 Apr. 1969:   Squad of Twenty-Two Players Selected to Play Rhodesia in Bulawayo:
Precious Kumbatira, George Linzie, Charles Kagwa, Robert Kutengule, Paul Morin, Henry Moyo, Oliver Nakhumwa, Roman Bwanali, Alex Mpinganjira, Titto Kelly, Chirambo, Yasin Osman, Robert Kalembo, Brian Griffin, Ben Phoya, Roy Cook, Kanjedza Kamwendo, Royee Maliwa, Mereka, James Thembulembu, Allaudin Osman, Shaba

30 Apr. 1969:   BAT Final: Malawi Police v. Yamaha Wanderers 2–1   Mboga, R. Kalembo, S. Chibambo
Malawi Police: Gwiramwendo, Mulera, Mwamsambo, Chimayo, Chilimba, Kwenje, Hudson Mleme, Samuel Kapalamula, Robert Kalembo, Zimba, Mboga
Yamaha Wanderers: William Green, James Kunyenge, Hamid Nazim, Kirby Thomson (sub Prince Nyirenda), Oliver Nakhumwa, Roy Cook, Allaudin Osman, Dick Nyirenda, Samson Chibambo, Cullen Mwase, Smile Kampeza

1 May 1969:   Final Squad of Fourteen Players and Six Officials to Play Rhodesia in Bulawayo.
Leader of delegation Football Association of Malawi Chairman Sydney Chikafa, Acting Secretary Egbert Mzandu, Chairman of Selection Committee Vic Brighton, Coach Ray Batchelor, Team Manager K. S. Hadyri, and referee Billie Phambala.
Precious Kumbatira, George Linzie, Charles Kagwa, Paul Morin, Oliver Nakhumwa, Alex Mpinganjira, Samson Chibambo, Yasin Osman, Brian Griffin, Ben Phoya, Roy Cook, Prescott Magaleta, P. Tindo, Green Malunga

4 May 1969: Bulawayo: Friendly: Rhodesia v. Malawi 4–1   S. Chibambo
Precious Kumbatira, Charles Kagwa, Prescott Magaleta, George Linzie, Oliver Nakhumwa, Paul Morin, Yasin Osman, Brian Griffin (Alex Mpinganjira), Samson Chibambo, Roy Cook, Ben Phoya   **Coach:**   Ray Batchelor

8 May 1969:   Zomba Town and National Player Frazer Chitenje Signs for Bata Bullets, and Malawi Schools Sign Henry Moyo

12 May 1969: **Squad of Twenty-One Players Selected to Represent Malawi against West Ham United Youth:**
Green Malunga, Oliver Nakhumwa, Samson Chibambo, Roy Cook, Hamid Nazim (Yamaha Wanderers), Ishmail Khamisa, Wales Nsewa (Michiru Castles), Charles Kagwa, Frazer Chitenje, Yasin Osman (Bata Bullets), George Linzie, Alex Mpinganjira, Paul Morin (Railways), John Vart, P. Tindo, Mereka (Limbe CC), James Thembulembu, Vali Tarmahomed (Chichiri Athletics), Samuel Kapalamula, Robert Kalembo (Malawi Police), Tito Ziwoya (Escom)

Squad of Twenty-Two Players for Malawi Schools to Play West Ham United Youth
Precious Kumbatira, Prescott Magaleta, G. Mofeking (Chichiri SS), Harry Mapondo, Tom Kazembe (Blantyre SS), Chris Kassia, G. Manda (HHI), Robert Kutengule, M. Kumilonde, Kanjedza Kamwendo, A. Nsaliwa, M. Mzungu (Zomba), Henry Moyo, Tony Mulela, J. Kanyuka (Likuni), L. Kamanga (Dedza), M. Chibambo, S. Liwewe (Mtendere), B. Jimusole (St. Patricks), John Phalula (CI), P. Chilalika (Malosa)

17 May 1969: Friendly: Kamuzu Stadium: Malawi v. West Ham United Youth 0–1
Green Malunga, Charles Kagwa, Hamid Nazim, George Linzie, Oliver Nakhumwa, Roman Bwanali, Robert Kalembo, Alex Mpinganjira, Samson Chibambo, Samuel Kapalamula (sub James Thembulembu), Roy Cook   **Coach:**   Ray Batchelor

18 May 1969: Friendly: Kamuzu Stadium: Malawi Schools v. West Ham United Youth 1–4   K. Kamwendo
Precious Kumbatira (sub Chris Kassia), Harry Mapondo, Robert Kutengule, M. Kumilonde, Henry Moyo, Prescott Magaleta, L. Kamanga (sub M. Chibambo), B. Jimusole, Kanjedza Kamwendo, George Mofeking, A. Nsaliwa

19 May 1969: **Malawi invites Swaziland to Play during the Independence Celebrations; Swaziland Also Invited to Play in Tananarive, Madagascar, in June during Their Republic Celebrations**

24 May 1969: Kamuzu Stadium: Chibuku Cup Final:
Yamaha Wanderers v. Bata Bullets 3–2 A. Osman, R. Cook, Smile Kampeza, Y. Osman, Mustafa Munshi
Yahama Wanderers: Green Malunga, Cullen Mwase, Hamid Nazim, Kirby Thomson, Oliver Nakhumwa, Prince Nyirenda, Allaudin Osman, Roy Cook, Samson Chibambo, Dick Nyirenda (sub James Mkwanda), Smile Kampeza
Bata Bullets: Henry Kapalamula (sub Greyson Simika), John Mpesi, Kaliati, Mustafa Munshi, Charles Kagwa, Ralph Stanley, Smart Thipa, Patrick Servana, Yasin Osman, Max Prien (sub Reggie Karim), Basil Malila

29 May 1969: **Squad of Thirty-One Players Selected for Madagascar Match to Be Played on 27 June 1969 in Tananarive:**
Green Malunga, Prince Nyirenda, Oliver Nakhumwa, Smile Kampeza, Roy Cook, Hamid Nazim (Yamaha Wanderers), Charles Kagwa, Henry Moyo, Frazer Chitenje, Yasin Osman, Mustafa Munshi (Bata Bullets), Roman Bwanali, George Linzie, Alex Mpinganjira (Railways), Precious Kumbatira, Kanjedza Kamwendo, Vali Tarmahomed, Ben Phoya, Prescott Magaleta (Chichiri Athletics), John Vart, P. Tindo, Don Quennell (Limbe CC), Ishmail Khamisa, Wales Nsewa (Michiru Castles), Samuel Kapalamula, Robert Kalembo (Malawi Police), Tito Ziwoya (Escom), Pearce, Winfred Mphande (University), Cliff Wintle (Blantyre SC), Shaba (Mithole Athletic)

23 Jun. 1969: **Malawi Selects Thirteen Players to Travel to Madagascar:**
Grcen Malunga, Oliver Nakhumwa, Samson Chibambo, Roy Cook, Hamid Nazim (Yamaha Wanderers), Charles Kagwa, Henry Moyo, Frazer Chitenje, Yasin Osman (Bata Bullets), Roman Bwanali, George Linzie, Alex Mpinganjira (Railways), Ben Phoya (Chichiri Athletics)

27 Jun. 1969: **Friendly: Tananarive: Madagascar v. Malawi   3–0**
Green Malunga, Hamid Nazim, George Linzie, Charles Kagwa, Oliver Nakhumwa (sub Henry Moyo), Frazer Chitenje, Roman Bwanali, Yasin Osman, Samson Chibambo, Roy Cook, Ben Phoya   **Coach:** Ray Batchelor

3 Jul. 1969:   Malawi Prepare for Swaziland Visit and Squad of Twenty-Two Players Selected, of Which the Final Squad Will Be Trimmed to Fifteen Players
Goaleepers: Green Malunga, Cliff Wintle, Precious Kumbatira   Full Backs: Charles Kagwa, John Vart, Hamid Nazim   Half Backs: Oliver Nakhumwa, Prince Nyirenda, George Linzie, Frazer Chitenje, Roman Bwanali, Henry Moyo   Forwards: Samson Chibambo, Alex Mpinganjira, Yasin Osman, Roy Cook, Robert Kalembo, Don Quennell, Ben Phoya, Mustafa Munshi, George Samati, Peter Tindo

6 Jul. 1969: Friendly: Kamuzu Stadium: Malawi v. Swaziland 3-0   S. Chibambo (2), R. Cook
(match abandoned after fifty-five minutes because of power failure)
Green Malunga, Charles Kagwa, Hamid Nazim, Prince Nyirenda, Oliver Nakhumwa, Frazer Chitenje, Samson Chibambo, Henry Moyo, Yasin Osman, Alex Mpinganjira, Roy Cook   **Coach:**   Ray Batchelor

9 Jul. 1969: Friendly: Kamuzu Stadium: Malawi v. Swaziland 1-1   S. Chibambo
Green Malunga, Peter Tindo (sub Charles Kagwa), John Vart, Prince Nyirenda, Oliver Nakhumwa, Frazer Chitenje, Samson Chibambo, Henry Moyo, Yasin Osman, Robert Kalembo (sub Alex Mpinganjira), Roy Cook

12 Jul. 1969:   Kamuzu Stadium: Castle Cup Final: University v. Yahama Wanderers 2-0 Mphande (2p)
University: Pierce, M. Mkandawire, Mhone, Nankhuni, Du Mhango, M. Mtawali, Mphande, Gondwe, Hezekaya Mkandawire, Mwabumba, G. Banda

Yamaha Wanderers: Green Malunga, James Kunyenge, Hamid Nazim, Kirby Thomson, Oliver Nakhumwa, Prince Nyirenda, Samson Chibambo, Cullen Mwase, Allaudin Osman, Roy Cook, Smile Kampeza (sub James Mkwanda)

Final Log Table

No.	Teams	P	W	D	L	F	A	PTS
1	Yamaha Wanderers	20	14	4	2	52	17	32
2	Bata Bullets	20	13	4	3	50	25	30
3	Chichiri Athletics	20	14	1	5	55	27	29
4	Railways	20	12	4	4	68	31	28
5	Michiru Castles	20	11	4	5	50	22	26
6	Limbe CC	20	6	6	8	44	46	18
7	Malawi Police	20	5	5	10	39	50	15
8	University	20	5	4	11	24	52	14
9	Malawi Army	20	6	2	12	32	69	14
10	Blantyre SC	20	2	2	16	25	64	6
11	Zomba Town*	20	1	6	13	30	66	4

Lilongwe Dynamos withdrew from the league, and all their results were null and void. At that time, they had played thirteen games and their record was W1 D3 L9 F17 A46, and they'd had 4 pointed deducted.

27 Jul. 1969: Kamuzu Stadium: Champions (Yamaha Wanderers) v. FAM Select 0-2   Don Quennell, ?
FAM Select XI: Pierce, John Vart, Frazer Chitenje, Wales Nsewa, Charles Kagwa, Albert Nsewa (sub Roman Bwanali), Yasin Osman, Alex Mpinganjira, Don Quennell, Winfred Mphande, Ben Phoya
Yamaha Wanderers: Green Malunga, James Kunyenge, Hamid Nazim, Cullen Mwase, Oliver Nakhumwa, Prince Nyirenda, Bob Van Guilder, Kirby Thomson, Samson Chibambo, Allaudin Osman, Smile Kampeza

29 Jul. 1969: **National Coach Ray Batchelor to Leave Tomorrow for England on a Two-Month Working Holiday**

2–3 Aug. 1969: **Duarte Silver Cup and Malawi Railways Trophy Involving a Four-Team Tournament: Clube Ferroviario, Malawi Railways, Bata Bullets, Yamaha Wanderers**
Malawi Railways: Manuel Lima, Ngwira, Saka, George Linzie, Roman Bwanali, John Phalula, Richard Lawrence, Paul Morin, Alex Mpinganjira, Ben Phoya, Victor Lawrence, Likagwa
Yamaha Wanderers: Green Malunga, Hamid Nazim, James Kunyenge, Prince Nyirenda, Oliver Nakhumwa, Cullen Mwase, Allaudin Osman, Kirby Thomson, Samson Chibambo, Bob Van Guilder, Smile Kampeza, James Mkwanda
Bata Bullets: George Trataris, Kaliati, Frazer Chitenje, John Mpesi, Mustafa Munshi, Charles Kagwa, Hanjahanja, Patrick Servana, Yasin Osman, Basil Malila, Smart Thipa, Ralph Stanley, Sattar Osman
SF: Bata Bullets beat Yamaha Wanderers
        Railways v. Clube Ferroviario de Mozambique 1–2

3/4 PO   Yamaha Wanderers v. Railways 3–2   J. Mkwanda, Karaja, Smile Chibambo, G, Linzie (p), Likagwa
Final   Clube Ferroviario de Mozambique v. Bata Bullets 1–0

Kamuzu Cup Final: Southern Region v. Northern Region (result still being researched)

12 Aug. 1969: **Malawi Invited to Play Three Games in Zambia with a Provisional Squad of 23 Players:**
Green Malunga, Precious Kumbatira, Chris Kassia, Nkata, Cliff Wintle, Hamid Nazim, Charles Kagwa, H. Chibambo, Robert Kutengule, Pat Mhone, John Vart, Store, Frazer Chitenje, Oliver Nakhumwa, Prince Nyirenda, P. Tindo, George Linzie, Kanjedza Kamwendo, Wales Nsewa, Stephen Gondwe, Robert Kalembo, Albert Nsewa, Winfred Mphande

14 Aug. 1969: **Travelling Squad for Zambia Tour Revised, as Malawi Schools Hosting Their Counterparts around the Same Time**
Green Malunga, Nkata, Cliff Wintle, Manuel Lima, Hamid Nazim, Charles Kagwa, H. Chibambo, Pat Mhone, John Vart, Store, Frazer Chitenje, Oliver Nakhumwa, Mustafa Munshi, Prince Nyirenda, Paul Morin, Roman Bwanali, P. Tindo, George Linzie, Cannock Munde, Bibo Chifukwa, Spy Msiska, Yasin Osman, Allaudin Osman, Samson Chibambo, Alex Mpinganjira, Robert Kalembo, James Mkwanda, Albert Nsewa, Smile Chibambo, Vali Tarmahomed, Joe Fernandes, Cullen Mwase, Basil Malila

22 Aug. 1969: **Malawi Invited to Participate in the East Africa Challenge Championship**

25 Aug. 1969: **Malawi Schools Squad Announced to Play against Zambia Schools**
Precious Kumbatira, Prescott Magaleta, Eric Namate, George Mofeking, Kelvin Mangisa, Ben Phoya (Chichiri SS), Chris Kassia (HHI), Robert Kutengule, Kanjedza Kamwendo, M. Kumilonde, A. Nsaliwa (Zomba), John Phalula (CI), Harry Mapondo, Tom Kazembe (Blantyre SS), Robert Gondwe, Chintola (Robert Blake), Henry Moyo, Tony Mulela (Likuni), Titus Nthara, Atlee Nkhonjera (Mzuzu)

27 Aug. 1969: The twenty-man squad for the Zambian tour was announced. George Nthukwa was the leader of the delegation, and other officials were George Nhelma, the acting FAM secretary; Frank Kapito, the team manager, and Nelson Chirwa as a referee.
Green Malunga, Precious Kumbatira, John Vart, Charles Kagwa, Prince Nyirenda, Pat Mhone, Hamid Nazim, Wales Nsewa, Oliver Nakhumwa (capt.), Cullen Mwase, Frazer Chitenje, Stephen Gondwe, Alex Mpinganjira, Mustafa Munshi, Cannock Munde, James Mkwanda, Smile Kampeza, Basil Malila, Robert Kalembo, Yasin Osman

28 Aug. 1969: At a meeting conducted by a commission of inquiry, it was found that the act of suspending Harold Humphreys by the chairman Sydney Chikafa was unconstitutional, as there was no provision in the constitution empowering the chairman.

It was also decided to dissolve both FAM and the FLM, with the new body to be known as the National Football Association (NFA). The leagues to be run at the regional level and the FLM were now to be known as the Southern Region Football League (SRFL). This was to be rectified at the AGM on 14 September, with the league to start in November.

In another development, Blantyre Sports Club, one of the oldest in the country as well as the founding member of the NFA in 1948, withdrew from the league.

29 Aug. 1969: Chichiri Athletics AGM:
Chairman E. Adamson, Vice Chairman: F. Davidson, Secretary I. Mojoo, Treasurer Jones   , committee members Harry Thomson, Magombo, Ikram Sheriff, Vali Tarmahomed

30 Aug. 1969: Peter Stuyvesant Trophy: Lusaka: Zambia v. Malawi 4–0
Green Malunga, Charles Kagwa, John Vart, Hamid Nazim, Oliver Nakhumwa, Prince Nyirenda, Mustafa Munshi, Wales Nsewa, Yasin Osman, Alex Mpinganjira, Basil Malila Substitutes: Stephen Gondwe, Robert Kalembo   **Team Manager:** Frank Kapito

30 Aug. 1969: Friendly: Lilongwe: Central Region Schools v. Zambia Schools 1–6   S. Bweya

31 Aug. 1969: Peter Stuyvesant Trophy: Ndola: Zambia v. Malawi 5–0
Green Malunga, Charles Kagwa, John Vart, Hamid Nazim (sub Mustafa Munshi), Oliver Nakhumwa, Frazer Chitenje, Pat Mhone (sub Prince Nyirenda), Robert Kalembo, Yasin Osman, Alex Mpinganjira, Cannock Munde   Team Manager: Frank Kapito

31 Aug. 1969: BAT Trophy: Lilongwe: Malawi Schools v. Zambia Schools 1–2   B. Phoya
Chris Kassia, Harry Mapondo, Eric Namate, Robert Gondwe, Henry Moyo, Prescott Magaleta, A. Nsaliwa, M. Kumilonde, Kanjedza Kamwendo, George Mofeking, Ben Phoya

2 Sep. 1969: Peter Stuyvesant Trophy: Kitwe: Zambia v. Malawi 7–0
Green Malunga, Charles Kagwa, Cullen Mwase, Hamid Nazim, Oliver Nakhumwa, Prince Nyirenda, Mustafa Munshi, James Mkwanda, Yasin Osman, Cannock Munde, Smile Kampeza   Substitutes: Alex Mpinganjira, Wales Nsewa   **Team Manager:** Frank Kapito

2 Sep. 1969: BAT Trophy: Kamuzu Stadium: Malawi Schools v. Zambia Schools   1–6 K. Kamwendo
Chris Kassia, Harry Mapondo, Eric Namate, Robert Gondwe, Henry Moyo (Tom Kazembe), Prescott Magaleta, Robert Kutengule, M. Kumilonde, Kanjedza Kamwendo, George Mofeking, Ben Phoya (A. Nkhonjera)

6 Sep. 1969: Friendly: Zomba: Zomba Town v. Zambia Schools 0–7
Ali (Kelvin Mangisa), Mwabile, Robert Kutengule, Lewis Chinula, Namwali, Chipeta, Mushani, Munde, Winfred Mphande, Khongwa, Chirwa

7 Sep. 1969: BAT Trophy: Kamuzu Stadium: Malawi Schools v. Zambia Schools   1–2 T. Kazembe
Chris Kassia, Harry Mapondo, Eric Namate, M. Kumilonde, Henry Moyo, Prescott Magaleta, Atlee Nkhonjera, Kanjedza Kamwendo, Titus Nthara, George Mofeking, Tom Kazembe

9 Sep. 1969: Yamaha Wanderers invited to play Lesotho Champions on 13 September

17 Oct. 1969: The Football Association of Malawi (FAM) was dissolved, to be overseen by a caretaker committee. Tom McClosky, the secretary; Jack Muwamba; and Lawrence Anthony constituted part of the committee members.

24 Oct. 1969: Risco, the 1969 Rhodesian Champions of Mines Arrive in the Country to Play Several Friendly Games as Scheduled Below:

26 October:	Kamuzu Stadium	v Limbe Toyota
28 October:	Cholo	v. Bata Bullets
30 October:	Zomba	v. Zomba Town or Michiru Castles
01 November:	Kamuzu Stadium	v. University
02 November:	Kamuzu Stadium	v. Yamaha Wanderers

10 Nov. 1969:   Caretaker Committee Selects a Squad of 25 Players for Future Fixtures with Two New Names—Nankhuni and G. Banda—and Recalls Raleigh M'manga.
Nankhuni, G. Banda, Raleigh M'manga, Paul Morin, Green Malunga, Frazer Chitenje, Hamid Nazim, Alex Mpinganjira, Robert Kutengule, John Vart, George Linzie, Yasin Osman, Cannock Munde, Ben Phoya, Roy Cook, Charles Kagwa, Precious Kumbatira, Cliff Wintle, Oliver Nakhumwa, Prince Nyirenda, Mustafa Munshi, Kanjedza Kamwendo, Winfred Mphande, Prescott Magaleta, M. Kumilonde

10 Nov. 1969:   Newly Elected Committee of the Blantyre and Districts League (BDL), under the Chairmanship of Lawrence Anthony, Secretary John Gilmore, and Committee Members Nyirenda, Brian Whitelaw, George Toyne, and Frank Kapito
With the new season yet to start, Railways became the second club to withdraw from the league. They were replaced by Escom United, reducing the league to ten clubs. Two clubs changed their names as a result of acquired sponsorships. Limbe Country Club was now to be known as Limbe Toyota, courtesy of Mobile Motors Limited, sole agents of Toyota vehicles, and the oldest football club, Michiru Castles, would henceforth be known as Michiru Blue Cross.
The composition of the three divisions was as follows:

Division One: Bata Bullets, Chichiri Athletics, Escom United, Limbe Toyota, Malawi Army, Malawi Police, Michiru Blue Cross, University, Yamaha Wanderers, Zomba Town
Division Two: Cholo, Farmers Marketing Board (FMB), Gold Leaf, Medicals, Mitole Athletics, Railways, Southern Bottlers, Times, United Transport of Malawi (UTM), Wenela
Division Three: Bangwe Black Stars, Barclays, Chalimbana, Imperial Tobacco Group (ITG), Malawi Housing Corporation (MHC), Mbami Kwela, Railways IT, Sunlight Rovers, Whiteaheads, Works & Supplies

13 Nov. 1969:   Malawi Invited to Participate during the Uhuru Celebrations in Kenya and to Play up to Four Games that would Include Other Countries between 10 and 12 December

18 Nov. 1969:   Trip to Kenya Cancelled by the Kenyan Football Authorities, Citing Financial Problems

Summary of the '60s

Malawi

Opposition	P	W	D	L	F	A	
Rhodesia	10	1	4	5	11	24	
Zambia	5	0	0	5	1	27	
Swaziland	3	1	1	1	4	3	
Madagascar	2	0	0	2	1	9	
Northern Rhodesia	2	0	0	2	1	10	(now Zambia)
Southern Rhodesia	2	0	1	1	3	5	(previously Rhodesia)
Basutoland	1	0	0	1	3	4	(now Lesotho)
Botswana	1	1	0	0	8	2	
Ghana	1	0	0	1	0	12	
Kenya	1	0	1	0	2	2	
Tanganyika	1	0	0	1	2	6	(nowTanzania)
	29	3	7	19	36	104	

Top Five Appearances (29)
22: Oliver Nakhumwa, Yasin Osman (including 1 sub)
12: Frazer Chitenje, Royee Maliwa, Charles Kagwa (including 2 subs)
11: Roy Cook, Paul Morin, Prince Nyirenda (including 2 subs)
10: Henry Kapalamula, Overton Mkandawire
9: Hamid (Jack) Nazim

Top Five Scorers (36)
6: Roy Cook, Samson Chibambo
5: Yasin Osman
4: Overton Mkandawire
3: Solomon Mkwapatira

Top Clean Sheets (3)
1: Henry Kapalamula, Giovanni Leotta, William Green

Malawi Select XI, U-23 against Club Sides

Opposition	P	W	D	L	F	A
Salisbury Callies	2	0	1	1	2	3
Salisbury City	2	1	1	0	3	0
Wankie	2	1	0	1	4	4
Copperbelt XI	1	0	0	1	4	5
Desportivo Tete	1	1	0	0	4	1
Ferroviario	1	0	0	1	1	5
Midlands	1	0	0	1	2	8
Oldham Athletics	1	0	0	1	2	3
Salisbury Dynamos	1	1	0	0	3	1
Sporting Club Tete	1	1	0	0	4	1
West Ham Youth	1	0	0	1	0	1
	14	5	2	7	29	32

Top Five Appearances (Malawi v. Club Sides) (14)
9: Oliver Nakhumwa
7: Henry Kapalamula, Overton Mkandawire
6: Frazer Chitenje, Hamid Nazim, Ray Wooley
5: Brian Griffin, James Mkwanda, Allaudin Osman, Yasin Osman
4: Wales Nsewa, Prince Nyirenda

Top Five Scorers (29—1 Unknown)
9: Overton Mkandawire
4: Brian Griffin
2: Emmanuel Gondwe, Samuel Kapalamula, Yasin Osman

Top Clean Sheets (3)
2: Henry Kapalamula
1: Green Malunga

Regional Select v. Club Sides

Opposition	P	W	D	L	F	A
Zomba						
Zambia Schools	1	1	0	0	3	2
Wankie	1	1	0	0	2	1
Salisbury Dynamos	1	0	0	1	2	7
Lilongwe						
Wankie	1	0	0	1	4	6
Chikwawa						
Wankie	1	0	0	1	1	2
Cholo						
Wankie	1	0	0	1	2	6

Malawi Schools

Opposition	P	W	D	L	F	A
Zambia Schools	8	1	0	7	6	32
Southern Province	1	0	0	1	1	4
Western Province	1	0	0	1	0	3
West Ham United	1	0	0	1	1	4
	11	1	0	10	8	43

Top Five Appearances (11)
11: Kanjedza Kamwendo, Prescott Magaleta
9: Harry Mapondo, Henry Moyo
8: Robert Kutengule, M. Kumilonde (including 2 subs)
7: Tom Kazembe (including 1 sub)
6: Chris Kassia (including 1 sub), B. Jimusole (including 2 subs)

Top Five Scorers (8)
3: Kanjedza Kamwendo
1: Five players with a goal each

Mario Antoine

Clean Sheets (1)
1: Mhango

NFA "A" Team

Opposition:	P	W	D	L	F	A
Southern Rhodesia	2	0	0	2	6	17

NFA "A" Team against Clubs

Opposition	P	W	D	L	F	A
Sport Lisboa e Beira	8	4	1	3	17	12
Alexandra FC	3	2	0	1	10	5
Clube de Tete	2	1	1	0	6	4
Salisbury Callies	2	0	1	1	1	10
Blackpool	1	0	0	1	1	6
De Sportivo de Tete	1	0	0	1	0	1
Dundee United	1	0	0	1	2	10
Quelimane	1	0	1	0	4	4
Railways Beira	1	0	1	0	2	2
Salisbury XI	1	1	0	0	3	2
Sporting Beira	1	0	0	1	0	3
West Ham United	1	0	0	1	0	4
	23	8	5	10	46	63

Top Five Appearances "A" (25)
20: Dennis Pritchard
19: Dennis Johnston, Brian Phillips, Jackie Cottingham (including 1 sub)
14: Sergio Nicholas
12: Max Prien
9: Brian Fox

Top Five Scorers (46—6 unknown)
13: Max Prien
8: Brian Phillips
3: Brian Fox, Dennis Pritchard
2: Terry Mills, Bob Rodgers

Most Clean Sheets (0)

NFA "B" Team

Opposition:	P	W	D	L	F	A
Alexandra FC	3	3	0	0	20	2
Salisbury Callies	2	1	0	1	2	3
	5	4	0	1	22	5

Top Five Appearances "B" Team (5)
3: Matt Hoyland, Peter Lewis, Ken Mansfield, Bob Power, George Trataris
2: Rui Bastos, Lorenco Colandria, Corb, Jackie Cottingham, Alan Geldard, J. Hoatson, Michel Melotte, Don Meintzies, Terry Mills, Vic Moss, Bob Rodgers, Rosenast

Top Five Scorers (22—9 unknown)
4: Vic Moss
3: Rui Bastos
2: Bob Rodgers

Top Clean Sheets (2)
1: A. Gafforio, George Trataris

Domestic scene–36 trophies: 6 Royle, 2 City and Suburban, 2 BDFL League, 8 Royle K/O, 8 Stanhope, 6 Franklin, 2 Castle Cup, 1 Chibuku, 1 BAT

Teams	League		Royle		Stanhope		Franklin		Castle		Chibuku		B.A.T.		Total	
	W	RU	W	RU	W	RU	W	RU	W	RU	W	RU	W	RU	W	RU
Blantyre SC	1	3	2	2	4	1		1	1						7	8
Y. Wanderers	4				1	1	1			1	1			1	7	3
Limbe CC	3		2	1	1			2							6	3
Olympia	1	2	2	1	2			1							6	3
Zomba	1	2	2		1		1	1							5	3
Railways				2			2								2	2
Chichiri Ath.						1		1	1						1	2
Mw. Police													1			1
Rovers							1								1	
University									1						1	
Callies		1		1	2											4
Bata Bullets		1		1								1				3
Cholo					2			1								3
Corona		1														1

For the Stanhope Cup final in 1965, Blantyre SC and Wanderers shared the trophy, as there was no available date for replay. Wanderers started as "Portuguese Wanderers" during the 1964–65 season, ended up as league champions, and shared the Stanhope Trophy as mentioned above. They dropped "Portuguese" the following year and won the double in 1966–67, winning the City & Suburban League and Franklin Cup.

In the 1967–68 season, the name "Wanderers" was changed to "Yamaha Wanderers" because of sponsorship from Yamaha Agents, Stansfield Motors. Yamaha Wanderers were champions of the Blantyre and Districts Football League (BDFL) in seasons 1967–68 and 1968–69, winning the league under three different names, and completed the double in 1968–69 by winning the Chibuku Cup. Blantyre City ended as runners-up in their first season, 1966–67, and changed their name to "Bata Bullets" in 1968–69. Bata Shoe Company sponsored the club, which ended as runners-up in both the BDFL and the Chibuku Cup.

CHAPTER NINE

SUMMARY OF MALAWI INTERNATIONAL PLAYERS

Full Internationals for Malawi and NFA games ares referred to as "Friendly", "Select", and "Regional"; "B" teams are referred to as "Others". Fixtures against club sides are identified as "Friendly Club".

Player Index

R. Kaliati	1949
E. Thondoya	1949
H. Jonga	1949
G. Jonas	1949
Kumkwenzu	1949
Chikwete	1949
K. Munthali	1949
W. Mbekeani	1949
Samson Manewa	1949–1950
Manyowa	1949
R. Jambo	1949
Smart Thipa	1950, 1962–1963
Costas Trataris	1954, 1956–1957, 1959–1960, 1963, 1965
James Kaminjolo	1957, 1964
Shonga	1957
Kumwenda	1957
Sazuze	1957
Kaunda	1957
Matinga	1957
Godfrey Kalitsiro	1957, 1962–1964
Thomas	1957
Kumwembwe	1957
Royee Maliwa	1957, 1962–1964, 1966, 1968–1969
Makwelero	1957
Kambuli	1957
Daudi	1957
Salamu	1957
James Sangala	1957, 1962–1964
Jackie Cottingham	1958–1965, 1967
Bob Power	1961–1963, 1967
Lennox Kishombe	1962–1963
Bright Gondwe	1962
Lewis Chinula	1962–1963

Oliver Nakhumwa	1962–1964, 1966–1969
Raleigh M'manga	1962–1964, 1968
Richard Banda	1962–1963, 1968
Nathan Gondwe	1962
Mobray de Thipa	1962–1963, 1966
Januaro de Maghalhaes	1962–1965
Allaudin Osman	1962–1963, 1965–1967, 1969
Joaquim Cunha	1962–1965
Noel Nthala	1963–1964, 1966–1967
F. Tembo	1963
Stanley Bweya	1963–1964, 1968
Emmanuel Gondwe	1963–1964, 1968
Lameck Phiri	1963
R. Kapote	1963
Joseph Leno (Chauluka)	1963, 1968
Mkalanyinga Sitoro	1963–1964
B. Phombeya	1963
Wesley Sangala	1963
John Brown	1963, 1965–1967
Franco Bregger	1963, 1968
George Linzie	1964, 1967–1969
D. Njema	1964
Roman Bwanali	1964, 1966–1967, 1969
Robert Kalembo	1964, 1969
Frazer Chitenje	1964, 1966 -1969
Samuel Kapalamula	1964, 1966–1969
Henry Nsewa	1964, 1967
Charles Nyirongo	1964
Overton Mkandawire	1964, 1966–1968
Shake	1964
Wales Juma	1964
Phillip Bradley	1964–1965
Ikram Sheriff	1964, 1968
Cliff Wintle	1965
Jerry Burns	1965
Harold Wrigley (jnr)	1965
Woods	1965
Henry Kapalamula	1966–1969
S. Bulla	1966–1967
Elijah Joshua	1966–1968
Paul Morin	1966–1969
Cullen Mwase (Continental)	1966, 1968–1969
Joe Gallagher	1966

Albert Nsewa	1966–1967
Solomon Mkwapatira	1966, 1968
Yasin Osman	1966–1969
Peter Chisasa	1966–1967
Prince Nyirenda	1966–1969
Crosby Chisasa	1966–1967
James Kuyenge	1967
Joe Fernandes	1967
Wales Nsewa	1967, 1969
John Raisbeck	1967
George Manda	1967–1968
Ray Wooley	1967–1968
Kirby Thomson	1967
Brian Griffin	1967–1969
Owen Kalitsiro	1967–1968
Crighton Msiya	1967
Balraj Bouri	1967
Losacco	1967
James Mkwanda	1967–1969
William Green Malunga	1967–1969
Gordon Brighton	1967
Hamid (Jack) Nazim	1967–1969
Julio Kamlaza	1967–1968
Katete	1967
Prescott Magaleta	1967–1969
Mustafa Munshi	1967–1969
Samson Chibambo	1967–1969
Smile Kampeza	1967, 1969
Zimba	1967
Samuel Chirwa	1968–1969
Roy Cook	1968–1969
Damiano Malefula	1968
Smile Chirambo	1968
Chidzero	1968
Henry Moyo	1968–1969
David Chirwa	1968–1969
James Thembulembu	1968–1969
Eric Watts	1968
Alex Mpinganjira (Poison)	1968–1969
Tito Kelly	1968
Ben Phoya	1968–1969
Chiwanda	1968
Uteka	1968

Ngwangwa	1968
Galatoni Njoka	1968
R. Pilato	1968
Antoine Madinga	1968
Kaipsya	1968
Katanga	1968
Fernando Araujo	1968
Horace Naming'ona	1968
Robert Gondwe	1968
Smart	1968
Fletcher	1968
Chirwa	1968
Chanasa	1968
Mwabile	1968
Kuyere	1968
Nagoli	1968
Namwali	1968
Carmichael	1968
Mheya	1968
Khumanje	1968
Masambera	1968
Chadza	1968
B. Mkandawire	1968
Chasweka	1968
Joza	1968
Mhango	1968
F. Mkwanda	1968
Shawa	1968
A. Kalitsiro	1968
Chikanda	1968
Kachokola	1968
Chikanda (jnr)	1968
Akara	1968
Malata	1968
Danger	1968
Mboga	1968
Chisambi	1968
Mashe	1968
Basil Malila	1968–1969
Giovanni Leotta	1968–1969
Precious Kumbatira	1969
Charles Kagwa	1969
Peter Tindo	1969

Robert Kutengule	1969	
John Vart	1969	
Pat Mhone	1969	
Kanjedza Kamwendo	1969	
Stephen Gondwe	1969	
C. Munde	1969	
Sparrow Malilo	1969	

1.   **R. Kaliati**

Year	Caps	Subs	Total	C/Sheets
1949	2	0	2	0

Summary of Games

Fixtures	P	W	D	L	F	A
Friendly Club	2	0	0	2	3	6
		0%	0%	100%	1.50	3.00

2.   **E. Thondoya**

Year	Caps	Subs	Total	Goals
1949	2	0	2	1

Summary of Games

Fixtures	P	W	D	L	F	A	GS
Friendly Club	2	0	0	2	3	6	1
		0%	0%	100%	1.50	3.00	33.3%

Notes: 1949: 1 unknown scorer v. Grupo Desportivo Rebenta Fogo in 1–2 defeat

3.   **H. Jonga**

Year	Caps	Subs	Total	Goals
1949	2	0	2	0

Summary of Games

Fixtures	P	W	D	L	F	A
Friendly Club	2	0	0	2	3	6
		0%	0%	100%	1.50	3.00

Notes: 1949: 1 unknown scorer v. Grupo Desportivo Rebenta Fogo in 1–2 defeat

4.   **G. Jonas**

Year	Caps	Subs	Total	Goals
1949	2	0	2	1

Summary of Games

Fixtures	P	W	D	L	F	A	GS
Friendly Club	2	0	0	2	3	6	1
		0%	0%	100%	1.50	3.00	33.3%

Notes: 1949: 1 unknown scorer v. Grupo Desportivo Rebenta Fogo in 1–2 defeat

5.   **Kumkwenzu**

Year	Caps	Subs	Total	Goals
1949	2	0	2	0

Summary of Games

Fixtures	P	W	D	L	F	A
Friendly Club	2	0	0	2	3	6
		0%	0%	100%	1.50	3.00

Notes: 1949: 1 unknown scorer v. Grupo Desportivo Rebenta Fogo in 1–2 defeat

6.   **Chikwete**

Year	Caps	Subs	Total	Goals
1949	2	0	2	0

Summary of Games

Fixtures	P	W	D	L	F	A
Friendly Club	2	0	0	2	3	6
		0%	0%	100%	1.50	3.00

Notes: 1949: 1 unknown scorer v. Grupo Desportivo Rebenta Fogo in 1–2 defeat

7.   **K. Munthali**

Year	Caps	Subs	Total	Goals
1949	2	0	2	0

Summary of Games

Fixtures	P	W	D	L	F	A
Friendly Club	2	0	0	2	3	6
		0%	0%	100%	1.50	3.00

Notes: 1949: 1 unknown scorer v. Grupo Desportivo Rebenta Fogo in 1–2 defeat

8.   **W. Mbekeani**

Year	Caps	Subs	Total	Goals
1949	2	0	2	0

Summary of Games

Fixtures	P	W	D	L	F	A
Friendly Club	2	0	0	2	3	6
		0%	0%	100%	1.50	3.00

Notes: 1949: 1 unknown scorer v. Grupo Desportivo Rebenta Fogo in 1–2 defeat

9.   **Samson Manewa**

Year	Caps	Subs	Total	Goals
1949	2	0	2	0
1950	1	0	1	1
	3	0	3	1

Summary of Games

Fixtures	P	W	D	L	F	A
Friendly Club	3	1	0	2	5	6
		33.3%	0%	66.7%	1.67	2.00

Notes: 1949: 1 unknown scorer v. Grupo Desportivo Rebenta Fogo in 1–2 defeat no details of second game v. Grupo Desportivo Rebenta Fogo in 1950

10.   **Manyowa**

Year	Caps	Subs	Total	Goals
1949	2	0	2	0

Summary of Games

Fixtures	P	W	D	L	F	A
Friendly Club	2	0	0	2	3	6
		0%	0%	100%	1.50	3.00

Notes: 1949: 1 unknown scorer v. Grupo Desportivo Rebenta Fogo in 1–2 defeat

11.   R. Jambo

Year	Caps	Subs	Total	Goals
1949	2	0	2	0

Summary of Games

Fixtures	P	W	D	L	F	A
Friendly Club	2	0	0	2	3	6
		0%	0%	100%	1.50	3.00

Notes: 1949: 1 unknown scorer v. Grupo Desportivo Rebenta Fogo in 1–2 defeat

12.   Smart Thipa

Year	Caps	Subs	Total	Goals
1950	1	0	1	1
1962	2	0	2	1
1963	2	0	2	0
	5	0	5	2

SMART THIPA who will skipper the Nyasaland African National team on their visit to Tanganyika this week.

Summary of Games

Fixtures	P	W	D	L	F	A	GS
Friendly	2	0	0	2	2	18	1
Friendly Club	3	2	0	1	7	7	1
	5	2	0	3	9	25	2
		40%	0%	60%	1.80	5.00	22.2%

Notes: no details of second game v. Grupo Desportivo Rebenta Fogo in 1950
1963: 1 unknown scorer v. Copperbelt XI in 4–5 defeat

13.   Costas Trataris

Year	Caps	Subs	Total	Goals	
1954*	3	0	3	1	(NFA)
1956*	3	0	3	5	(NFA)
1957*	3	0	3	0	(NFA)
1959*	2	0	2	0	(NFA)
1960*	2	0	2	1	(NFA)
1963*	0	1	1	0	(NFA)
1965	1	0	1	0	
	14	1	15	7	

Summary of Games

Fixtures	P	W	D	L	F	A	GS	
Friendly Club	1	0	0	1	1	5	0	
Oury Cup*	1	1	0	0	5	0	2	(NFA)
Trataris Cup*	1	1	0	0	4	1	0	(NFA)
Friendly Club*	5	1	1	3	8	24	0	(NFA)
Bruss Cup*	4	2	1	1	7	7	2	(NFA)
Friendly Club B*	3	1	0	2	5	6	3	(NFA)
	15	6	2	7	30	43	7	
		40%	13%	47%	2.00	2.87	23.3%	

Notes: 1959: 2 unknown scorers v. Alexandra FC "B" in 2–3 defeat

14.   James Kaminjolo

Year	Caps	Subs	Total	Goals	
1957	0	0	0	0	
1964	2	0	2	0	
1964*	2	0	2	0	(NFA)
	4	0	4	0	

Summary of Games

Fixtures	P	W	D	L	F	A	
Friendly	2	0	1	1	2	7	
Oury Cup*	1	0	0	1	1	2	(NFA)
Friendly Club*	1	1	0	0	4	1	(NFA)
	4	1	1	2	7	10	
		25%	25%	50%	1.75	2.50	

Notes: 1957 was in squad and played 6 games in South Africa and Southern Rhodesia: W1 D2 L4 F16 A29

15.   Shonga

Year	Caps	Subs	Total	Goals
1957	0	0	0	0

Summary of Games

Fixtures	P	W	D	L	F	A
Friendly Club	0	0	0	0	0	0
		0%	0%	0%	0.00	0.00

Notes: 1957 was in squad and played 6 games in South Africa and Southern Rhodesia: W1 D2 L4 F16 A29

16.   Kumwenda

Year	Caps	Subs	Total	Goals
1957	0	0	0	0

Summary of Games

Fixtures	P	W	D	L	F	A
Friendly Club	0	0	0	0	0	0
		0%	0%	0%	0.00	0.00

Notes: 1957 was in squad and played 6 games in South Africa and Southern Rhodesia: W1 D2 L4 F16 A29

17.   Sazuze

Year	Caps	Subs	Total	c/sheets
1957	0	0	0	0

Summary of Games

Fixtures	P	W	D	L	F	A
Friendly Club	0	0	0	0	0	0
		0%	0%	0%	0.00	0.00

Notes: 1957 was in squad and played 6 games in South Africa and Southern Rhodesia: W1 D2 L4 F16 A29

18.   Kaunda

Year	Caps	Subs	Total	Goals
1957	0	0	0	0

Summary of Games

Fixtures	P	W	D	L	F	A
Friendly Club	0	0	0	0	0	0
		0%	0%	0%	0.00	0.00

Notes: 1957 was in squad and played 6 games in South Africa and Southern Rhodesia: W1 D2 L4 F16 A29

19.   **Matinga**

Year	Caps	Subs	Total	Goals
1957	0	0	0	0

Summary of Games

Fixtures	P	W	D	L	F	A
Friendly Club	0	0	0	0	0	0
		0%	0%	0%	0.00	0.00

Notes: 1957 was in squad and played 6 games in South Africa and Southern Rhodesia: W1 D2 L4 F16 A29

20.   **Godfrey Kalitsiro**

Year	Caps	Subs	Total	Goals
1957	0	0	0	0
1962	2	0	2	1
1963	1	0	1	0
1964	2	0	2	0
	5	0	5	1

Summary of Games

Fixtures	P	W	D	L	F	A
Friendly	4	0	1	3	4	25
Friendly Club	1	1	0	0	3	2
	5	1	1	3	7	27
	20%	20%	60%		1.40	5.40

Notes: 1957 was in squad and played 6 games in South Africa and Southern Rhodesia: W1 D2 L4 F16 A29

21.   **Thomas**

Year	Caps	Subs	Total	Goals
1957	0	0	0	0

Summary of Games

Fixtures	P	W	D	L	F	A
Friendly Club	0	0	0	0	0	0
0%	0%	0%	0%	0.00	0.00	

Notes:	1957 was in squad and played 6 games in South Africa and Southern Rhodesia: W1 D2 L4 F16 A29

22. **Kumwembe**

Year	Caps	Subs	Total	Goals
1957	0	0	0	0

Summary of Games

Fixtures	P	W	D	L	F	A
Friendly Club	0	0	0	0	0	0
0%	0%	0%	0.00	0.00		

Notes:	1957 was in squad and played 6 games in South Africa and Southern Rhodesia: W1 D2 L4 F16 A29

23. **Royee Maliwa**

Year	Caps	Subs	Total	Goals
1957	0	0	0	0
1962	2	0	2	0
1963	4	0	4	0
1964	2	0	2	0
1966	3	0	3	0
1968	3	0	3	0
1969	1	0	1	0
	15	0	15	0

Summary of Games

Fixtures	P	W	D	L	F	A
Friendly	12	1	3	8	18	54
Friendly Club	3	1	0	2	9	15
	15	2	3	10	27	69
		13.3%	20%	66.7%	1.80	4.60

Notes:	1957 was in squad and played 6 games in South Africa and Southern Rhodesia: W1 D2 L4 F16 A29
	1963: 1 unknown scorer v. Copperbelt XI in 4–5 defeat

24. **Makwelero**

Year	Caps	Subs	Total	Goals
1957	0	0	0	0

Summary of Games

Fixtures	P	W	D	L	F	A
Friendly Club	0	0	0	0	0	0
		0%	0%	0%	0.00	0.00

Notes: 1957 was in squad and played 6 games in South Africa and Southern Rhodesia: W1 D2 L4 F16 A2

25. **Kambuli**

Year	Caps	Subs	Total	Goals
1957	0	0	0	0

Summary of Games

Fixtures	P	W	D	L	F	A
Friendly Club	0	0	0	0	0	0
		0%	0%	0%	0.00	0.00

Notes: 1957 was in squad and played 6 games in South Africa and Southern Rhodesia: W1 D2 L4 F16 A29

26. **Daudi**

Year	Caps	Subs	Total	Goals
1957	0	0	0	0

Summary of Games

Fixtures	P	W	D	L	F	A
Friendly Club	0	0	0	0	0	0
		0%	0%	0%	0.00	0.00

Notes: 1957 was in squad and played 6 games in South Africa and Southern Rhodesia W1 D2 L4 F16 A29

27. **Salamu**

Year	Caps	Subs	Total	Goals
1957	0	0	0	0

Summary of Games

Fixtures	P	W	D	L	F	A
Friendly Club	0	0	0	0	0	0
		0%	0%	0%	0.00	0.00

Notes: 1957 was in squad and played 6 games in South Africa and Southern Rhodesia: W1 D2 L4 F16 A29

28. **James Sangala**

Year	Caps	Subs	Total	Goals
1957	0	0	0	0
1962	2	0	2	0
1963	4	0	4	2
1964	1	0	1	0
	7	0	7	2

Summ ary of Games

Fixtures	P	W	D	L	F	A	GS
Friendly	3	0	0	3	3	23	0
Other	1	0	0	1	1	3	0
Friendly Club	3	1	0	2	9	15	2
	7	1	0	6	13	41	2
		14.3%	0%	85.7%	1.86	5.86	15.4%

Notes: 1957 was in squad and played 6 games in South Africa and Southern Rhodesia: W1 D2 L4 F16 A29

1963: 1 unknown scorer v. Copperbelt XI in 4–5 defeat

29. **Jackie Cottingham**

Year	Caps	Subs	Total	Goals	
1958*	3	0	3	0	(NFA)
1959*	4	0	4	0	(NFA)
1960*	8	0	8	0	(NFA)
1961*	4	0	4	0	(NFA)
1962*	4	0	4	0	(NFA)
1963*	2	1	3	0	(NFA)
1964*	2	0	2	0	(NFA)
1965	1	0	1	0	
1967	1	0	1	0	
	29	1	30	0	

Summary of Games

Fixtures	P	W	D	L	F	A	
Others	1	0	0	1	2	5	
Friendly Club	1	0	0	1	1	5	
Friendly*	2	0	0	2	6	17	(NFA)

Oury Cup*	7	3	0	4	11	12	(NFA)
Trataris Cup*	4	2	0	2	8	9	(NFA)
Friendly Club*	13	3	4	6	29	42	(NFA)
Friendly Club B*	2	1	0	1	2	3	(NFA)
	30	9	4	17	59	93	
		30%	13%	57%	1.97	3.10	

Notes: 1961: 3 unknown scorers v. Alexandra FC in 6–1 win

1962: 1 unknown scorer v. Salisbury Callies "B" in 1–3 defeat

30.   **Bob Power**

Year	Caps	Subs	Total	Goals	
1961*	4	0	4	0	NFA)
1962*	2	0	2	0	NFA)
1963*	1	0	1	0	NFA)
1967	1	0	1	0	
	8	0	8	0	

Summary of Games

Fixtures	P	W	D	L	F	A	
Friendly Club	1	0	0	1	2	3	
Oury Cup*	2	2	0	0	6	2	(NFA)
Friendly Club*	2	0	1	1	2	5	(NFA)
Friendly Club B*	3	2	0	1	18	4	(NFA)
	8	4	1	3	28	14	
		50%	12.5%	37.5%	3.50	1.75	

Notes: 1962: 8 unknown scorers v. Alexandra FC "B" in 8–0 win

1962: 1 unknown scorer v. Salisbury Callies "B" in 1–3 defeat

31.   **Llewellen Kishombe**

Year	Caps	Subs	Total	C/Sheets
1962	2	0	2	0
1963	1	0	1	0
	3	0	3	0

Summary of Games

Fixtures	P	W	D	L	F	A
Friendly	2	0	0	2	2	18
Other	1	0	0	1	1	3
	3	0	0	3	3	21
		0%	0%	100%	1.00	7.00

32.   **Bright Gondwe**

Year	Caps	Subs	Total	Goals
1962	2	0	2	0

Summary of Games

Fixtures	P	W	D	L	F	A
Friendly	2	0	0	2	2	18
		0%	0%	100%	1.00	9.00

33.   **Lewis Chinula**

Year	Caps	Subs	Total	Goals
1962	2	0	2	0
1963	1	0	1	0
	3	0	3	0

Summary of Games

Fixtures	P	W	D	L	F	A
Friendly	2	0	0	2	2	18
Friendly Club	1	1	0	0	3	2
	3	1	0	2	5	20
		33.3%	0%	66.7%	1.67	6.67

34.   **Oliver Nakhumwa**

Oliver Nankhumwa

Year	Caps	Subs	Total	Goals
1962	2	0	2	0
1963	3	0	3	0
1964	2	0	2	0
1966	4	0	4	0
1967	7	0	7	0
1968	4	0	4	0
1969	9	0	9	0
	31	0	31	0

Summary of Games

Fixtures	P	W	D	L	F	A
Friendly	22	3	5	14	29	84
Club Friendly	9	4	1	4	22	20
	31	7	6	18	51	104
		22.5%	19.4%	58.1%	1.65	3.35

Notes: 1963: 1 unknown scorer v. Copperbelt XI in 4–5 defeat

35.   Raleigh M'manga

Year	Caps	Subs	Total	Goals	
1962	2	0	2	0	
1963	3	0	3	0	
1964	2	0	2	1	
1968	1	0	1	0	
	8	0	8	1	

Summary of Games

Fixtures	P	W	D	L	F	A	GS
Friendly	5	0	1	4	5	30	1
Friendly Club	2	0	0	2	6	13	0
Others	1	0	0	1	2	7	0
	8	0	1	7	13	50	1
		0%	12.5%	87.5%	1.63	6.25	7.7

Notes: 1963: 1 unknown scorer v. Copperbelt XI in 4–5 defeat

        1968: 2 unknown scorers v. Salisbury Dynamos in 2–7 defeat

36.   Richard Banda

Year	Caps	Subs	Total	Goals	
1962	2	0	2	0	
1963	4	0	4	3	
1968	1	0	1	0	
	7	0	7	3	

Summary of Games

Fixtures	P	W	D	L	F	A	GS
Friendly	3	0	0	3	3	23	0
Friendly Club	4	2	0	2	12	16	3
	7	2	0	5	15	39	3
		28.6%	0%	71.4%	2.14	5.57	20%

Notes: 1963: 1 unknown scorer v. Copperbelt XI in 4–5 defeat

36.   Nathan Gondwe

Year	Caps	Subs	Total	Goals
1962	1	0	1	0

Summary of Games

Fixtures	P	W	D	L	F	A
Friendly	1	0	0	1	0	12
		0%	0%	100%	0.00	12.00

38.   Mobray De Thipa

de M. THIPA — Smart's brother, who is brought in to fill the outside right position in the National side.

Year	Caps	Subs	Total	Goals
1962	1	0	1	0
1963	4	0	4	1
1966	3	0	3	0
	8	0	8	1

Summary of Games

Fixtures	P	W	D	L	F	A	GS
Friendly	5	0	0	5	5	28	0
Club Friendly	3	1	0	2	9	15	1
	8	1	0	7	14	43	1
		12.5%	0%	87.5%	1.75	5.38	7.1%

Notes: 1963: 1 unknown scorer v. Copperbelt XI in 4–5 defeat

39.   Januaro De Maghalhaes

Year	Caps	Subs	Total	Goals	
1962*	2	0	2	0	(NFA)
1963*	1	0	1	0	(NFA)

Year	Caps	Subs	Total	Goals	
1964*	1	0	1	1	(NFA)
1965	1	0	1	0	
	5	0	5	1	

Summary of Games

Fixtures	P	W	D	L	F	A	**GS**
Friendly Club	1	0	0	1	1	5	0
Friendly Club*	4	2	1	1	10	6	1
	5	2	1	2	11	11	1
		40%	20%	40%	2.20	2.20	9.1%

Notes: missing 3 goals v. Clube de Tete in 1962

40.   Allaudin Osman

Year	Caps	Subs	Total	Goals	
1962*	2	0	2	0	(NFA)
1963*	2	0	2	1	(NFA)
1965	1	0	1	0	
1966	4	0	4	0	
1967	5	0	5	2	
1969	1	0	1	0	
	15	0	15	3	

Summary of Games

Fixtures	P	W	D	L	F	A	GS	
Friendly	6	0	1	5	9	28	1	
Friendly Club	5	3	0	2	14	10	1	
Friendly Club*	4	1	1	2	8	15	1	(NFA)
	15	4	2	9	31	53	3	
		26.7%	13.3%	60%	2.07	3.53	9.7%	

41.   Joaquim Cunha

Year	Caps	Subs	Total	Goals	
1962*	4	0	4	1 (NFA)	
1963*	1	0	1	0 (NFA)	
1964	1	0	1	0 (NFA)	
1965	1	0	1	0	
	7	0	7	1	

Summary of Games

Fixtures	P	W	D	L	F	A	G
Friendly Club	1	0	0	1	1	5	0
Oury Cup*	1	0	0	1	1	2	0 (NFA)
Friendly Club*	5	1	2	2	7	15	1 (NFA)
	7	1	2	4	9	22	1
		14.3%	28.6%	57.1%	1.29	3.14	11.1%

42.   **Noel Nthala**

Year	Caps	Subs	Total	C/Sheets
1963	2	0	2	0
1964	2	0	2	0
1966	1	0	1	0
1967	1	0	1	0
	6	0	6	0

Summary of Games

Fixtures	P	W	D	L	F	A
Friendly	4	0	1	3	4	17
Friendly Club	2	0	0	2	4	11
	6	0	1	5	8	28
		0%	16.7%	83.3%	1.33	4.67

43.   **F. Tembo**

Year	Caps	Subs	Total	Goals
1963	2	0	2	0

Summary of Games

Fixtures	P	W	D	L	F	A
Friendly	1	0	0	1	1	5
Friendly Club	1	0	0	1	2	8
	2	0	0	2	3	13
		0%	0%	100%	1.50	6.50

44.   **Stanley Bweya**

Year	Caps	Subs	Total	Goals
1963	3	0	3	1
1964	2	0	2	0
1968	1	0	1	0
	6	0	6	1

Summary of Games

Fixtures	P	W	D	L	F	A	GS
Friendly	3	0	1	2	3	12	1
Friendly Club	2	0	0	2	6	13	0
Others	1	0	0	1	4	6	0
	6	0	1	5	13	31	1
		0%	16.7%	83.3%	2.17	5.17	7.7%

Notes: 1963: 1 unknown scorer v. Copperbelt XI in 4–5 defeat

45.   **Emmanuel Gondwe**

Year	Caps	Subs	Total	Goals
1963	3	0	3	2
1964	2	0	2	1
1968	1	0	1	2
	6	0	6	5

Summary of Games

Fixtures	P	W	D	L	F	A	GS
Friendly	3	0	1	2	3	12	1
Friendly Club	2	0	0	2	6	13	2
Othersl	1	0	0	1	4	6	2
	6	0	1	5	13	31	5
		0%	16.7%	83.3%	2.17	5.17	38.5%

Notes: 1963: 1 unknown scorer v. Copperbelt XI in 4–5 defeat

46.   **Lameck Phiri**

Year	Caps	Subs	Total	Goals
1963	2	0	2	0

Summary of Games

Fixtures	P	W	D	L	F	A
Friendly	1	0	0	1	1	5
Friendly Club	1	0	0	1	2	8
	2	0	0	2	3	13
		0%	0%	100%	1.50	6.50

47.   **R. Kapote**

Year	Caps	Subs	Total	C/Sheets
1963	1	0	1	0

Summary of Games

Fixtures	P	W	D	L	F	A
Friendly Club	1	1	0	0	3	2
		100%	0%	0%	3.00	2.00

48.   **Joseph Leno (Chauluka)**

JOSEPH LENO........known
as Chauluka when in football

Year	Caps	Subs	Total	C/Sheets
1963	1	0	1	0
1968	2	0	2	1
	3	0	3	1

Summary of Games

Fixtures	P	W	D	L	F	A	GS
Friendly	2	1	0	1	8	4	1
Friendly Club	1	0	0	1	4	5	0
	3	1	0	2	12	9	1
		33.3%	0%	66.7%	4.00	3.00	8.3%

49.   **Mkalanyinga Sitoro**

Year	Caps	Subs	Total	Goals
1963	2	0	2	0
1964	1	0	1	0
	3	0	3	0

Summary of Games

Fixtures	P	W	D	L	F	A
Other	1	0	0	1	1	3
Friendly Club	2	1	0	1	7	7
	3	1	0	2	8	10
		33.3%	0%	66.7%	2.67	3.33

50.   **B. Phombeya**

Year	Caps	Subs	Total	Goals
1963	1	0	1	0

Summary of Games

Fixtures	P	W	D	L	F	A
Friendly Club	1	1	0	0	3	2
		100%	0%	0%	3.00	2.00

51.   **Wesley Sangala**

Year	Caps	Subs	Total	Goals
1963	1	0	1	0

Summary of Games

Fixtures	P	W	D	L	F	A
Friendly Club	1	1	0	0	3	2
		100%	0%	0%	3.00	2.00

52.   **John Brown**

Year	Caps	Subs	Total	Goals
1963*	2	1	3	0 (NFA)
1965	1	0	1	0
1966	3	0	3	0
1967	1	0	1	0
	7	1	8	0

Summary of Games

Fixtures	P	W	D	L	F	A
Friendly	3	0	0	3	2	17
Others	1	0	0	1	2	5
Friendly Club	1	0	0	1	1	5
Oury Cup*	1	0	0	1	1	2
Friendly Club*	2	0	0	2	2	11
	8	0	0	8	8	40
		0%	0%	100%	1.00	5.00

53.   **Franco Bregger**

Year	Caps	Subs	Total	Goals
1963*	1	0	1	0 (NFA)
1968	1	0	1	0
	2	0	2	0

Summary of Games

Fixtures	P	W	D	L	F	A
Others	1	0	0	1	2	6
Friendly Club*	1	0	1	0	2	2
	2	0	1	1	4	8
		0%	50%	50%	2.00	4.00

54.   George Linzie

GEORGE LINZIE, Railways

Year	Caps	Subs	Total	Goals
1964	1	0	1	0
1967	3	0	3	0
1968	1	0	1	0
1969	6	0	6	0
	11	0	11	0

Summary of Games

Fixtures	P	W	D	L	F	A
Friendly	6	1	1	4	3	13
Other	2	0	1	1	1	3
Friendly Club	3	1	0	2	5	5
	11	2	2	7	9	21
		18.2%	18.2%	63.6%	0.82	1.91

55.   D. Njema

Year	Caps	Subs	Total	Goals
1964	1	0	1	0

Summary of Games

Fixtures	P	W	D	L	F	A
Other	1	0	0	1	1	3
		0%	0%	100%	1.00	3.00

56.   Roman Bwanali

Year	Caps	Subs	Total	Goals
1964	2	0	2	0
1966	0	1	1	0
1967	2	0	2	0
1969	4	1	5	0
	8	2	10	0

Summary of Games

Fixtures	P	W	D	L	F	A
Friendly	7	0	2	5	9	25
Other	1	0	1	0	0	0
Friendly Club	2	0	0	2	2	4
	10	0	3	7	11	29
		0%	30%	70%	1.10	2.90

57.   **Robert Kalembo**

Year	Caps	Subs	Total	Goals
1964	1	0	1	0
1969	4	2	6	0
	5	2	7	0

Summary of Games

Fixtures	P	W	D	L	F	A
Friendly	6	0	2	2	2	11
Other	2	0	1	1	1	3
Friendly Club	1	0	0	1	0	1
	7	0	3	4	3	15
		0%	42.9%	57.1%	0.43	2.14

58.   **Frazer Chitenje**

Year	Caps	Subs	Total	Goals
1964	2	0	2	0
1966	1	0	1	0
1967	9	0	9	0
1968	3	0	3	0
1969	4	0	4	0
	19	0	19	0

Summary of Games

Fixtures	P	W	D	L	F	A
Friendly	11	2	4	5	16	29
Friendly Club	6	4	1	1	16	6
Others	2	1	0	1	4	6
	19	7	5	7	36	41
		36.8%	26.4%	36.8%	1.89	2.16

59.   **Samuel Kapalamula**

Year	Caps	Subs	Total	Goals
1964	1	0	1	0
1966	1	0	1	0
1967	3	0	3	2
1968	1	0	1	1
1969	1	0	1	0
	7	0	7	3

Summary of Games

Fixtures	P	W	D	L	F	A	GS
Friendly	2	0	0	2	6	10	0
Friendly Club	3	2	0	1	7	2	2
Others	2	1	0	1	3	4	1
	7	3	0	4	16	16	3
		42.9%	0%	57.1%	2.29	2.29	18.8%

Notes: 1968: 2 unknown scorers v. Salisbury Dynamos in 2–7 defeat

60.   **Henry Nsewa**

Year	Caps	Subs	Total	Goals
1964	1	0	1	0
1967	2	0	2	0
	3	0	3	0

Summary of Games

Fixtures	P	W	D	L	F	A
Others	1	0	0	1	1	3
Friendly Club	2	1	1	0	4	1
	3	1	1	1	5	4
		33.4%	33.3%	33.3%	1.67	1.33

61.   **Charles Nyirongo**

Year	Caps	Subs	Total	Goals
1964	1	0	1	0

Summary of Games

Fixtures	P	W	D	L	F	A
Others	1	0	0	1	1	3
		0%	0%	100%	1.00	3.00

62. **Overton Mkandawire**

Year	Caps	Subs	Total	Goals
1964	2	0	2	0
1966	4	0	4	1
1967	10	0	10	10
1968	2	0	2	2
	18	0	18	13

Summary of Games

Fixtures	P	W	D	L	F	A	GS
Friendly	9	1	2	6	12	35	3
Friendly Club	7	4	1	2	18	9	9
Others	2	1	0	2	3	6	1
	18	6	3	9	34	50	13
		33.3%	16.7%	50%	1.89	2.78	38.2%

63. **Shake**

Year	Caps	Subs	Total	Goals
1964	1	0	1	0

Summary of Games

Fixtures	P	W	D	L	F	A
Others	1	0	0	1	1	3
		0%	0%	100%	1.00	3.00

64. **Wales Juma**

Year	Caps	Subs	Total	Goals
1964	1	0	1	1

Summary of Games

Fixtures	P	W	D	L	F	A	GS
Others	1	0	0	1	1	3	1
		0%	0%	100%	1.00	3.00	100%

65. **Phillip Bradley**

Year	Caps	Subs	Total	Goals
1964*	1	0	1	0 (NFA)
1965	1	0	1	1
	2	0	2	1

Summary of Games

Fixtures	P	W	D	L	F	A	GS
Friendly Club	1	0	0	1	1	5	1
Oury Cup*	1	0	0	1	1	2	0 (NFA)
	2	0	0	2	2	7	1
		0%	0%	100%	1.00	3.50	50%

66.	**Ikram Sheriff**			
Year	Caps	Subs	Total	Goals
1964*	2	0	2	1
1968	1	0	1	0
	3	0	3	1

(NFA)

IKRAM SHERRIF

Summary of Games

Fixtures	P	W	D	L	F	A	G
Friendly Club	1	1	0	0	3	1	0
Oury Cup*	1	0	0	1	1	2	0 (NFA)
Friendly Club*	1	1	0	0	4	1	1 (NFA)
	3	2	0	1	8	4	1
		66.7%	0%	33.3%	2.67	1.33	12.5%

67.	**Cliff Wintle**			
Year	Caps	Subs	Total	C/Sheets
1965	1	0	1	0

Summary of Games

Fixtures	P	W	D	L	F	A
Friendly Club	1	0	0	1	1	5
		0%	0%	100%	1.00	5.00

68.	**Jerry Burns**			
Year	Caps	Subs	Total	Goals
1965	1	0	1	0

Summary of Games

Fixtures	P	W	D	L	F	A
Friendly Club	1	0	0	1	1	5
		0%	0%	100%	1.00	5.00

69. **Harold Wrigley (Jnr)**

Year	Caps	Subs	Total	Goals
1965	1	0	1	0

Summary of Games

Fixtures	P	W	D	L	F	A
Friendly Club	1	0	0	1	1	5
		0%	0%	100%	1.00	5.00

70. **Woods**

Year	Caps	Subs	Total	Goals
1965	1	0	1	0

Summary of Games

Fixtures	P	W	D	L	F	A
Friendly Club	1	0	0	1	1	5
		0%	0%	100%	1.00	5.00

71. **Henry Kapalamula**

Year	Caps	Subs	Total C/ Sheets	
1966	3	0	3	0
1967	8	0	8	3
1968	5	0	5	0
1969	2	0	2	0
	18	0	18	3

Summary of Games

Fixtures	P	W	D	L	F	A	CS
Friendly	9	1	2	6	12	29	1
Friendly Club	7	5	1	1	19	7	2
Others	2	1	0	1	4	6	0
	18	7	3	8	35	42	3
		38.9%	16.7%	44.4%	1.94	2.33	16.7%

72. **S. Bulla**

Year	Caps	Subs	Total	Goals
1966	1	0	1	0
1967	2	0	2	0
	3	0	3	0

Summary of Games

Fixtures	P	W	D	L	F	A
Friendly	1	0	0	1	3	4
Friendly Club	2	1	1	0	4	5
	3	1	1	1	7	9
		33.4%	33.3%	33.3%	2.33	3.00

73.   **Elijah Joshua**

Year	Caps	Subs	Total	Goals
1966	1	0	1	0
1967	2	0	2	0
1968	2	0	2	0
	5	0	5	0

Summary of Games

Fixtures	P	W	D	L	F	A
Friendly	2	0	0	2	6	10
Friendly Club	1	1	0	0	4	1
Regional	2	0	0	2	4	8
	5	1	0	4	14	19
		20%	0%	80%	2.80	3.80

Notes: 1968: 2 unknown goals v. Salisbury Dynamos in 2–7 defeat

74.   **Paul Morin**

Year	Caps	Subs	Total	Goals
1966	3	0	3	0
1967	2	0	2	0
1968	4	0	4	0
1969	4	0	4	0
	13	0	13	0

Summary of Games

Fixtures	P	W	D	L	F	A
Friendly	10	1	1	8	18	37
Others	1	0	0	1	2	5
Friendly Club	2	1	0	1	4	4
	13	2	1	10	24	46
		15.4%	7.7%	76.9%	1.85	3.54

75.   **Cullen Mwase (Continental)**

Year	Caps	Subs	Total	Goals
1966	1	0	1	0
1968	1	0	1	0
1969	1	0	1	0
	3	0	3	0

Summary of Games

Fixtures	P	W	D	L	F	A
Friendly	2	0	0	2	1	12
Friendly Club	1	1	0	0	3	1
	3	1	0	2	4	13
		33.3%	0%	66.7%	1.33	4.33

76.   **Joe Gallagher**

Year	Caps	Subs	Total	Goals
1966	2	0	2	0

Summary of Games

Fixtures	P	W	D	L	F	A
Friendly	2	0	0	2	1	12
		0%	0%	100%	1.00	6.00

77.   **Albert Nsewa**

Year	Caps	Subs	Total	Goals
1966	1	0	1	0
1967	1	0	1	0
	2	0	2	0

Summary of Games

Fixtures	P	W	D	L	F	A
Friendly	1	0	0	1	1	5
Friendly Club	1	0	1	0	0	0
	2	0	1	1	1	5
		0%	50%	50%	0.50	2.50

78. **Solomon Mkwapatira**

Year	Caps	Subs	Total	Goals
1966	1	0	1	3
1968	1	0	1	1
	2	0	2	4

Summary of Games

Fixtures	P	W	D	L	F	A	GS
Friendly	1	0	0	1	3	4	3
Regional	1	0	0	1	4	6	1
	2	0	0	2	7	10	4
		0%	0%	100%	3.50	5.00	57.1%

79. **Yasin Osman**

Year	Caps	Subs	Total	Goals
1966	4	0	4	0
1967	7	1	8	2
1968	4	0	4	4
1969	11	0	11	1
	26	1	27	7

Summary of Games

Fixtures	P	W	D	L	F	A	GS
Friendly	21	3	5	13	28	66	5
Others	1	0	0	1	2	5	0
Friendly Club	5	3	1	1	12	5	2
	27	6	6	15	42	76	7
		22.2%	22.2%	55.6%	1.56	2.81	16.7%

80. **Peter Chisasa**

P. CHISASA

Year	Caps	Subs	Total	Goals
1966	3	0	3	1
1967	1	0	1	0
	4	0	4	1

Summary of Games

Fixtures	P	W	D	L	F	A	GS
Friendly	3	0	0	3	2	17	1
Friendly Club	1	0	1	0	0	0	0
	4	0	1	3	2	17	1
		0%	25%	75%	0.50	4.25	50%

81.   **Prince Nyirenda**

Year	Caps	Subs	Total	Goals
1966	0	1	1	0
1967	4	0	4	0
1968	4	0	4	0
1969	5	1	6	0
	13	2	15	0

Summary of Games

Fixtures	P	W	D	L	F	A
Friendly	11	3	3	5	20	29
Friendly Club	4	2	2	0	6	1
	15	5	5	5	26	30
		33.3%	33.4%	33.3%	1.73	2.00

82.   **Crosby Chisasa**

Year	Caps	Subs	Total	Goals
1966	0	1	1	0
1967	1	0	1	0
	1	1	2	0

Summary of Games

Fixtures	P	W	D	L	F	A
Friendly	1	0	0	1	3	4
Friendly Club	1	0	1	0	0	0
	2	0	1	1	3	4
		0%	50%	50%	1.50	2.00

83.   **James Kuyenge**

Year	Caps	Subs	Total	Goals
1967	1	0	1	0

Summary of Games

Fixtures	P	W	D	L	F	A
Friendly	1	0	0	1	3	6
		0%	0%	100%	3.00	6.00

84.   **Joe Fernandes**

Year	Caps	Subs	Total	Goals
1967	1	0	1	0

Summary of Games

Fixtures	P	W	D	L	F	A
Others	1	0	0	1	2	5
		0%	0%	100%	2.00	5.00

85. | **Wales Nsewa**

Year	Caps	Subs	Total	Goals
1967	4	0	4	0
1969	1	1	2	0
	5	1	6	0

Summary of Games

Fixtures	P	W	D	L	F	A
Friendly	3	0	1	2	1	11
Friendly Club	3	2	1	0	8	2
	6	2	2	2	9	13
		33.3%	33.4%	33.3%	1.50	2.17

86. | **John Raisbeck**

Year	Caps	Subs	Total	Goals
1967	1	0	1	0

Summary of Games

Fixtures	P	W	D	L	F	A
Friendly	1	1	0	0	1	0
		100%	0%	0%	1.00	0.00

87. | **George Manda**

Year	Caps	Subs	Total	Goals
1967	1	0	1	0
1968	2	0	2	0
	3	0	3	0

Summary of Games

Fixtures	P	W	D	L	F	A
Friendly	2	0	2	0	3	3
Friendly Club	1	0	0	1	1	3
	3	0	2	1	4	6
		0%	66.7%	33.3%	1.33	2.00

88. **Ray Wooley**

Year	Caps	Subs	Total	Goals
1967	5	0	5	0
1968	2	0	2	0
	7	0	7	0

Summary of Games

Fixtures	P	W	D	L	F	A
Friendly	1	1	0	0	1	0
Friendly Club	6	4	1	1	15	6
	7	5	1	1	16	6
		71.4%	14.3%	14.3%	2.29	0.86

89. **Kirby Thomson**

Year	Caps	Subs	Total	Goals
1967	1	0	1	0

Summary of Games

Fixtures	P	W	D	L	F	A
Friendly	1	0	0	1	3	6
		0%	0%	100%	3.00	6.00

90. **Brian Griffin**

Year	Caps	Subs	Total	Goals
1967	6	0	6	4
1968	1	0	1	1
1969	5	0	5	0
	12	0	12	5

Summary of Games

Fixtures	P	W	D	L	F	A	GS
Friendly	6	1	2	3	5	12	0
Others	1	0	0	1	2	5	1
Friendly Club	5	4	0	1	13	6	4
	12	5	2	5	20	23	5
		41.7%	16.6%	41.7%	1.67	1.92	25%

91.   **Owen Kalitsiro**

Year	Caps	Subs	Total	Goals
1967	2	0	2	0
1968	1	0	1	0
	3	0	3	0

Summary of Games

Fixtures	P	W	D	L	F	A
Friendly	2	0	2	0	3	3
Friendly Club	1	0	1	0	0	0
	3	0	3	0	3	3
		0%	100%	0%	1.00	1.00

92.   **Crighton Msiya**

Year	Caps	Subs	Total	Goals
1967	1	0	1	0

Summary of Games

Fixtures	P	W	D	L	F	A
Friendly	1	0	1	0	1	1
		0%	100%	0%	0.50	0.50

93.   **Balraj Bouri**

Year	Caps	Subs	Total	Goals
1967	2	0	2	1

Summary of Games

Fixtures	P	W	D	L	F	A	GS
Friendly	1	0	1	0	1	1	1
Other	1	0	0	1	2	5	0
	2	0	1	1	3	6	1
		0%	50%	50%	0.50	0.50	33.3%

94.   **Losacco**

Year	Caps	Subs	Total	Goals
1967	1	0	1	0

Summary of Games

Fixtures	P	W	D	L	F	A
Other	1	0	0	1	2	5
		0%	0%	100%	2.00	5.00

95.   **James Mkwanda**

Year	Caps	Subs	Total	Goals
1967	6	0	6	0
1968	2	0	2	0
1969	1	0	1	0
	9	0	9	0

Summary of Games

Fixtures	P	W	D	L	F	A
Friendly	4	2	1	1	10	10
Friendly Club	5	2	1	2	11	8
	9	4	2	3	21	18
		44.5%	22.2%	33.3%	2.33	2.00

96.   **William Green Malunga**

Year	Caps	Subs	Total	C/Sheets
1967	2	0	2	1
1968	1	0	1	0
1969	7	0	7	1
	10	0	10	2

Summary of Games

Fixtures	P	W	D	L	F	A	CS
Friendly	7	2	1	4	12	22	1
Friendly Club	3	0	1	2	2	4	1
	10	2	2	6	14	26	2
		20%	20%	60%	1.40	2.60	20%

97.   **Gordon Brighton**

Year	Caps	Subs	Total	C/Sheets
1967	1	0	1	0

Summary of Games

Fixtures	P	W	D	L	F	A
Friendly	1	0	1	0	1	1
		0%	100%	0%	1.00	1.00

98. **Hamid (Jack) Nazim**

Year	Caps	Subs	Total	Goals
1967	4	0	4	0
1968	4	0	4	0
1969	7	0	7	0
	15	0	15	0

Summary of Games

Fixtures	P	W	D	L	F	A
Friendly	9	2	2	5	15	27
Friendly Club	6	2	0	4	12	11
	15	4	2	9	27	38
		26.7%	13.3%	60%	1.80	2.53

99. **Julio Kamlaza**

Year	Caps	Subs	Total	Goals
1967	1	0	1	0
1968	1	0	1	0
	2	0	2	0

Summary of Games

Fixtures	P	W	D	L	F	A
Friendly Club	1	0	0	1	2	3
Regional	1	0	0	1	4	6
	2	0	0	2	6	9
		0%	0%	100%	3.00	4.50

100. **Katete**

Year	Caps	Subs	Total	Goals
1967	1	0	1	0

Summary of Games

Fixtures	P	W	D	L	F	A
Friendly Club	1	0	1	0	0	0
		0%	50%	50%	0.00	0.00

101. **Prescott Magaleta**

Prescot Magaleta for Malawi Schools team

Year	Caps	Subs	Total	Goals
1967	1	0	1	0
1968	1	0	1	0
1969	1	0	1	0
	3	0	3	0

Summary of Games

Fixtures	P	W	D	L	F	A
Friendly Club	3	0	0	3	4	10
		0%	0%	100%	1.33	3.33

102. **Mustafa Munshi**

Year	Caps	Subs	Total	Goals
1967	1	0	1	0
1968	1	0	1	0
1969	2	1	3	0
	4	1	5	0

Summary of Games

Fixtures	P	W	D	L	F	A
Friendly	3	0	0	3	0	16
Friendly Club	2	0	1	1	1	3
	5	0	1	4	1	19
		0%	20%	80%	0.20	3.80

103. **Samson Chibambo**

Year	Caps	Subs	Total	Goals
1967	1	0	1	1
1968	4	0	4	2
1969	7	0	7	4
	12	0	12	7

Summary of Games

Fixtures	P	W	D	L	F	A	GS
Friendly	9	2	3	4	17	17	6
Friendly Club	3	0	0	3	3	7	1
	12	2	3	7	20	24	7
		16.7%	25%	58.3%	1.67	2.00	35%

104. **Smile Kampeza**

Year	Caps	Subs	Total	Goals
1967	1	0	1	0
1969	1	0	1	0
	2	0	2	0

Summary of Games

Fixtures	P	W	D	L	F	A
Friendly	1	0	0	1	0	7
Friendly Club	1	0	0	1	2	3
	2	0	0	2	2	10
		0%	0%	100%	1.00	5.00

105. **Zimba**

Year	Caps	Subs	Total	Goals
1967	1	0	1	0

Summary of Games

Fixtures	P	W	D	L	F	A
Friendly Club	1	0	1	0	0	0
		0%	100%	0%	0.00	0.00

106. **Samuel Chirwa**

Year	Caps	Subs	Total	Goals
1968	2	0	2	0
1969	1	1	2	0
	3	1	4	0

Summary of Games

Fixtures	P	W	D	L	F	A
Friendly	2	0	1	1	2	4

Friendly Club	2	0	1	1	2	4
	4	0	2	2	4	8
		0%	50%	50%	1.00	2.00

107. **Roy Cook**

Year	Caps	Subs	Total	Goals
1968	4	0	4	5
1969	9	0	9	2
	13	0	13	7

Summary of Games

Fixtures	P	W	D	L	F	A	GS
Friendly	11	2	4	5	18	22	6
Friendly Club	2	1	0	1	3	2	1
	13	3	4	6	21	24	7
		23.1%	30.8%	46.2%	1.62	1.85	33.3%

108. **Damiano Malefula**

Year	Caps	Subs	Total	Goals
1968	2	1	3	1

Summary of Games

Fixtures	P	W	D	L	F	A	GS
Friendly	1	0	1	0	2	2	0
Friendly Club	1	0	0	1	1	3	0
Regional	1	1	0	0	2	1	1
	3	1	1	1	5	6	1
		33.4%	33.3%	33.3%	1.67	2.00	20%

109. **Smile Chirambo**

Year	Caps	Subs	Total	Goals
1968	0	1	1	0

Summary of Games

Fixtures	P	W	D	L	F	A
Friendly	1	0	0	1	0	2
		0%	0%	100%	0.00	2.00

110.   **Chidzero**

Year	Caps	Subs	Total	C/Sheets
1968	1	0	1	0

Summary of Games

Fixtures	P	W	D	L	F	A
Friendly Club	1	0	0	1	1	3
		0%	0%	100%	1.00	3.00

111.   **Henry Moyo**

Year	Caps	Subs	Total	Goals
1968	1	0	1	0
1969	6	2	8	0
	7	2	9	0

Summary of Games

Fixtures	P	W	D	L	F	A
Friendly Club	8	2	3	3	10	13
Other	1	0	0	1	0	0
	9	2	4	3	10	13
		22.3%	44.4%	33.3%	1.11	1.44

112.   **David Chirwa**

Year	Caps	Subs	Total	Goals
1968	1	0	1	0
1969	1	0	1	0
	2	0	2	0

Summary of Games

Fixtures	P	W	D	L	F	A
Friendly Club	1	0	0	1	1	3
Other	1	0	1	0	0	0
	2	0	1	1	1	3
		0%	50%	50%	0.50	1.50

113.   **James Thembulembu**

Year	Caps	Subs	Total	Goals
1968	1	0	1	0
1969	1	1	2	0
	2	1	3	0

Summary of Games

Fixtures	P	W	D	L	F	A
Others	1	0	1	0	0	0
Friendly Club	2	1	0	1	3	2
	3	1	1	1	3	2
		33.4%	33.3%	33.3%	1.00	0.67

114. **Eric Watts**

Year	Caps	Subs	Total	Goals
1968	1	0	1	0

Summary of Games

Fixtures	P	W	D	L	F	A
Friendly Club	1	1	0	0	3	1
		100%	0%	0%	3.00	1.00

115. **Alex "Poison" Mpinganjira**

Year	Caps	Subs	Total	Goals
1968	1	0	1	1
1969	7	3	10	0
	8	3	11	1

Summary of Games

Fixtures	P	W	D	L	F	A	GS
Friendly	9	1	2	6	7	28	0
Friendly Club	2	1	0	1	3	2	1
	11	2	2	7	10	30	1
		18.2%	18.2%	63.6%	0.91	2.73	10%

116. **Titto Kelly**

Year	Caps	Subs	Total	Goals
1968	1	0	1	0

Summary of Games

Fixtures	P	W	D	L	F	A
Friendly Club	1	0	0	1	1	3
		0%	0%	100%	1.00	3.00

117. **Ben Phoya**

Year	Caps	Subs	Total	Goals
1968	1	0	1	0
1969	4	0	4	0
	5	0	5	0

Summary of Games

Fixtures	P	W	D	L	F	A
Friendly Club	4	1	1	2	5	9
Other	1	0	1	0	0	0
	5	1	2	2	5	9
		20%	40%	40%	1.00	1.80

118. **Chiwanda**

Year	Caps	Subs	Total C/ Sheets	
1968	1	0	1	0

Summary of Games

Fixtures	P	W	D	L	F	A
Regional	1	0	0	1	4	6
		0%	0%	100%	4.00	6.00

119. **Uteka**

Year	Caps	Subs	Total	Goals
1968	1	0	1	0

Summary of Games

Fixtures	P	W	D	L	F	A
Others	1	0	0	1	4	6
		0%	0%	100%	4.00	6.00

120. **Ngwangwa**

Year	Caps	Subs	Total	Goals
1968	1	0	1	0

Mario Antoine

Summary of Games

Fixtures	P	W	D	L	F	A
Others	1	0	0	1	4	6
		0%	0%	100%	4.00	6.00

121.　　**Galatoni Njoka**

Year	Caps	Subs	Total	Goals
1968	1	0	1	0

Summary of Games

Fixtures	P	W	D	L	F	A
Others	1	0	0	1	4	6
		0%	0%	100%	4.00	6.00

122.　　**R. Pilato**

Year	Caps	Subs	Total	Goals
1968	1	0	1	0

Summary of Games

Fixtures	P	W	D	L	F	A
Others	1	0	0	1	4	6
		0%	0%	100%	4.00	6.00

123.　　**Antoine Madinga**

Year	Caps	Subs	Total	Goals
1968	1	0	1	0

Summary of Games

Fixtures	P	W	D	L	F	A
Others	1	0	0	1	4	6
		0%	0%	100%	4.00	6.00

124.　　**Kaipsya**

Year	Caps	Subs	Total	Goals
1968	1	0	1	0

Summary of Games

Fixtures	P	W	D	L	F	A
Others	1	0	0	1	4	6
		0%	0%	100%	4.00	6.00

125. **Katanga**

Year	Caps	Subs	Total	Goals
1968	0	1	1	1

Summary of Games

Fixtures	P	W	D	L	F	A	GS
Others	1	0	0	1	4	6	1
		0%	0%	100%	4.00	6.00	25%

126. **Fernando Araujo**

Year	Caps	Subs	Total	Goals
1968	0	1	1	0

Summary of Games

Fixtures	P	W	D	L	F	A
Others	1	0	0	1	4	6
		0%	0%	100%	4.00	6.00

127. **Horace Naming'ona**

Year	Caps	Subs	Total	C/Sheets
1968	1	0	1	0

Summary of Games

Fixtures	P	W	D	L	F	A
Others	1	0	0	1	2	7
		0%	0%	100%	2.00	7.00

128. **Robert Gondwe**

Year	Caps	Subs	Total	Goals
1968	1	0	1	0

Summary of Games

Fixtures	P	W	D	L	F	A
Others	1	0	0	1	2	7
		0%	0%	100%	2.00	7.00

Notes: 1968: 2 unknown scorers v. Salisbury Dynamos in 2–7 defeat

129.	Smart			
Year	Caps	Subs	Total	Goals
1968	1	0	1	0

Summary of Games

Fixtures	P	W	D	L	F	A
Others	1	0	0	1	2	7
		0%	0%	100%	2.00	7.00

Notes: 1968: 2 unknown scorers v. Salisbury Dynamos in 2–7 defeat

130.	Fletcher			
Year	Caps	Subs	Total	Goals
1968	1	0	1	0

Summary of Games

Fixtures	P	W	D	L	F	A
Others	1	0	0	1	2	7
		0%	0%	100%	2.00	7.00

Notes: 1968: 2 unknown scorers v. Salisbury Dynamos in 2–7 defeat

131.	Chirwa			
Year	Caps	Subs	Total	Goals
1968	1	0	1	0

Summary of Games

Fixtures	P	W	D	L	F	A
Others	1	0	0	1	2	7
		0%	0%	100%	2.00	7.00

Notes: 1968: 2 unknown scorers v. Salisbury Dynamos in 2–7 defeat

132.   Chanasa

Year	Caps	Subs	Total	Goals
1968	1	0	1	0

Summary of Games

Fixtures	P	W	D	L	F	A
Others	1	0	0	1	2	7
		0%	0%	100%	2.00	7.00

Notes: 1968: 2 unknown scorers v. Salisbury Dynamos in 2–7 defeat

133.   Mwabile

Year	Caps	Subs	Total	Goals
1968	1	0	1	0

Summary of Games

Fixtures	P	W	D	L	F	A
Others	1	1	0	0	2	1
		100%	0%	0%	2.00	1.00

134.   Kuyere

Year	Caps	Subs	Total	Goals
1968	1	0	1	0

Summary of Games

Fixtures	P	W	D	L	F	A
Others	1	1	0	0	2	1
		100%	0%	0%	2.00	1.00

135.   Nagoli

Year	Caps	Subs	Total	Goals
1968	2	0	2	0

Summary of Games

Fixtures	P	W	D	L	F	A
Others	2	1	0	1	4	8
		50%	0%	50%	2.00	4.00

Notes: 1968: 2 unknown scorers v. Salisbury Dynamos in 2–7 defeat

136. **Namwali**

Year	Caps	Subs	Total	Goals
1968	2	0	2	0

Summary of Games

Fixtures	P	W	D	L	F	A
Others	2	1	0	1	4	8
		50%	0%	50%	2.00	4.00

Notes: 1968: 2 unknown scorers v. Salisbury Dynamos in 2–7 defeat

137. **Carmichael**

Year	Caps	Subs	Total	Goals
1968	2	0	2	0

Summary of Games

Fixtures	P	W	D	L	F	A
Others	2	1	0	1	4	8
		50%	0%	50%	2.00	4.00

Notes: 1968: 2 unknown scorers v. Salisbury Dynamos in 2–7 defeat

138. **Mheya**

Year	Caps	Subs	Total	C/Sheets
1968	1	0	1	0

Summary of Games

Fixtures	P	W	D	L	F	A
Others	1	0	0	1	1	2
		0%	0%	100%	1.00	2.00

139. **Khumanje**

Year	Caps	Subs	Total	Goals
1968	1	0	1	0

Summary of Games

Fixtures	P	W	D	L	F	A
Others	1	0	0	1	1	2
		0%	0%	100%	1.00	2.00

140.   **Masambera**

Year	Caps	Subs	Total	Goals
1968	1	0	1	0

Summary of Games

Fixtures	P	W	D	L	F	A
Others	1	0	0	1	1	2
		0%	0%	100%	1.00	2.00

141.   **Chadza**

Year	Caps	Subs	Total	Goals
1968	1	0	1	0

Summary of Games

Fixtures	P	W	D	L	F	A
Others	1	0	0	1	1	2
		0%	0%	100%	1.00	2.00

142.   **B. Mkandawire**

Year	Caps	Subs	Total	Goals
1968	1	0	1	0

Summary of Games

Fixtures	P	W	D	L	F	A
Others	1	0	0	1	1	2
		0%	0%	100%	1.00	2.00

143.   **Chasweka**

Year	Caps	Subs	Total	Goals
1968	1	0	1	0

Summary of Games

Fixtures	P	W	D	L	F	A
Others	1	0	0	1	1	2
		0%	0%	100%	1.00	2.00

144.   **Joza**

Year	Caps	Subs	Total	Goals
1968	1	0	1	0

Summary of Games

Fixtures	P	W	D	L	F	A
Others	1	0	0	1	1	2
		0%	0%	100%	1.00	2.00

145.   **Mhango**

Year	Caps	Subs	Total	Goals
1968	1	0	1	1

Summary of Games

Fixtures	P	W	D	L	F	A	GS
Others	1	0	0	1	1	2	1
		0%	0%	100%	1.00	2.00	100%

146.   **F. Mkwanda**

Year	Caps	Subs	Total	Goals
1968	1	0	1	0

Summary of Games

Fixtures	P	W	D	L	F	A
Others	1	0	0	1	1	2
		0%	0%	100%	1.00	2.00

147.   **Shawa**

Year	Caps	Subs	Total	Goals
1968	1	0	1	0

Summary of Games

Fixtures	P	W	D	L	F	A
Others	1	0	0	1	1	2
		0%	0%	100%	1.00	2.00

148. **A. Kalitsiro**

Year	Caps	Subs	Total	Goals
1968	1	0	1	0

Summary of Games

Fixtures	P	W	D	L	F	A
Others	1	0	0	1	1	2
		0%	0%	100%	1.00	2.00

149. **Chikanda**

Year	Caps	Subs	Total	Goals
1968	1	0	1	0

Summary of Games

Fixtures	P	W	D	L	F	A
Others	1	0	0	1	2	6
		0%	0%	100%	2.00	6.00

150. **Kachokola**

Year	Caps	Subs	Total	Goals
1968	1	0	1	0

Summary of Games

Fixtures	P	W	D	L	F	A
Others	1	0	0	1	2	6
		0%	0%	100%	2.00	6.00

151. **Chikanda (Jnr)**

Year	Caps	Subs	Total	Goals
1968	1	0	1	0

Summary of Games

Fixtures	P	W	D	L	F	A
Others	1	0	0	1	2	6
		0%	0%	100%	2.00	6.00

152.   Akara

Year	Caps	Subs	Total	Goals
1968	1	0	1	0

Summary of Games

F	A					
Others	1	0	0	1	2	6
		0%	0%	100%	2.00	6.00

153.   Malata

Year	Caps	Subs	Total	Goals
1968	1	0	1	0

Summary of Games

Fixtures	P	W	D	L	F	A
Others	1	0	0	1	2	6
		0%	0%	100%	2.00	6.00

154.   Danger

Year	Caps	Subs	Total	Goals
1968	1	0	1	0

Summary of Games

Fixtures	P	W	D	L	F	A
Others	1	0	0	1	2	6
		0%	0%	100%	2.00	6.00

155.   Mboga

Year	Caps	Subs	Total	Goals
1968	1	0	1	1

Summary of Games

Fixtures	P	W	D	L	F	A	GS
Others	1	0	0	1	2	6	1
		0%	0%	100%	2.00	6.00	50%

156. **Chisambi**

Year	Caps	Subs	Total	Goals
1968	1	0	1	0

Summary of Games

Fixtures	P	W	D	L	F	A
Others	1	0	0	1	2	6
		0%	0%	100%	2.00	6.00

157. **Mashe**

Year	Caps	Subs	Total	Goals
1968	1	0	1	0

Summary of Games

Fixtures	P	W	D	L	F	A
Others	1	0	0	1	2	6
		0%	0%	100%	2.00	6.00

158. **Basil Malila**

Year	Caps	Subs	Total	Goals
1968	0	1	1	1
1969	1	0	1	0
	1	1	2	1

Summary of Games

Fixtures	P	W	D	L	F	A	GS
Friendly	1	0	0	1	0	4	0
Others	1	0	0	1	2	6	1
	2	0	0	2	2	10	1
		0%	0%	100%	1.00	5.00	50%

159. **Giovanni Leotta**

Year	Caps	Subs	Total	C/Sheets
1968	1	0	1	0
1969	2	1	3	1
	3	1	4	1

Summary of Games

Fixtures	P	W	D	L	F	A	CS
Friendly	3	0	1	2	0	5	1
Others	1	0	0	1	2	6	0
	4	0	1	3	2	11	1
		0%	25%	75%	0.50	2.75	25%

160. **Precious Kumbatira**

Year	Caps	Subs	Total	C/Sheets
1969	2	0	2	0

Summary of Games

Fixtures	P	W	D	L	F	A
Friendly	2	0	1	1	2	5
		0%	50%	50%	1.00	2.50

161. **Charles Kagwa**

Year	Caps	Subs	Total	Goals
1969	11	2	13	0

Summary of Games

Fixtures	P	W	D	L	F	A
Friendly	11	1	3	7	8	32
Others	1	0	1	0	0	0
Friendly Club	1	0	0	1	0	1
	13	1	4	8	8	33
		7.7%	30.8%	61.5%	0.62	2.54

162. **Peter Tindo**

Year	Caps	Subs	Total	Goals
1969	1	0	1	0

Summary of Games

Fixtures	P	W	D	L	F	A
Friendly	1	0	1	0	1	1
		0%	100%	0%	1.00	1.00

163.   **Robert Kutengule**

Year	Caps	Subs	Total	Goals
1969	4	0	4	0

Summary of Games

Fixtures	P	W	D	L	F	A
Friendly	3	0	1	2	1	6
Others	1	0	1	0	0	0
	4	0	2	2	1	6
		0%	50%	50%	0.25	1.50

164.   **John Vart**

Year	Caps	Subs	Total	Goals
1969	3	0	3	0

Summary of Games

Fixtures	P	W	D	L	F	A
Friendly	3	0	1	2	1	10
		0%	33.3%	66.7%	0.33	3.33

165.   **Pat Mhone**

Year	Caps	Subs	Total	Goals
1969	1	0	1	0

Summary of Games

Fixtures	P	W	D	L	F	A
Friendly	1	0	0	1	0	5
		0%	0%	100%	0.00	5.00

166.   **Kanjedza Kamwendo**

Year	Caps	Subs	Total	Goals
1969	1	1	2	0

KAMWENDO

Summary of Games

Fixtures	P	W	D	L	F	A
Friendly	2	0	0	2	0	5
		0%	0%	100%	0.00	2.50

167. **Stephen Gondwe**

Year	Caps	Subs	Total	Goals
1969	1	1	2	0

Summary of Games

Fixtures	P	W	D	L	F	A
Friendly	1	0	0	1	0	4
Others	1	0	1	0	0	0
	2	0	1	1	0	4
		0%	50%	50%	0.00	2.00

168. **C. Munde**

Year	Caps	Subs	Total	Goals
1969	2	0	2	0

Summary of Games

Fixtures	P	W	D	L	F	A
Friendly	2	0	0	2	0	12
		0%	0%	100%	0.00	6.00

169. **Sparrow Malilo**

Year	Caps	Subs	Total	Goals
1969	0	1	1	0

Summary of Games

Fixtures	P	W	D	L	F	A
Friendly	1	0	0	1	0	4
		0%	0%	100%	0.00	4.00

Of the 169 players mentioned above, 18 won further caps during the '70s, which will be covered in the second volume of this series. The players are as listed below until the listed ends of their careers.

Name of Player	Current Status	End of International Career
Frazer Chitenje	19 caps	1972
Roy Cook	13 caps–7 goals	1971
Brian Griffin	12 caps–5 goals	1971
Charles Kagwa	13 caps (2 subs)	1976
Kanjedza Kamwendo	2 caps (1 sub)	1970
Henry Kapalamula	18 caps–3 c/sheets	1974
Precious Kumbatira	2 caps	1972
Robert Kutengule	4 caps	1971
Damiano Malefula	3 caps (1 sub)	1978
William Green Malunga	10 caps–2 c/sheets	1971
George Manda	3 caps	1974
Paul Morin	13 caps	1971
Henry Moyo	9 caps (2 subs)	1974
Mustafa Munshi	5 caps (1 sub)	1972
Hamid Nazim	15 caps	1974
Prince Nyirenda	15 caps (2 subs)	1971
Yasin Osman	27 caps (1 sub)–7 goals	1975
Ben Phoya	5 caps	1975

Top Fives

Following are lists of the top five players in various segments. Players need to have played in five games minimum from 1949 to 1969 to be considered.

Wins

Player	Games played	Percentage
Ray Wooley	7	71.4%
James Mkwanda	9	44.5%
Samuel Kapalamula	7	42.9%
Brian Griffin	12	41.7%
Smart Thipa	5	40.0%

Draws

Player	Games played	Percentage
Henry Moyo	9	44.4%
Robert Kalembo	7	42.9%

Ben Phoya	5	40.0%
Prince Nyirenda	15	33.4%
Wales Nsewa	6	33.4%

Losses

Player	Games played	Percentage
Ray Wooley	7	14.3%
Prince Nyirenda	15	33.3%
James Mkwanda	9	33.3%
Henry Moyo	9	33.3%
Wales Nsewa	6	33.3%

Average Goals Scored Per Game

Player	Games played	Average
Elijah Joshua	5	2.80
James Mkwanda	9	2.33
Samuel Kapalamula	9	2.29
Ray Wooley	7	2.29
Stanley Bweya	6	2.17
Emmanuel Gondwe	6	2.17

Average Goals Conceded Per Game

Player	Games played	Average
Ray Wooley	7	0.86
Henry Moyo	9	1.44
Ben Phoya	5	1.80
Roy Cook	13	1.85
James Sangala	7	1.86

Top Five Appearances

Player	Games played
Oliver Nakhumwa	31
Yasin Osman	27 (including 1 sub)

Frazer Chitenje	19	
Henry Kapalamula	18	
Overton Mkandawire	18	

Top Five Scorers

Player	Games played	Goals
Overton Mkandawire	18	12
Samson Chibambo	12	7
Roy Cook	13	7
Yasin Osman	27	7
Emmanuel Gondwe	6	5
Brian Griffin	12	5

Top Clean Sheets

Player	Games played	C/Sheets
Henry Kapalamula	18	3
William Green Malunga	10	2
Giovanni Leotta	4	1

CHAPTER TEN

ANALYSIS OF MALAWI COACHES

Index of Coaches

1.   **Dennis Johnston**

Year	Games
1962	2

Summary of Games

Fixtures	P	W	D	L	F	A
Friendly	2	0	0	2	2	18
		0%	0%	100%	1.00	9.00

2.   **K. Thipa, Sydney Chikafa, P. Muwamba**

Year	Games
1963	3

Summary of Games

Fixtures	P	W	D	L	F	A
Friendly	1	0	0	1	1	5
Friendly Club	2	0	0	2	6	13
	3	0	0	3	7	18
		0%	0%	100%	2.33	6.00

3.   **Augustine Chavura**

Year	Games
1964	3

Summary of Games

Fixtures	P	W	D	L	F	A
Friendly	3	0	1	2	3	10
		0%	33.3%	66.7%	1.00	3.3

4.   **Ron Meades**

Year	Games
1966	3

Summary of Games

Fixtures	P	W	D	L	F	A
Friendly	3	0	0	3	2	17
		0%	0%	100%	0.67	5.67

5.   **F. Munthali**

Year	Games
1966	1

Summary of Games

Fixtures	P	W	D	L	F	A
Friendly	1	0	0	1	3	4
		0%	0%	100%	3.00	4.00

6.   **Brian Griffin**

Year	Games
1967	7

Summary of Games

Fixtures	P	W	D	L	F	A
Friendly	2	0	0	2	5	11
Friendly Club	5	3	1	1	13	5
	7	3	1	3	18	16
		42.9%	14.2%	42.9%	2.57	2.29

7.   **Ray Batchelor**

Year	Games
1967	4
1968	6
1969	10
	20

Summary of Games

Fixtures	P	W	D	L	F	A
Friendly	14	3	6	5	20	23
Friendly Club	6	2	1	3	9	9
	20	5	7	8	29	32
		25%	35%	40%	1.45	1.60

8.   **Frank Kapito**

Year	Games
1969	3

Summary of Games

Fixtures	P	W	D	L	F	A
Friendly	3	0	0	3	0	16
		0%	0%	100%	0.00	5.33

CHAPTER ELEVEN

ANALYSIS OF NFA INTERNATIONAL PLAYERS

Index of NFA International Players

Harry Middleton	1935–1938
J. MacDonald	1935
S. Robertson	1935, 1937, 1940, 1946
N. Carr	1935–1936, 1938–1939
G. Francis	1935–1936, 1938–1939
V. Smithyman	1935
Lionel Hayes	1935–1937, 1939–1940
George Summers	1935–1937, 1946
H. Fox	1935
R. Neil	1935–1940
G. Longfield	1935
Thomson	1936–1938, 1940, 1945
Russell-Jones	1936–1940, 1945, 1947–1948
Forrest	1936–1940, 1945–1946, 1949–1950
Puttock	1936, 1938–1939
Bemister	1936
R. Grant	1936–1940, 1945–1947
Roberts	1937
Hoey	1937–1938
Campbell	1937, 1939
Mackinnon	1937, 1939
Brooking	1937
Smith	1937–1938
Malcolm Alexander Phillips	1937, 1945
Leach	1937
Clarke	1937–1939, 1947
Tots Bishop	1937, 1945–1946
Irwin	1937
Galloway	1937, 1940
Survana	1937
T. Carroll	1938

Hood	1938
Glass	1939
Van Horsten	1939
Saunders	1939–1940, 1945–1946
Bingham	1939–1940
Cameron	1939
Woodall	1940
Whiting	1945
Milward	1945
Johns	1945
Cliff Allin	1945–1946, 1948
Boot	1946
Hodgson	1946
Stubbs	1946–1947
Longden	1946
Hamment	1947
Nash	1947
Fairley	1947–1948
Roger Royle	1947, 1953
Millar	1947
McIntosh	1947
Archie Muir	1947–1949, 1952–1953, 1955–1957
George Sophos	1947–1948, 1951
Ian Royan	1948–1950, 1952, 1955
Bright	1948
Young	1948–1949
Kirby	1948–1950
John Patterson	1948–1952, 1954
White	1948–1949
Jimmy Kongialis	1949–1953, 1955
Rose	1949
Alan Flowerdew	1949
Imlah	1949
Albert Hall	1950
R. Payne	1950–1951
Edmonds	1950
Dennis Nock	1950–1952, 1954–1955
Don Armstrong	1950, 1954–1955
Jimmy Smith	1950–1957

R. Bennett	1951
Dennis Johnston	1951–1963
Tommy Allen	1951–1955, 1957–1958, 1960
Harry Levy	1951
William Harvey	1951, 1953
Sergio Nicholas	1952–1954, 1956–1962
Sullivan	1952
Roberts	1952–1953
Khuda Bax	1952, 1954
Houston	1952
Cruickshank	1952
Micky Megraw	1952–1954, 1956–1957
Alan Taylor	1952, 1954–1957
Pengelly	1953
Harold Wrigley	1953–1954
Dipple	1953
Morris	1953
Ricky Robertson	1954–1957
Ken Thomson	1954–1956
Entwhistle	1954–1955
Brian Phillips	1954–1955, 1957–1963
Humphries	1954
Ken Mansfield	1954–1962
Bob Marrinan	1954–1956
Pipes	1954–1955
Da Cruz	1954
Peter Gurney	1954, 1956
Fred Taylor	1954–1955
Kabul	1954
Brian Fox	1955–1963
Les Doran	1955–1960
Van Arenthals	1955
George Trataris	1955, 1957, 1960–1961, 1963–1964
Peter Parker (snr)	1955, 1960
Dennis Harris	1955–1956
Stockman	1956, 1958
Don Harper	1956
Brian Burgess	1956
Colin Findlay	1956–1957

Shergold	1956
Wilson	1956
F. de Vito	1956
Matt Hoyland	1956, 1958, 1960–1962
Pat Saunders	1957
Ian Strachan	1957, 1960
Alan Geldard	1957, 1959–1961
Pat Kelly	1957
Godfrey Keys	1957, 1960–1961
G. Hindaugh	1957
Pat Lorimer	1957
Billy Pillans	1957
Brooks	1957
Grant	1957
George Barley	1957–1960
John Trataris	1957
Harold Wrigley (snr)	1957
Reid	1957
John Hoatson	1957, 1961
Stellious	1958
A. Marr	1958
Johnny Hawthorne	1958–1960
Alfio Vatteroni	1958
Archie Carver	1958–1961
Dennis Pritchard	1958–1964
Amilcare Comminetti	1958
Buchan	1958–1959
Archie Cottingham	1958–1960
Jack Lowery	1958–1959
Colandria Lorenco	1958–1959
Jim Cottingham	1959
John Cotton	1959–1960, 1962–1963
Vic Moss	1959–1961
Preen	1959
Cominas Yiannakis	1959–1960, 1962–1964
Peter Lewis	1959–1961
Peter Crossan	1959–1960, 1963
T. Donaldson	1959
Acconci	1959

Mike Bowery	1959–1960
Jack Stuart	1960
Fletcher	1960
Harold Davies	1960
Ken Burns	1960
J. Kopanakis	1960
Max Prien	1960–1962
Colley	1960
Bob Rodgers	1960–1962
I. Grilli	1960, 1962
Crawford	1960
Monteiro	1960
Mann	1961–1962
Corb	1961
French	1961
Peter Parker (jnr)	1961
MacDonald	1961
Rosenast	1961
Rui Bastos	1961–1962
A. Gafforio	1962
Tommy Prentice	1962
Johnnie Ruprecht	1962
Ronnie King	1962
Michel Melotte	1962–1963
Bill Keddie	1962–1964
S. Damalakis	1962
J. Pietersie	1962
Terry Mills	1962
Haroon Karim	1962
Peter West	1962
Tommy Ballantyne	1962
Don Mientjies	1962–1963
B. McArdle	1962
Jim Yiannakis	1962
Dettmar	1962
Hugh Smith	1963–1964
L. Ferguson	1963
Chalmers	1964
Santokh Singh	1964

1.   **Harry Middleton**

Year	Caps	C/Sheets
1935	1	0
1936	2	0
1937	1	0
1938	1	1
	5	1

Summary of Games

Fixtures	P	W	D	L	F	A	CS
Oury Cup	2	1	0	1	1	1	1
Friendly Club	3	1	0	2	7	10	0
	5	2	0	3	8	11	1
		40%	0%	60%	1.60	2.20	20%

2.   **J. Macdonald**

Year	Caps	Goals
1935	1	0

Summary of Games

Fixtures	P	W	D	L	F	A
Friendly Club	1	0	0	1	1	4
		0%	0%	100%	1.00	4.00

3.   **S. Robertson**

Year	Caps	Goals
1935	1	0
1937	1	0
1940	2	0
1946	1	0
	5	0

Summary of Games

Fixtures	P	W	D	L	F	A
Oury Cup	3	1	0	2	5	6
Friendly Club	2	0	0	2	2	7
	5	1	0	4	7	13
		20%	0%	80%	1.40	2.60

Notes: 1940: 2 unknown scorers v. Sport Lisboa e Beira (1 in 3–2 win and 1–3 defeat)

4.   **N. Carr**

Year	Caps	Goals
1935	1	0
1936	2	0
1938	2	0
1939	1	0
	6	0

Summary of Games

Fixtures	P	W	D	L	F	A
Oury Cup	2	1	0	1	1	6
Friendly Club	4	1	0	3	8	13
	6	2	0	4	9	19
		33.3%	0%	66.7%	1.50	3.17

5.   **G. Francis**

Year	Caps	Goals
1935	1	0
1936	1	0
1938	2	0
1939	1	0
	5	0

Summary of Games

Fixtures	P	W	D	L	F	A
Oury Cup	2	1	0	1	1	6
Friendly Club	3	1	0	2	5	8
	5	2	0	3	6	14
		40%	0%	60%	1.20	2.80

6.   **V. Smithyman**

Year	Caps	Goals
1935	1	0

Summary of Games

Fixtures	P	W	D	L	F	A
Friendly Club	1	0	0	1	1	4
		0%	0%	100%	1.00	4.00

7. **Lionel Hayes**

Year	Caps	Goals	
1935	1	0	
1936	2	1	
1937	2	0	(C/sheets)
1939	2	0	
1940	2	0	(C/sheets)
	9	1	

Summary of Games

Fixtures	P	W	D	L	F	A	GS
Oury Cup	2	1	0	1	3	8	0
Friendly Club	5	1	0	4	8	16	1
	7	2	0	5	11	24	1
		28.6%	0%	71.4%	1.57	3.43	9.1%

Notes: 1937: 2 unknown results v. Alexandra FC

8. **George Summers**

Year	Caps	Goals
1935	1	1
1936	2	1
1937	1	0
1946	1	0
	5	2

Summary of Games

Fixtures	P	W	D	L	F	A	GS
Oury Cup	2	0	0	2	2	4	0
Friendly Club	3	1	0	2	7	10	2
	5	1	0	4	9	14	2
		20%	0%	80%	1.80	2.80	22.2%

9. **H. Fox**

Year	Caps	Goals
1935	1	0

Summary of Games

Fixtures	P	W	D	L	F	A
Friendly Club	1	0	0	1	1	4
		0%	0%	100%	1.00	4.00

10. **R. Neil**

Year	Caps	Goals
1935	1	0
1936	2	2
1937	1	0
1938	2	0
1939	1	0
1940	2	0
	9	2

Summary of Games

Fixtures	P	W	D	L	F	A	GS
Oury Cup	2	2	0	0	4	2	0
Friendly Club	7	1	0	6	9	20	2
	9	3	0	6	13	22	2
		33.3%	0%	66.7%	1.44	2.44	15.4%

Notes:	1940: 2 unknown scorers v. Sport Lisboa e Beira (1 in 3–2 win and 1–3 defeat)

11. **G. Longfield**

Year	Caps	Goals
1935	1	0

Summary of Games

Fixtures	P	W	D	L	F	A
Friendly Club	1	0	0	1	1	4
		0%	0%	100%	1.00	4.00

12. **Thomson**

Year	Caps	Goals
1936	2	0
1937	3	0
1938	1	0
1940	2	0

1945	2	0
	10	0

Summary of Games

Fixtures	P	W	D	L	F	A
Oury Cup	4	2	0	2	5	7
Friendly Club	3	1	0	2	7	9
	7	3	0	4	12	16
		42.9%	0%	57.1%	1.71	2.29

Notes:	1937: 2 unknown results v. Alexandra FC
	1940: 2 unknown scorers v. Sport Lisboa e Beira (1 in 3–2 win and 1–3 defeat)
	1945: 1 unknown result v. Sport Lisboa e Beira

13. Russell-Jones

Year	Caps	Goals
1936	2	0
1937	3	0
1938	2	1
1939	2	0
1940	2	0
1945	2	0
1947	2	0
1948	1	0
	16	1

Summary of Games

Fixtures	P	W	D	L	F	A	GS
Oury Cup	7	2	0	5	6	25	0
Friendly Club	6	1	0	5	8	18	1
	13	3	0	10	14	43	1
		23.1%	0%	76.9%	1.08	3.31	7.1%

Notes:	1937: 2 unknown results v. Alexandra FC
	1940: 2 unknown scorers v. Sport Lisboa e Beira (1 in 3–2 win and 1–3 defeat)
	1945: 1 unknown result v. Sport Lisboa e Beira

14. Forrest

Year	Caps	Goals
1936	2	0

1937	3	0
1938	2	0
1939	2	0
1940	2	2
1945	2	0
1946	1	0
1949	2	1
1950	1	0
	17	3

Summary of Games

Fixtures	P	W	D	L	F	A	GS
Oury Cup	7	3	1	3	15	22	3
Friendly Club	7	1	0	6	9	21	0
	14	4	1	9	24	43	3
		28.6%	7.1%	64.3%	1.71	3.07	12.5%

Notes:
1937: 2 unknown results v. Alexandra FC
1940: 2 unknown scorers v. Sport Lisboa e Beira (1 in 3–2 win and 1–3 defeat)
1945: 1 unknown result v. Sport Lisboa e Beira
1949: 1 unknown scorer v. Beira Select XI in 1–5 defeat

15. **Puttock**

Year	Caps	Goals
1936	1	0
1938	2	0
1939	2	0
	5	0

Summary of Games

Fixtures	P	W	D	L	F	A
Oury Cup	2	1	0	1	1	6
Friendly Club	3	0	0	3	4	11
	5	1	0	4	5	17
		20%	0%	80%	1.00	3.40

16. **Bemister**

Year	Caps	Goals
1936	2	1

Summary of Games

Fixtures	P	W	D	L	F	A	GS
Friendly Club	2	1	0	1	6	6	1
		50%	0%	50%	3.00	3.00	14.%

17.   **R. Grant**

Year	Caps	Goals
1936	2	1
1937	3	0
1938	2	1
1939	2	0
1940	2	0
1945	2	0
1946	1	1
1947	2	0
	16	3

Summary of Games

Fixtures	P	W	D	L	F	A	GS
Oury Cup	7	2	0	5	7	26	2
Friendly Club	6	1	0	5	8	18	1
	13	3	0	10	15	44	3
		23.1%	0%	76.9%	1.15	3.38	20%

Notes: 1937: 2 unknown results v. Alexandra FC

1940: 2 unknown scorers v. Sport Lisboa e Beira (1 in 3–2 win and 1–3 defeat)

1945: 1 unknown result v. Sport Lisboa e Beira

18.   **Roberts**

Year	Caps	Goals
1937	1	0

Summary of Games

Fixtures	P	W	D	L	F	A
Oury Cup	1	0	0	1	0	1
		0%	0%	100%	0.00	1.00

19.   **Hoey**

Year	Caps	Goals
1937	1	0
1938	1	0
	2	0

Summary of Games

Fixtures	P	W	D	L	F	A
Friendly Club	1	0	0	1	1	3
		0%	0%	100%	1.00	3.00

Notes: 1937: 1 unknown result v. Alexandra FC

20.   **Campbell**

Year	Caps	Goals
1937	1	0
1939	1	0
	2	0

Summary of Games

Fixtures	P	W	D	L	F	A
Friendly Club	1	0	0	1	0	3
		0%	0%	100%	0.00	3.00

Notes: 1937: 1 unknown result v. Alexandra FC

21.   **Mackinnon**

Year	Caps	Goals
1937	1	0
1939	1	0
	2	0

Summary of Games

Fixtures	P	W	D	L	F	A
Oury Cup	1	0	0	1	0	6
Friendly Club	0	0	0	0	0	0
	1	0	0	1	0	6
		0%	0%	100%	0.00	6.00

Notes: 1937: 1 unknown result v. Alexandra FC

22. **Brooking**

Year	Caps	Goals
1937	1	0

Summary of Games

Fixtures	P	W	D	L	F	A
Friendly Club	0	0	0	0	0	0
		0%	0%	0%	0.00	0.00

Notes: 1937: 1 unknown result v. Alexandra FC

23. **Smith**

Year	Caps	Goals
1937	2	0
1938	1	0
	3	0

Summary of Games

Fixtures	P	W	D	L	F	A
Friendly Club	1	0	0	1	1	3
		0%	0%	100%	1.00	3.00

Notes: 1937: 2 unknown results v. Alexandra FC

24. **Malcolm Alexander Phillips**

Year	Caps	Goals
1937	1	0
1945	2	0
	3	0

Summary of Games

Fixtures	P	W	D	L	F	A
Oury Cup	1	0	0	1	1	4
Friendly Club	0	0	0	0	0	0
	1	0	0	1	1	4
		0%	0%	100%	1.00	4.00

Notes: 1937: 1 unknown result v. Alexandra FC

1945: 1 unknown result v. Sport Lisboa e Beira

25. **Leach**

Year	Caps	Goals
1937	2	0

Summary of Games

Fixtures	P	W	D	L	F	A
Friendly Club	0	0	0	0	0	0
		0%	0%	0%	0.00	0.00

Notes: 1937: 2 unknown results v. Alexandra FC

26. **Clarke**

Year	Caps	Goals
1937	1	0
1938	1	0
1939	1	0
1947	2	0
	5	0

Summary of Games

Fixtures	P	W	D	L	F	A
Oury Cup	3	1	0	2	1	16
Friendly Club	1	0	0	1	0	3
	4	1	0	3	1	19
		25%	0%	75%	0.25	4.75

Notes: 1937: 1 unknown result v. Alexandra FC

27. **Tots Bishop**

Year	Caps	Goals
1937	1	0
1945	2	0
1946	1	0
	4	0

Summary of Games

Fixtures	P	W	D	L	F	A
Oury Cup	2	0	0	2	3	7
Friendly Club	0	0	0	0	0	0
	2	0	0	2	3	7
		0%	0%	100%	1.50	3.50

Notes: 1937: 1 unknown result v. Alexandra FC

1945: 1 unknown result v. Sport Lisboa e Beira

28.	**Irwin**	
Year	Caps	Goals
1937	1	0

Summary of Games

Fixtures	P	W	D	L	F	A
Friendly Club	0	0	0	0	0	0
		0%	0%	0%	0.00	0.00

Notes: 1937: 1 unknown result v. Alexandra FC

29.	**Galloway**	
Year	Caps	Goals
1937	1	0
1940	2	0
	3	0

Summary of Games

Fixtures	P	W	D	L	F	A
Oury Cup	1	1	0	0	3	2
Friendly Club	1	0	0	1	1	3
	2	1	0	1	4	5
		50%	0%	50%	2.00	2.50

Notes: 1937: 1 unknown result v. Alexandra FC

1940: 2 unknown scorers v. Sport Lisboa e Beira (1 in 3–2 win and 1–3 defeat)

30.	**Survana**	
Year	Caps	Goals
1937	1	0

Summary of Games

Fixtures	P	W	D	L	F	A
Oury Cup	1	0	0	1	0	1
		0%	0%	100%	0.00	1.00

31.   **T. Carroll**

Year	Caps	Goals
1938	1	0

Summary of Games

Fixtures	P	W	D	L	F	A
Friendly Club	1	0	0	1	1	3
		0%	0%	100%	1.00	3.00

32.   **Hood**

Year	Caps	Goals
1938	2	0

Summary of Games

Fixtures	P	W	D	L	F	A
Oury Cup	1	1	0	0	1	0
Friendly Club	1	0	0	1	1	3
	2	1	0	1	2	3
		50%	0%	50%	1.00	1.50

33.   **Glass**

Year	Caps	C/Sheets
1939	1	0

Summary of Games

Fixtures	P	W	D	L	F	A
Oury Cup	1	0	0	1	0	6
		0%	0%	100%	0.00	6.00

34.   **Van Horsten**

Year	Caps	C/Sheets
1939	1	0

Summary of Games

Fixtures	P	W	D	L	F	A
Friendly Club	1	0	0	1	0	3
		0%	0%	100%	0.00	3.00

35.   **Saunders**

Year	Caps	Goals
1939	1	0
1940	2	0
1945	2	0
1946	1	0
	6	0

Summary of Games

Fixtures	P	W	D	L	F	A
Oury Cup	3	1	0	2	6	9
Friendly Club	2	0	0	2	1	6
	5	1	0	4	7	15
		20%	0%	80%	1.40	3.00

Notes:	1940: 2 unknown scorers v. Sport Lisboa e Beira (1 in 3–2 win and 1–3 defeat)
	1945: 1 unknown result v. Sport Lisboa e Beira

36.   **Bingham**

Year	Caps	Goals
1939	1	0
1940	2	0
	3	0

Summary of Games

Fixtures	P	W	D	L	F	A
Oury Cup	1	1	0	0	3	2
Friendly Club	2	0	0	2	1	6
	3	1	0	2	4	8
		33.3%	0%	66.7%	1.33	2.67

Notes:	1940: 2 unknown scorers v. Sport Lisboa e Beira (1 in 3–2 win and 1–3 defeat)

37.   **Cameron**

Year	Caps	Goals
1939	2	0

Summary of Games

Fixtures	P	W	D	L	F	A
Oury Cup	1	0	0	1	0	6
Friendly Club	1	0	0	1	0	3
	2	0	0	3	0	9
		0%	0%	100%	0.00	4.50

38.   **Woodall**

Year	Caps	Goals
1940	2	0

Summary of Games

Fixtures	P	W	D	L	F	A
Oury Cup	1	1	0	0	3	2
Friendly Club	1	0	0	1	1	3
	2	1	0	1	4	5
		50%	0%	50%	2.00	2.50

Notes: 1940: 2 unknown scorers v. Sport Lisboa e Beira (1 in 3–2 win and 1–3 defeat)

39.   **Whiting**

Year	Caps	C/Sheets
1945	2	0

Summary of Games

Fixtures	P	W	D	L	F	A
Oury Cup	1	0	0	1	1	4
Friendly Club	0	0	0	0	0	0
	1	0	0	1	1	4
		0%	0%	100%	1.00	4.00

Notes: 1945: 1 unknown result v. Sport Lisboa e Beira

40.   **Milward**

Year	Caps	Goals
1945	2	0

Summary of Games

Fixtures	P	W	D	L	F	A
Oury Cup	1	0	0	1	1	4
Friendly Club	0	0	0	0	0	0
	1	0	0	1	1	4
		0%	0%	100%	1.00	4.00

Notes: 1945: 1 unknown result v. Sport Lisboa e Beira

41.   **Johns**

Year	Caps	Goals
1945	2	0

Summary of Games

Fixtures	P	W	D	L	F	A
Oury Cup	1	0	0	1	1	4
Friendly Club	0	0	0	0	0	0
	1	0	0	1	1	4
		0%	0%	100%	1.00	4.00

Notes: 1945: 1 unknown result v. Sport Lisboa e Beira

42.   **Cliff Allin**

Year	Caps	Goals
1945	2	1
1946	1	1
1948	1	0
	4	2

Summary of Games

Fixtures	P	W	D	L	F	A	GS
Oury Cup	3	0	0	3	4	9	2
Friendly Club	0	0	0	0	0	0	0
	3	0	0	3	4	9	2
		0%	0%	100%	1.33	3.00	50%

Notes: 1945: 1 unknown result v. Sport Lisboa e Beira

43. **Boot**

Year	Caps	C/Sheets
1946	1	0

Summary of Games

Fixtures	P	W	D	L	F	A
Oury Cup	1	0	0	1	2	3
		0%	0%	100%	2.00	3.00

44. **Hodgson**

Year	Caps	Goals
1946	1	0

Summary of Games

Fixtures	P	W	D	L	F	A
Oury Cup	1	0	0	1	2	3
		0%	0%	100%	2.00	3.00

45. **Stubbs**

Year	Caps	Goals
1946	1	0
1947	2	0
	3	0

Summary of Games

Fixtures	P	W	D	L	F	A
Oury Cup	2	0	0	2	2	13
Friendly Club	1	0	0	1	0	3
	3	0	0	3	2	16
		0%	0%	100%	0.67	5.33

46. **Longden**

Year	Caps	Goals
1946	1	0

Summary of Games

Fixtures	P	W	D	L	F	A
Oury Cup	1	0	0	1	2	3
		0%	0%	100%	2.00	3.00

47.　　　　**Hamment**

Year	Caps	C/Sheets
1947	1	0

Summary of Games

Fixtures	P	W	D	L	F	A
Oury Cup	1	0	0	1	0	10
		0%	0%	100%	0.00	10.00

48.　　　　**Nash**

Year	Caps	C/Sheets
1947	1	0

Summary of Games

Fixtures	P	W	D	L	F	A
Friendly Club	1	0	0	1	0	3
		0%	0%	100%	0.00	3.00

49.　　　　**Fairley**

Year	Caps	Goals
1947	2	0
1948	1	0
	3	0

Summary of Games

Fixtures	P	W	D	L	F	A
Oury Cup	2	0	0	2	1	12
Friendly Club	1	0	0	1	0	3
	3	0	0	3	1	15
		0%	0%	100%	0.33	5.00

50.   **Roger Royle**

Year	Caps	Goals
1947	2	0
1953	2	0
	4	0

Summary of Games

Fixtures	P	W	D	L	F	A
Oury Cup	2	1	0	1	1	10
Friendly Club	2	0	0	2	0	4
	4	1	0	3	1	14
		25%	0%	75%	0.25	3.50

51.   **Millar**

Year	Caps	Goals
1947	2	0

Summary of Games

Fixtures	P	W	D	L	F	A
Oury Cup	1	0	0	1	0	10
Friendly Club	1	0	0	1	0	3
	2	0	0	2	0	13
		0%	0%	100%	0.00	6.50

52.   **Mcintosh**

Year	Caps	Goals
1947	2	0

Summary of Games

Fixtures	P	W	D	L	F	A
Oury Cup	1	0	0	1	0	10
Friendly Club	1	0	0	1	0	3
	2	0	0	2	0	13
		0%	0%	100%	0.00	6.50

53.   **Archie Muir**

Year	Caps	Goals
1947	2	0
1948	1	0

1949	2	0
1952	2	0
1953	2	0
1955	4	3
1956	2	0
1957	1	1
	16	4

Summary of Games

Fixtures	P	W	D	L	F	A	GS
Oury Cup	6	1	1	4	6	27	0
Trataris Cup	2	1	0	1	3	4	0
Friendly Club	7	3	0	4	13	17	3
Bruss Cup "B"	1	1	0	0	6	1	1
	16	6	1	9	28	49	4
		37.5%	6.2%	56.3%	1.75	3.06	14.3%

Notes: 1949: 1 unknown scorer v. Beira Select XI in 1–5 defeat

1952: Four unknown scorers v. Sport Lisboa e Beira in 4–3 win

54. George Sophos

Year	Caps	Goals
1947	2	0
1948	1	0
1951	1	1
	4	1

Summary of Games

Fixtures	P	W	D	L	F	A	GS
Oury Cup	3	1	0	2	3	13	1
Friendly Club	1	0	0	1	0	3	0
	4	1	0	3	3	16	1
		25%	0%	75%	0.75	4.00	33.3%

55. Ian Royan

Year	Caps	C/Sheets
1948	1	0
1949	2	0
1950	1	0
1952	1	0

1955	4	0
	9	0

Summary of Games

Fixtures	P	W	D	L	F	A
Oury Cup	5	1	1	3	10	21
Trataris Cup	1	1	0	0	3	2
Friendly Club	3	2	0	1	8	8
	9	4	1	4	21	31
		44.4%	11.2%	44.4%	2.33	3.44

56.   **Bright**

Year	Caps	Goals
1948	1	0

Summary of Games

Fixtures	P	W	D	L	F	A
Oury Cup	1	0	0	1	1	2
		0%	0%	100%	1.00	2.00

57.   **Young**

Year	Caps	Goals
1948	1	0
1949	2	0
	3	0

Summary of Games

Fixtures	P	W	D	L	F	A
Oury Cup	2	0	1	1	4	5
Friendly Club	1	0	0	1	1	5
	3	0	1	2	5	10
		0%	33.3%	66.7%	1.67	3.33

Notes: 1949: 1 unknown scorer v. Beira Select XI in 1–5 defeat

58.   **Kirby**

Year	Caps	Goals
1948	1	0
1949	2	1

Mario Antoine

1950	1	0
	4	1

Summary of Games

Fixtures	P	W	D	L	F	A	GS
Oury Cup	3	1	1	1	9	9	1
Friendly Club	1	0	0	1	1	5	0
	4	1	1	2	10	14	1
		25%	25%	50%	2.50	3.50	10%

Notes: 1949: 1 unknown scorer v. Beira Select XI in 1–5 defeat

59.   **John Patterson**

Year	Caps	Goals
1948	1	1
1949	2	0
1950	1	2
1951	1	0
1952	2	1
1954	3	2
	10	6

Summary of Games

Fixtures	P	W	D	L	F	A	GS
Oury Cup	6	3	1	2	17	14	5
Trataris Cup	1	0	0	1	1	4	1
Friendly Club	3	1	0	2	6	11	0
	10	4	1	5	24	29	6
		40%	10%	50%	2.40	2.90	25%

Notes: 1949: 1 unknown scorer v. Beira Select XI in 1–5 defeat

1952: 4 unknown scorers v. Sport Lisboa e Beira in 4–3 win

60.   **White**

Year	Caps	Goals
1948	1	0
1949	2	0
	3	0

Summary of Games

Fixtures	P	W	D	L	F	A
Oury Cup	2	0	1	1	4	5
Friendly Club	1	0	0	1	1	5
	3	0	1	2	5	10
		0%	33.3%	66.7%	1.67	3.33

Notes: 1949: 1 unknown scorer v. Beira Select XI in 1–5 defeat

61.   Jimmy Kongialis

Year	Caps	Goals
1949	2	0
1950	1	0
1951	1	0
1952	1	0
1953	4	0
1955	3	0
	12	0

Summary of Games

Fixtures	P	W	D	L	F	A
Oury Cup	6	3	1	2	16	22
Trataris Cup	2	1	0	1	4	6
Friendly Club	4	2	0	2	11	13
	12	6	1	5	31	41
		50%	8.3%	41.7%	2.58	3.42

Notes: 1949: 1 unknown scorer v. Beira Select XI in 1–5 defeat

62.   Rose

Year	Caps	Goals
1949	2	0

Summary of Games

Fixtures	P	W	D	L	F	A
Oury Cup	1	0	1	0	3	3
Friendly Club	1	0	0	1	1	5
	2	0	1	1	4	8
		0%	50%	50%	2.00	4.00

Notes: 1949: 1 unknown scorer v. Beira Select XI in 1–5 defeat

63.   Alan Flowerdew

Year	Caps	Goals
1949	2	0

Summary of Games

Fixtures	P	W	D	L	F	A
Oury Cup	1	0	1	0	3	3
Friendly Club	1	0	0	1	1	5
	2	0	1	1	4	8
		0%	50%	50%	2.00	4.00

Notes: 1949: 1 unknown scorer v. Beira Select XI in 1–5 defeat

64.   Imlah

Year	Caps	Goals
1949	2	1

Summary of Games

Fixtures	P	W	D	L	F	A	GS
Oury Cup	1	0	1	0	3	3	1
Friendly Club	1	0	0	1	1	5	0
	2	0	1	1	4	8	1
		0%	50%	50%	2.00	4.00	25%

Notes: 1949: 1 unknown scorer v. Beira Select XI in 1–5 defeat

65.   Albert Hall

Year	Caps	Goals
1950	1	0

Summary of Games

Fixtures	P	W	D	L	F	A
Oury Cup	1	1	0	0	5	4
		100%	0%	0%	5.00	4.00

66.   R. Payne

Year	Caps	Goals

1950	1	0
1951	1	0
	2	0

Summary of Games

Fixtures	P	W	D	L	F	A
Oury Cup	2	2	0	0	7	5
		100%	0%	0%	3.50	2.50

67.   **Edmonds**

Year	Caps	Goals
1950	1	0

Summary of Games

Fixtures	P	W	D	L	F	A
Oury Cup	1	1	0	0	5	4
		100%	0%	0%	5.00	4.00

68.   **Dennis Nock**

Year	Caps	Goals
1950	1	1
1951	1	1
1952	2	0
1954	2	0
1955	2	1
	8	3

Summary of Games

Fixtures	P	W	D	L	F	A	GS
Oury Cup	3	2	0	1	8	7	2
Friendly Club	1	1	0	0	4	3	0
Bruss Cup "B"	2	1	0	1	3	5	0
Friendly Club B	2	1	0	1	2	2	1
	8	5	0	3	17	17	3
		62.5%	0%	37.5%	2.13	2.13	17.6%

Notes: 1952: 4 unknown scorers v. Sport Lisboa e Beira in 4–3 win

69.   **Don Armstrong**

Year	Caps	Goals
1950	1	2
1954	3	0
1955	4	0
	8	2

Summary of Games

Fixtures	P	W	D	L	F	A	GS
Oury Cup	2	1	0	1	5	14	2
Trataris Cup	1	1	0	0	3	2	0
Friendly	3	3	0	0	11	6	0
Bruss Cup "B"	1	1	0	0	2	1	0
Friendly Club B	1	0	0	1	0	2	0
	8	6	0	2	21	25	2
		75%	0%	25%	2.63	3.13	9.5%

70.   **Jimmy Smith**

Year	Caps	Goals
1950	1	0
1951	1	0
1952	2	0
1953	1	0
1954	1	0
1955	2	0
1956	3	0
1957	2	2
	13	2

Summary of Games

Fixtures	P	W	D	L	F	A	GS
Oury Cup	5	4	0	1	13	8	0
Trataris Cup	1	1	0	0	4	1	2
Friendly Club	2	1	0	1	5	5	0
Bruss Cup "B"	3	1	1	1	3	5	0
Friendly Club B	2	2	0	0	5	1	0
	13	9	1	3	30	20	2
		69.2%	7.7%	23.1%	2.31	1.54	6.7%

Notes: 1952: 4 unknown scorers v. Sport Lisboa e Beira in 4–3 win

71. **R. Bennett**

Year	Caps	C/Sheets
1951	1	0

Summary of Games

Fixtures	P	W	D	L	F	A
Oury Cup	1	1	0	0	2	1
		100%	0%	0%	2.00	1.00

72. **Dennis Johnston**

Year	Caps	Goals
1951	1	0
1952	2	0
1953	2	0
1954	4	0
1955	3	0
1956	4	0
1957	4	0
1958	3	0
1959	2	0
1960	6	0
1961	4	0
1962	5	0
1963	4	0
	44	0

Summary of Games

Fixtures	P	W	D	L	F	A
Oury Cup	12	8	0	4	28	24
Trataris Cup	8	4	0	4	16	18
Friendly Club	24	7	4	13	46	75
	44	19	4	21	90	117
		43.2%	9.1%	47.7%	2.05	2.66

Notes:
1952: 4 unknown scorers v. Sport Lisboa e Beira in 4–3 win
1957: 1 unknown scorer v. Alexandra FC in 1–8 defeat
1959: 1 unknown scorer v. Alexandra FC in 1–3 defeat
1961: 3 unknown scorers v. Alexandra FC in 6–1 win

73.   **Tommy Allen**

Year	Caps	Goals	
1951	1	0	
1952	2	0	
1953	2	0	
1954	4	0	
1955	4	0	
1957	4	1	
1958	3	0	
1960	1	0	
	21	1	

Summary of Games

Fixtures	P	W	D	L	F	A	GS
Oury Cup	8	5	0	3	16	20	1
Trataris Cup	4	3	0	1	10	7	0
Friendly Club	9	5	0	4	20	24	0
	21	13	0	8	46	51	1
		61.9%	0%	38.1%	2.19	2.43	2.2%

Notes:	1952: 4 unknown scorers v. Sport Lisboa e Beira in 4–3 win
	1957: 1 unknown scorer v. Alexandra FC in 1–8 defeat

74.   **Harry Levy**

Year	Caps	Goals
1951	1	0

Summary of Games

Fixtures	P	W	D	L	F	A
Oury Cup	1	1	0	0	2	1
	100%	0%	0%	2.00	1.00	

75.   **William Harvey**

Year	Caps	Goals	
1951	1	0	
1953	3	0	(C/Sheets)
	4	0	

Summary of Games

Fixtures	P	W	D	L	F	A
Oury Cup	1	1	0	0	2	1
Friendly Club	1	1	0	0	4	3
Bruss Cup (B)	1	1	0	0	2	1
Friendly Club B	1	0	0	1	0	2
	4	3	0	1	8	7
		75%	0%	25%	2.00	1.75

76.   **Sergio Nicholas**

Year	Caps	C/Sheets
1952	1	0
1953	2	1
1954	3	0
1956	3	1
1957	3	0
1958	3	1
1959	4	0
1960	5	0
1961	4	0
1962	4	0
	32	3

Summary of Games

Fixtures	P	W	D	L	F	A	CS
Oury Cup	9	7	0	2	24	11	2
Trataris Cup	7	3	0	4	13	16	1
Friendly Club	16	4	4	8	29	43	0
	32	14	4	14	66	70	3
		43.8%	12.5%	43.8%	2.06	2.19	9.4%

77.   **Sullivan**

Year	Caps	Goals
1952	1	0

Summary of Games

Fixtures	P	W	D	L	F	A
Friendly Club	1	1	0	0	4	3
		100%	0%	0%	4.00	3.00

Notes: 1952: 4 unknown scorers v. Sport Lisboa e Beira in 4–3 win

78. **Roberts**

Year	Caps	Goals
1952	1	0
1953	2	0
	3	0

Summary of Games

Fixtures	P	W	D	L	F	A
Oury Cup	2	1	0	1	2	2
Friendly Club	1	0	0	1	0	1
	3	1	0	2	2	3
		33.3%	0%	66.7%	0.67	1.00

79. **Khuda Bax**

Year	Caps	Goals
1952	1	0
1954	1	0
	2	0

Summary of Games

Fixtures	P	W	D	L	F	A
Friendly Club	1	1	0	0	4	3
Friendly Club B	1	0	0	1	0	2
	2	1	0	1	4	5
		50%	0%	50%	2.00	2.50

Notes: 1952: 4 unknown scorers v. Sport Lisboa e Beira in 4–3 win

80. **Houston**

Year	Caps	Goals
1952	1	0

Summary of Games

Fixtures	P	W	D	L	F	A
Oury Cup	1	0	0	1	1	2
		0%	0%	100%	1.00	2.00

81.   **Cruickshank**

Year	Caps	Goals
1952	1	0

Summary of Games

Fixtures	P	W	D	L	F	A
Friendly Club	1	1	0	0	4	3
		100%	0%	0%	4.00	3.00

Notes: 1952: 4 unknown scorers v. Sport Lisboa e Beira in 4–3 win

82.   **Micky Megraw**

Year	Caps	Goals
1952	1	0
1953	2	0
1954	2	0
1956	3	0
1957	1	0
	9	0

Summary of Games

Fixtures	P	W	D	L	F	A
Oury Cup	3	2	0	1	7	2
Trataris Cup	3	1	0	2	5	7
Friendly Club	3	0	0	3	4	8
	9	3	0	6	16	17
		33.6%	0%	66.7%	1.78	1.89

83.   **Alan Taylor**

Year	Caps	Goals
1952	1	0
1954	3	1
1955	4	0
1956	3	1
1957	1	0
	12	1

Summary of Games

Fixtures	P	W	D	L	F	A	GS
Oury Cup	2	1	0	1	5	10	1

Trataris Cup	2	1	0	1	3	4	0
Friendly Club	5	3	0	2	13	11	0
Bruss Cup "B"	2	2	0	0	8	2	1
Friendly Club B	1	0	0	1	0	2	0
	12	7	0	5	29	29	2
		58.3%	0%	41.7%	2.42	2.42	6.9%

Notes: 1952: 4 unknown scorers v. Sport Lisboa e Beira in 4–3 win

84. **Pengelly**

Year	Caps	Goals
1953	2	0

Summary of Games

Fixtures	P	W	D	L	F	A
Oury Cup	1	1	0	0	1	0
Friendly Club	1	0	0	1	0	1
	2	1	0	1	1	1
		50%	0%	50%	0.50	0.50

85. **Harold Wrigley**

Year	Caps	Goals
1953	2	0
1954	2	0
	4	0

Summary of Games

Fixtures	P	W	D	L	F	A
Oury Cup	2	2	0	0	6	2
Trataris Cup	1	0	0	1	1	4
Friendly Club	1	0	0	1	0	1
	4	2	0	2	7	7
		50%	0%	50%	1.75	1.75

86. **Dipple**

Year	Caps	Goals
1953	2	0

Summary of Games

Fixtures	P	W	D	L	F	A	GS
Oury Cup	1	1	0	0	1	0	1
Friendly Club	1	0	0	1	0	1	0
	2	1	0	1	1	1	1
		50%	0%	50%	0.50	0.50	100%

87.   **Morris**

Year	Caps	Goals
1953	1	0

Summary of Games

Fixtures	P	W	D	L	F	A
Friendly Club	1	0	0	1	0	1
		0%	0%	100%	0.00	1.00

88.   **Ricky Robertson**

Year	Caps	Goals
1954	3	0
1955	3	0
1956	3	0
1957	4	3
	13	3

Summary of Games

Fixtures	P	W	D	L	F	A	GS
Oury Cup	3	3	0	0	14	3	0
Trataris Cup	3	1	0	2	5	7	1
Friendly Club	5	3	0	2	10	15	2
Bruss Cup	1	0	0	1	1	4	0
Friendly Club B	1	1	0	0	2	0	0
	13	8	0	5	32	29	3
		61.5%	0%	38.5%	2.46	2.23	9.4%

Notes: 1957: 1 unknown scorer v. Alexandra FC in 1–8 defeat

89.   **Ken Thomson**

Year	Caps	Goals
1954	3	0

Mario Antoine

Year	Caps	Goals
1955	2	0
1956	2	0
	7	0

Summary of Games

Fixtures	P	W	D	L	F	A
Oury Cup	1	1	0	0	5	2
Bruss Cup "B"	3	1	1	1	3	5
Friendly Club "B"	3	2	0	1	5	3
	7	4	1	2	13	10
		57.1%	14.3%	28.6%	1.86	1.43

90.   **Entwhistle**

Year	Caps	Goals
1954	1	0
1955	1	0
	2	0

Summary of Games

Fixtures	P	W	D	L	F	A
Friendly Club	1	1	0	0	4	3
Bruss Cup "B"	1	0	0	1	1	4
	2	1	0	1	5	7
		50%	0%	50%	2.50	3.50

91.   **Brian Phillips**

Year	Caps	Goals
1954	4	1
1955	4	2
1957	4	2
1958	2	0
1959	4	1
1960	8	5
1961	4	0
1962	5	0
1963	2	0
	37	11

Summary of Games

Fixtures	P	W	D	L	F	A	GS
Friendly	2	0	0	2	6	17	2
Oury Cup	7	4	0	3	15	19	1
Trataris Cup	5	2	0	3	11	14	2
Friendly Club	20	6	5	9	40	68	4
Bruss Cup "B"	2	0	0	2	4	9	1
Friendly Club B	1	1	0	0	2	0	1
	37	13	5	19	78	127	11
		35.1%	13.5%	51.4%	2.11	3.43	14.1%

Notes:	1957: 1 unknown scorer v. Alexandra FC in 1–8 defeat
	1959: 1 unknown scorer v. Alexandra FC in 1–2 defeat
	1961: 3 unknown scorers v. Alexandra FC in 6–1 win

92.   **Humphries**

Year	Caps	Goals
1954	2	0

Summary of Games

Fixtures	P	W	D	L	F	A
Friendly Club	1	1	0	0	4	3
Bruss Cup "B"	1	1	0	0	2	1
	2	2	0	0	6	4
		100%	0%	0%	3.00	2.00

93.   **Ken Mansfield**

Year	Caps	Subs	Total	Goals
1954	4	0	4	4
1955	4	0	4	1
1956	4	0	4	2
1957	2	0	2	1
1958	3	0	3	1
1959	3	0	3	0
1960	1	0	1	0
1961	0	1	1	0
1962	3	0	3	0
	24	1	25	9

Summary of Games

Fixtures	P	W	D	L	F	A	GS
Oury Cup	6	4	0	2	17	17	5
Trataris Cup	3	1	0	2	4	8	0
Friendly Club	11	5	1	5	24	23	4
Bruss Cup "B"	3	1	0	2	8	11	0
Friendly Club "B"	2	1	0	1	2	3	0
	25	12	1	12	55	62	9
		488%	4%	48%	2.20	2.48	16.4%

Notes:	1962: 1 unknown scorer v. Salisbury Callies "B" in 1–3 defeat

94. **Bob Marrinan**

Year	Caps	Goals
1954	4	3
1955	1	3
1956	2	0
	7	6

Summary of Games

Fixtures	P	W	D	L	F	A	GS
Oury Cup	1	1	0	0	5	2	1
Trataris Cup	3	1	0	2	4	8	3
Friendly Club	3	1	0	2	6	8	2
	7	3	0	4	15	18	6
		42.9%	0%	57.1%	2.14	2.57	40%

95. **Pipes**

Year	Caps	Goals
1954	1	0
1955	2	0
	3	0

Summary of Games

Fixtures	P	W	D	L	F	A
Bruss Cup "B"	2	1	0	1	3	5
Friendly "B"	1	1	0	0	2	0
	3	2	0	1	5	5
		66.7%	0%	33.3%	1.67	1.67

96.   **Da Cruz**

Year	Caps	Goals
1954	1	0

Summary of Games

Fixtures	P	W	D	L	F	A
Friendly Club B	1	0	0	1	0	2
		0%	0%	100%	0.00	2.00

97.   **Peter Gurney**

Year	Caps	Goals
1954	2	0
1956	3	0
	5	0

Summary of Games

Fixtures	P	W	D	L	F	A
Friendly Club	1	0	0	1	1	2
Bruss Cup "B"	2	1	1	0	2	1
Friendly Club B	2	1	0	1	3	3
	5	2	1	2	6	6
		40%	20%	40%	1.20	1.20

98.   **Fred Taylor**

Year	Caps	Goals
1954	2	0
1955	2	0
	4	0

Summary of Games

Fixtures	P	W	D	L	F	A
Bruss Cup "B"	2	1	0	1	3	5
Friendly Club B	2	1	0	1	2	2
	4	2	0	2	5	7
		50%	0%	50%	1.25	1.75

99.   **Kabul**

Year	Caps	Goals
1954	1	0

Summary of Games

Fixtures	P	W	D	L	F	A
Friendly Club B	1	0	0	1	0	2
		0%	0%	100%	0.00	2.00

100.   **Brian Fox**

Year	Caps	Goals
1955	3	3
1956	3	0
1957	4	0
1958	3	0
1959	2	0
1960	7	0
1961	4	0
1962	5	3
1963	3	0
	34	6

Summary of Games

Fixtures	P	W	D	L	F	A	GS
Friendly	2	0	0	2	6	17	0
Oury Cup	7	5	0	2	19	9	1
Trataris Cup	6	3	0	3	12	12	0
Friendly Club	18	6	2	10	32	58	5
Friendly Club B	1	1	0	0	2	0	0
	34	15	2	17	71	96	6
		44.1%	5.9%	50%	2.09	2.82	8.5%

Notes:	1957: 1 unknown scorer v. Alexandra FC in 1–8 defeat
	1961: 3 unknown scorers v. Alexandra FC in 6–1 win

101.   **Les Doran**

Year	Caps	Goals
1955	4	0
1956	3	1
1957	2	0
1958	2	0
1959	1	0
1960	4	0
	16	1

Summary of Games

Fixtures	P	W	D	L	F	A	GS
Friendly	1	0	0	1	3	13	0
Oury Cup	5	2	0	3	8	16	1
Trataris Cup	3	2	0	1	5	4	0
Friendly Club	5	2	1	2	13	15	0
Bruss Cup "B"	1	1	0	0	6	1	0
Friendly Club "B"	1	0	1	0	2	2	0
	16	7	2	7	37	51	1
		43.8%	12.4%	43.8%	2.31	3.19	2.7%

Notes: 1957: 2 unknown scorers v. Alexandra FC in 2–2 draw

102. **Van Arenthals**

Year	Caps	Goals
1955	4	0

Summary of Games

Fixtures	P	W	D	L	F	A
Oury Cup	1	0	0	1	0	10
Trataris Cup	1	1	0	0	3	2
Friendly Club	2	2	0	0	7	3
	4	3	0	1	10	15
		75%	0%	25%	2.50	3.75

103. **George Trataris**

Year	Caps C/ Sheets	
1955	2	1
1957	2	0
1960	4	0
1961	2	1
1963	3	0
1964	1	0
	14	2

Summary of Games

Fixtures	P	W	D	L	F	A	CS
Friendly	1	0	0	1	3	4	0

Oury Cup	2	0	0	2	2	4	0
Friendly Cup	4	0	2	2	7	20	0
Bruss Cup "B"	4	3	0	1	19	7	0
Friendly Club B	3	2	1	0	12	2	2
	14	5	3	6	43	37	2
		35.7%	21.4%	42.9%	3.07	2.64	14.3%

104.   **Peter Parker (Snr)**

Year	Caps	Goals
1955	2	0
1960	2	1
	4	1

Summary of Games

Fixtures	P	W	D	L	F	A	GS
Friendly	2	0	0	2	6	17	1
Bruss Cup "B"	1	0	0	1	1	4	0
Friendly Club B	1	1	0	0	2	0	1
	4	1	0	3	9	21	1
		25%	0%	75%	2.25	5.25	11.1%

105.   **Dennis Harris**

Year	Caps	Goals
1955	2	0
1956	3	0
	5	0

Summary of Games

Fixtures	P	W	D	L	F	A
Friendly Club	1	0	0	1	1	2
Bruss Cup "B"	2	0	1	1	1	4
Friendly Club B	2	2	0	0	5	1
	5	2	1	2	7	7
		40%	20%	40%	1.40	1.40

106.   **Stockman**

Year	Caps	C/Sheets
1956	3	0
1958	1	0
	4	0

Summary of Games

Fixtures	P	W	D	L	F	A	CS
Friendly Club	1	0	0	1	1	2	0
Bruss Cup "B"	2	0	1	1	3	5	1
Friendly Club B	1	1	0	0	3	1	0
	4	1	1	2	7	8	1
		25%	25%	50%	1.75	2.00	25%

107.   **Don Harper**

Year	Caps	Goals
1956	4	1

Summary of Games

Fixtures	P	W	D	L	F	A	GS
Oury Cup	1	1	0	0	5	0	0
Friendly Club	1	0	0	1	1	2	1
Bruss Cup "B"	1	0	1	0	0	0	0
Friendly Club B	1	1	0	0	3	1	0
	4	2	1	1	9	3	1
		50%	25%	25%	2.25	0.75	11.1%

108.   **Burgess**

Year	Caps	Goals
1956	2	0

Summary of Games

Fixtures	P	W	D	L	F	A
Friendly Club	1	0	0	1	1	2
Bruss Cup "B"	1	0	1	0	0	0
	2	0	1	1	1	2
		0%	50%	50%	0.50	1.00

109.   **Colin Findlay**

Year	Caps	Goals
1956	3	0
1957	3	5
	6	5

Summary of Games

Fixtures	P	W	D	L	F	A	GS
Friendly Club	2	1	0	1	3	3	0
Bruss Cup "B"	2	1	1	0	6	1	5
Friendly Club B	2	1	1	0	5	3	0
	6	3	2	1	14	7	5
		50%	33.3%	16.7%	2.33	1.17	35.7%

Notes: 1957: 2 unknown scorers v. Alexandra FC in 2–2 draw

110. Shergold

Year	Caps	Goals
1956	3	0

Summary of Games

Fixtures	P	W	D	L	F	A
Friendly Club	1	0	0	1	1	2
Bruss Cup "B"	1	0	1	0	0	0
Friendly Club B	1	1	0	0	3	1
	3	1	1	1	4	3
		33.4%	33.3%	33.3%	1.33	1.00

111. Wilson

Year	Caps	Goals
1956	4	0

Summary of Games

Fixtures	P	W	D	L	F	A
Oury Cup	1	1	0	0	5	0
Trataris Cup	1	0	0	1	0	2
Friendly Club	2	0	0	2	2	4
	4	1	0	3	7	6
		25%	0%	75%	1.75	1.50

112. F. De Vito

Year	Caps	Goals
1956	2	0

Summary of Games

Fixtures	P	W	D	L	F	A
Bruss Cup "B"	1	0	1	0	0	0
Friendly Club B	1	1	0	0	3	1
	2	1	1	0	3	1
		50%	50%	0%	1.50	0.50

113. **Matt Hoyland**

Year	Caps	Goals
1956	1	0
1958	1	0
1960	3	0
1961	4	0
1962	1	1
	10	1

Summary of Games

Fixtures	P	W	D	L	F	A	GS
Friendly	1	0	0	1	3	4	0
Oury Cup	1	1	0	0	4	1	0
Friendly Club	3	0	1	2	3	11	0
Bruss Cup "B"	1	0	0	1	3	5	0
Friendly Club B	4	4	0	0	21	2	1
	10	5	1	4	34	23	1
		50%	10%	40%	3.40	2.30	2.9%

Notes:	1961: 8 unknown scorers v. Alexandra FC "B" in 8–0 win

114. **Pat Saunders**

Year	Caps C/ Sheets	
1957	1	0

Summary of Games

Fixtures	P	W	D	L	F	A
Friendly Club	1	0	0	1	1	8
		0%	0%	100%	1.00	8.00

115.   **Ian Strachan**

Year	Caps	Goals
1957	1	0
1960	1	0
	2	0

Summary of Games

Fixtures	P	W	D	L	F	A
Friendly Club	2	0	1	1	3	10
		0%	50%	50%	1.50	5.00

Notes: 1957: 1 unknown scorer v. Alexandra FC in 1–8 defeat

116.   **Alan Geldard**

Year	Caps	Goals
1957	4	0
1959	2	0
1960	1	0
1961	2	0
	9	0

Summary of Games

Fixtures	P	W	D	L	F	A
Friendly	1	0	0	1	3	13
Oury Cup	1	1	0	0	4	1
Friendly Club	1	1	0	0	2	1
Bruss Cup "B"	2	1	0	1	8	6
Friendly Club B	4	2	1	1	21	6
	9	5	1	3	38	27
		55.6%	11.1%	33.3%	4.22	3.00

Notes: 1957: 2 unknown scorers v. Alexandra FC in 2–2 draw
1961: 8 unknown scorers v. Alexandra FC "B" in 8–0 win

117.   **Pat Kelly**

Year	Caps	Goals
1957	3	0

Summary of Games

Fixtures	P	W	D	L	F	A
Oury Cup	1	1	0	0	4	1
Trataris Cup	1	1	0	0	4	1
Friendly Club	1	0	0	1	1	8
	3	2	0	1	9	10
		66.7%	0%	33.3%	3.00	3.33

Notes: 1957: 1 unknown scorer v. Alexandra FC in 1–8 defeat

118. **Godfrey Keys**

Year	Caps	Goals
1957	3	0
1960	1	0
1961	2	0
	6	0

Summary of Games

Fixtures	P	W	D	L	F	A	GS
Friendly	1	0	0	1	3	4	0
Oury Cup	1	1	0	0	4	1	1
Trataris Cup	2	2	0	0	7	2	0
Friendly Club	2	2	0	0	8	2	0
	6	5	0	1	22	9	1
		83.3%	0%	16.7%	3.67	1.50	4.5%

Notes: 1961: 3 unknown scorers v. Alexandra FC in 6–1 win

119. **G. Hindaugh**

Year	Caps	Goals
1957	1	0

Summary of Games

Fixtures	P	W	D	L	F	A
Friendly Club	1	0	0	1	1	8
		0%	0%	100%	1.00	8.00

Notes: 1957: 1 unknown scorer v. Alexandra FC in 1–8 defeat

120.   **Pat Lorimer**

Year	Caps	Goals
1957	1	0

Summary of Games

Fixtures	P	W	D	L	F	A
Friendly Club	1	0	0	1	1	8
		0%	0%	100%	1.00	8.00

Notes: 1957: 1 unknown scorer v. Alexandra FC in 1–8 defeat

121.   **Billy Pillans**

Year	Caps	Goals
1957	2	0

Summary of Games

Fixtures	P	W	D	L	F	A
Bruss Cup "B"	1	1	0	0	6	1
Friendly Club B	1	0	1	0	2	2
	2	1	1	0	8	3
		50%	50%	0%	4.00	1.50

Notes: 1957: 2 unknown scorers v. Alexandra FC in 2–2 draw

122.   **Brooks**

Year	Caps	Goals
1957	2	0

Summary of Games

Fixtures	P	W	D	L	F	A
Bruss Cup "B"	1	1	0	0	6	1
Friendly Club B	1	0	1	0	2	2
	2	1	1	0	8	3
		50%	50%	0%	4.00	1.50

Notes: 1957: 2 unknown scorers v. Alexandra FC in 2–2 draw

123.   **Grant**

Year	Caps	Goals
1957	2	0

Summary of Games

Fixtures	P	W	D	L	F	A
Bruss Cup "B"	1	1	0	0	6	1
Friendly Club B	1	0	1	0	2	2
	2	1	1	0	8	3
		50%	50%	0%	4.00	1.50

Notes: 1957: 2 unknown scorers v. Alexandra FC in 2–2 draw

124.   **George Barley**

Year	Caps	Goals
1957	1	0
1958	2	0
1959	4	0
1960	1	0
	8	0

Summary of Games

Fixtures	P	W	D	L	F	A
Oury Cup	1	0	0	1	0	2
Trataris Cup	1	0	0	1	2	5
Friendly Club	3	0	1	2	5	7
Bruss Cup "B"	3	2	0	1	12	7
	8	2	1	5	19	21
		25%	12.5%	62.5%	2.38	2.63

125.   **John Trataris**

Year	Caps	Goals
1957	1	0

Summary of Games

Fixtures	P	W	D	L	F	A
Friendly Club B	1	0	1	0	2	2
		0%	100%	0%	2.00	2.00

Notes: 1957: 2 unknown scorers v. Alexandra FC in 2–2 draw

126.   **Harold Wrigley (Snr)**

Year	Caps	Goals
1957	1	0

Summary of Games

Fixtures	P	W	D	L	F	A
Bruss Cup "B"	1	1	0	0	6	1
		100%	0%	0%	6.00	1.00

127.   **Reid**

Year	Caps	Goals
1957	1	0

Summary of Games

Fixtures	P	W	D	L	F	A
Friendly Club B	1	0	1	0	2	2
		0%	100%	0%	2.00	2.00

Notes: 1957: 2 unknown scorers v. Alexandra FC in 2–2 draw

128.   **J. Hoatson**

Year	Caps	Goals
1957	1	0
1961	2	0
	3	0

Summary of Games

Fixtures	P	W	D	L	F	A
Friendly Club B	3	2	1	0	19	3
		66.7%	33.3%	0%	6.33	1.00

Notes: 1957: 2 unknown scorers v. Alexandra FC "B" in 2–2 draw

                1961: 8 unknown scorers v. Alexandra FC "B" in 8–0 win

129.   **Stellious**

Year	Caps	Goals
1958	2	0

Summary of Games

Fixtures	P	W	D	L	F	A
Oury Cup	1	1	0	0	3	2
Trataris Cup	1	1	0	0	2	0
	2	2	0	0	5	2
		100%	0%	0%	2.50	1.00

130.   **A. Marr**

Year	Caps	Goals
1958	3	3

Summary of Games

Fixtures	P	W	D	L	F	A	GS
Oury Cup	1	1	0	0	3	2	1
Trataris Cup	1	1	0	0	2	0	1
Friendly Club	1	0	0	1	1	2	1
	3	2	0	1	6	4	3
		66.7%	0%	33,3%	2.00	1.33	50%

131.   **Johnny Hawthorne**

Year	Caps	Goals
1958	2	1
1959	2	0
1960	2	0
	6	1

Summary of Games

Fixtures	P	W	D	L	F	A	GS
Oury Cup	1	1	0	0	3	2	0
Trataris Cup	2	1	0	1	4	5	1
Friendly Club	3	0	1	2	6	12	0
	6	2	1	3	13	19	1
		33.3%	16.7%	50%	2.17	3.17	7.7%

132.   **Alfio Vatteroni**

Year	Caps	Goals
1958	1	0

Mario Antoine

Summary of Games

Fixtures	P	W	D	L	F	A
Friendly Club B	1	1	0	0	2	0
		100%	0%	0%	2.00	0.00

133. **Archie Carver**

Year	Caps	Goals
1958	3	0
1959	1	0
1960	1	0
1961	2	0
	7	0

Summary of Games

Fixtures	P	W	D	L	F	A
Oury Cup	2	2	0	0	7	3
Friendly Club	3	0	1	2	3	7
Bruss Cup "B"	1	0	0	1	3	5
Friendly Club "B"	1	0	0	1	2	3
	7	2	1	4	15	18
		28.6%	14.3%	57.1%	2.14	2.57

Notes: 1959: 2 unknown scorers v. Alexandra FC "B" in 2–3 defeat

134. **Dennis Pritchard**

Year	Caps	Goals
1958	2	0
1959	4	1
1960	8	0
1961	2	0
1962	5	1
1963	3	1
1964	2	1
	26	4

Summary of Games

Fixtures	P	W	D	L	F	A	GS
Friendly	2	0	0	2	6	17	0

Oury Cup	5	1	0	4	4	9	2
Trataris Cup	4	2	0	2	8	9	1
Friendly Club	15	4	5	6	34	50	1
	26	7	5	14	52	85	4
		26.9%	19.3%	53.8%	2.00	3.27	7.7%

Notes: 1959: 2 unknown scorers v. Alexandra FC in 1–3 defeat

1961: 3 unknown scorers v. Alexandra FC in 6–1 win

135.   **Amilcare Cominetti**

Year	Caps	Goals
1958	1	0

Summary of Games

Fixtures	P	W	D	L	F	A
Bruss Cup "B"	1	0	0	1	3	5
		0%	0%	100%	3.00	5.00

136.   **Buchan**

Year	Caps	Goals
1958	1	0
1959	3	0
	4	0

Summary of Games

Fixtures	P	W	D	L	F	A
Oury Cup	1	0	0	1	0	2
Bruss Cup "B"	2	0	0	2	5	10
Friendly Club "B"	1	0	0	1	2	3
	4	0	0	4	7	15
		0%	0%	100%	1.75	3.75

Notes: 1959: 2 unknown scorers v. Alexandra FC "B" in 2–3 defeat

137.   **Archie Cottingham**

Year	Caps	Goals
1958	1	0
1959	3	1
1960	1	0
	5	1

Summary of Games

Fixtures	P	W	D	L	F	A	GS
Friendly Club	1	0	1	0	3	3	1
Bruss Cup "B"	3	1	0	2	8	11	0
Friendly Club "B"	1	0	0	1	2	3	0
	5	1	1	3	13	17	1
		20%	20%	60%	2.60	3.40	7.7%

Notes: 1959: 2 unknown scorers v. Alexandra FC "B" in 2–3 defeat

138.   **Jack Lowery**

Year	Caps	Goals
1958	1	0
1959	2	0
	3	0

Summary of Games

Fixtures	P	W	D	L	F	A
Bruss Cup "B"	2	0	0	2	5	10
Friendly Club "B"	1	0	0	1	2	3
	3	0	0	3	7	13
		0%	0%	100%	2.33	4.33

Notes: 1959: 2 unknown scorers v. Alexandra FC "B" in 2–3 defeat

139.   **Colandria Lorenco**

Year	Caps	Goals
1958	1	0
1959	2	0
1962	4	0
1963	1	0
	8	0

Summary of Games

Fixtures	P	W	D	L	F	A
Oury Cup	1	0	0	1	0	2
Friendly Club	4	1	2	1	9	8
Bruss Cup "B"	1	0	0	1	3	5

Friendly Club "B"	2	1	0	1	2	3
	8	2	2	4	14	18
		25%	25%	50%	1.75	2.25

Notes: 1962: 3 unknown scorers v. Club de Tete" in 3–3 draw

1962: 1 unknown scorer v. Salisbury Callies "B" in 1–3 defeat

140.   **Jim Cottingham**

Year	Caps	Goals
1959	1	0

Summary of Games

Fixtures	P	W	D	L	F	A
Friendly Club	1	0	1	0	3	3
		0%	100%	0%	3.00	3.00

141.   **John Cotton**

Year	Caps	Goals
1959	4	0
1960	2	0
1962	3	0
1963	4	0
	13	0

Summary of Games

Fixtures	P	W	D	L	F	A
Oury Cup	3	1	0	2	3	5
Trataris Club	2	0	0	2	3	8
Friendly Club	7	2	2	3	15	21
Friendly Club "B"	1	0	0	1	1	3
	13	3	2	8	22	37
		23.1%	15.4%	61.5%	1.69	2.85

Notes: 1959: 1 unknown scorer v. Alexandra FC in 1–2 defeat

1962: 1 unknown scorer v. Salisbury Callies "B" in 1–3 defeat

142.   **Vic Moss**

Year	Caps	Goals
1959	4	0
1960	5	0

Mario Antoine

1961	4	4
	13	4

Summary of Games

Fixtures	P	W	D	L	F	A	GS
Oury Cup	3	1	0	2	4	5	0
Trataris Club	2	0	0	2	3	8	0
Friendly Club	6	1	3	2	13	16	0
Friendly Club "B"	2	2	0	0	17	1	4
	13	4	3	6	37	30	4
		30.7%	23.1%	46.2%	2.85	2.31	10.8%

Notes: 1959: 1 unknown scorer v. Alexandra FC in 1–2 defeat
1962: 8 unknown scorers v. Alexandra FC "B" in 8–0 win

143.   **Preen**

Year	Caps	Goals
1959	2	0

Summary of Games

Fixtures	P	W	D	L	F	A
Trataris Cup	1	0	0	1	2	5
Friendly Club	1	0	0	1	1	2
	2	0	0	2	3	7
		0%	0%	100%	1.50	3.50

Notes: 1959: 1 unknown scorer v. Alexandra FC in 1–2 defeat

144.   **Cominas Yiannakis**

Year	Caps	C/Sheets
1959	2	0
1960	1	0
1962	2	0
1963	1	0
1964	1	0
	7	0

Summary of Games

Fixtures	P	W	D	L	F	A
Friendly	1	0	0	1	3	13
Friendly Club	4	2	1	1	10	6
Bruss Cup "B"	1	0	0	1	2	5
Friendly Club "B"	1	0	0	1	2	3
	7	2	1	4	17	27
		28.6%	14.3%	57.1%	2.43	3.86

145. **Peter Lewis**

Year	Caps	Goals
1959	2	0
1960	4	0
1961	4	1
	10	1

Summary of Games

Fixtures	P	W	D	L	F	A	GS
Oury Cup	1	1	0	0	4	1	1
Friendly Club	4	0	2	2	7	15	0
Bruss Cup "B"	2	1	0	1	5	6	0
Friendly Club "B"	3	2	0	1	19	4	0
	10	4	2	4	35	26	1
		40%	30%	40%	3.50	2.60	2.9%

Notes:	1959: 2 unknown scorers v. Alexandra FC "B" in 2–3 defeat
	1962: 8 unknown scorers v. Alexandra FC "B" in 8–0 win

146. **Peter Crossan**

Year	Caps	Goals
1959	1	2
1960	5	2
1963	1	0
	7	4

Summary of Games

Fixtures	P	W	D	L	F	A	GS
Friendly	1	0	0	1	3	4	1
Oury Cup	2	0	0	2	1	4	0

Trataris Cup	1	0	0	1	1	3	0
Friendly Club	2	1	1	0	5	4	1
Bruss Cup "B"	1	0	0	1	2	5	2
	7	1	1	5	12	20	4
		14.3%	14.3%	71.4%	1.71	2.86	33.3%

147. **T. Donaldson**

Year	Caps	Goals
1959	1	0

Summary of Games

Fixtures	P	W	D	L	F	A
Friendly Club "B"	1	0	0	1	2	3
		0%	0%	100%	2.00	3.00

Notes: 1959: 2 unknown scorers v. Alexandra FC "B" in 2–3 defeat

148. **Acconci**

Year	Caps	Goals
1959	2	0

Summary of Games

Fixtures	P	W	D	L	F	A
Bruss Cup "B"	1	0	0	1	2	5
Friendly Club "B"	1	0	0	1	2	3
	2	0	0	2	4	8
		0%	0%	100%	2.00	4.00

Notes: 1959: 2 unknown scorers v. Alexandra FC "B" in 2–3 defeat

149. **Mike Bowery**

Year	Caps	Goals
1959	2	0
1960	2	1
	4	1

Summary of Games

Fixtures	P	W	D	L	F	A	GS
Friendly Club	1	0	1	0	2	2	1

Bruss Cup "B"	2	1	0	1	5	6	0
Friendly Club "B"	1	0	0	1	2	3	0
	4	1	1	2	9	11	1
		25%	25%	50%	2.25	2.75	11.1%

Notes: 1959: 2 unknown scorers v. Alexandra FC "B" in 2–3 defeat

150. **Jack Stuart**

Year	Caps	Goals
1960	4	0

Summary of Games

Fixtures	P	W	D	L	F	A
Friendly	1	0	0	1	3	13
Friendly Club	2	0	2	0	6	6
Bruss Cup "B"	1	1	0	0	3	1
	4	1	2	1	12	20
		25%	50%	25%	3.00	5.00

151. **Fletcher**

Year	Caps	Goals
1960	1	0

Summary of Games

Fixtures	P	W	D	L	F	A
Friendly Club	1	0	1	0	2	2
		0%	100%	0%	2.00	2.00

152. **Harold Davies**

Year	Caps	Goals
1960	1	0

Summary of Games

Fixtures	P	W	D	L	F	A
Friendly	1	0	0	1	3	4
		0%	0%	100%	3.00	4.00

153. **Ken Burns**

Year	Caps	Goals
1960	1	0

Summary of Games

Fixtures	P	W	D	L	F	A
Friendly Club	1	0	1	0	2	2
		0%	100%	0%	2.00	2.00

154. **J. Kopanakis**

Year	Caps	Goals
1960	2	0

Summary of Games

Fixtures	P	W	D	L	F	A
Trataris Cup	1	0	0	1	1	3
Friendly Club	1	1	0	0	3	2
	2	1	0	1	4	5
		50%	0%	50%	2.00	2.50

155. **Max Prien**

Year	Caps	Goals
1960	7	7
1961	2	6
1962	3	0
	12	13

Summary of Games

Fixtures	P	W	D	L	F	A	GS
Friendly	1	0	0	1	3	13	0
Oury Cup	1	0	0	1	0	2	0
Trataris Cup	2	1	0	1	5	4	4
Friendly Club	8	2	3	3	17	29	9
	12	3	3	6	25	48	13
		25%	25%	50%	2.08	4.00	52%

156. **Colley**

Year	Caps	Goals
1960	1	0

Summary of Games

Fixtures	P	W	D	L	F	A
Friendly Club	1	0	1	0	2	2
		0%	100%	0%	2.00	2.00

157. **Bob Rodgers**

Year	Caps	Goals
1960	2	0
1961	2	2
1963	3	1
	7	3

Summary of Games

Fixtures	P	W	D	L	F	A	GS
Friendly	2	0	0	2	6	17	0
Oury Cup	1	0	0	1	1	2	1
Friendly Club	2	0	1	1	2	3	0
Friendly Club "B"	2	2	0	0	17	1	2
	7	2	1	4	26	23	3
		28.6%	14.3%	57.1%	3.71	3.29	11.5%

Notes: 1962: 8 unknown scorers v. Alexandra FC "B" in 8–0 win

158. **I. Grilli**

Year	Caps	Goals
1960	3	1
1962	2	0
	5	1

Summary of Games

Fixtures	P	W	D	L	F	A	GS
Friendly Club	4	0	3	1	5	14	0
Bruss Cup "B"	1	1	0	0	3	1	1
	5	1	3	1	8	15	1
		20%	60%	20%	1.60	3.00	12.5%

159. **Crawford**

Year	Caps	Goals
1960	1	0

Summary of Games

Fixtures	P	W	D	L	F	A
Bruss Cup "B"	1	1	0	0	3	1
		100%	0%	0%	3.00	1.00

160.   **Monteiro**

Year	Caps	Goals
1960	1	0

Summary of Games

Fixtures	P	W	D	L	F	A
Bruss Cup "B"	1	1	0	0	3	1
		100%	0%	0%	3.00	1.00

161.   **Mann**

Year	Caps	Subs	Total	Goals
1961	2	1	3	0
1962	2	0	2	0
	4	1	5	0

Summary of Games

Fixtures	P	W	D	L	F	A
Oury Cup	1	1	0	0	2	1
Trataris Cup	1	1	0	0	3	1
Friendly Club	2	1	0	1	6	4
Friendly Club "B"	1	1	0	0	1	0
	5	4	0	1	12	6
		80%	0%	20%	2.40	1.20

Notes: 1961: 3 unknown scorers v. Alexandra FC in 6–1 win

162.   **Corb**

Year	Caps	Goals
1961	2	0

Summary of Games

Fixtures	P	W	D	L	F	A
Friendly Club "B"	2	2	0	0	17	1
		100%	0%	0%	8.50	0.50

163.   **French**

Year	Caps	Goals
1961	2	0

Summary of Games

Fixtures	P	W	D.	L	F	A
Trataris Cup	1	1	0	0	3	1
Friendly Club	1	1	0	0	6	1
	2	2	0	0	9	2
		100%	0%	0%	4.50	1.00

Notes: 1961: 3 unknown scorers v. Alexandra FC in 6–1 win

164.   **Peter Parker (Jnr)**

Year	Caps	Goals
1961	4	0

Summary of Games

Fixtures	P	W	D	L	F	A
Oury Cup	1	1	0	0	4	1
Trataris Cup	1	1	0	0	3	1
Friendly Club	2	1	0	1	6	4
	4	3	0	1	13	6
		100%	0%	0%	4.50	1.00

Notes: 1961: 3 unknown scorers v. Alexandra FC in 6–1 win

165.   **Macdonald**

Year	Caps	Subs	Total	Goals
1961	0	1	1	0

Summary of Games

Fixtures	P	W	D	L	F	A
Friendly Club	1	0	0	1	0	3
		0%	0%	100%	0.00	3.00

166.   **Rosenast**

Year	Caps	Goals
1961	2	0

Summary of Games

Fixtures	P	W	D	L	F	A
Friendly Club "B"	2	2	0	0	17	1
		100%	0%	0%	8.50	0.50

167. **Rui Bastos**

Year	Caps	Goals
1961	2	0
1962	3	1
	5	1

Summary of Games

Fixtures	P	W	D	L	F	A	GS
Friendly Club	3	0	1	2	1	14	1
Friendly Club "B"	2	2	0	0	17	1	3
	5	2	1	2	18	15	4
		40%	20%	40%	3.60	3.00	22.2%

Notes: 1962: 8 unknown scorers v. Alexandra FC "B" in 8–0 win

168. **A. Gafforio**

Year	Caps	C/Sheet
1962	2	1

Summary of Games

Fixtures	P	W	D	L	F	A	CS
Friendly Club	1	1	0	0	4	1	0
Friendly Club "B"	1	1	0	0	1	0	1
	2	2	0	0	5	1	1
		100%	0%	0%	2.50	0.50	50%

169. **Tommy Prentice**

Year	Caps	Goals
1962	1	0

Summary of Games

Fixtures	P	W	D	L	F	A
Friendly Club	1	0	0	1	0	4
		0%	0%	100%	0.00	4.00

170. **Johnnie Ruprecht**

Year	Caps	Goals
1962	2	0

Summary of Games

Fixtures	P	W	D	L	F	A
Friendly Club	2	1	1	0	6	4
		50%	50%	0%	3.00	2.00

Notes: 1962: 3 unknown scorers v. Club de Tete" in 3–3 draw

171. **Ronnie King**

Year	Caps	Goals
1962	1	0

Summary of Games

Fixtures	P	W	D	L	F	A
Friendly Club	1	1	0	0	3	1
		100%	0%	0%	3.00	1.00

172. **Michel Melotte**

Year	Caps	Goals
1962	5	0
1963	4	0
	9	0

Summary of Games

Fixtures	P	W	D	L	F	A
Oury Cup	1	0	0	1	1	2
Friendly Club	6	2	2	2	14	18
Friendly Club "B"	2	1	0	1	2	3
	9	3	2	4	17	23
		33.3%	22.3%	44.4%	1.89	2.56

Notes: 1962: 3 unknown scorers v. Club de Tete" in 3–3 draw
1962: 1 unknown scorer v. Salisbury Callies "B" in 1–3 defeat

173.   **Bill Keddie**

Year	Caps	Goals
1962	4	0
1963	1	0
1964	2	1
	7	1

Summary of Games

Fixtures	P	W	D	L	F	A	GS
Oury Cup	2	1	0	1	3	3	0
Friendly Club	5	2	1	2	11	22	1
	7	3	1	3	14	25	1
		42.9%	14.2%	42.9%	2.00	3.57	7.1%

174.   **S. Damalakis**

Year	Caps	Goals
1962	2	0

Summary of Games

Fixtures	P	W	D	L	F	A
Friendly Club	2	1	1	0	6	4
		50%	50%	0%	3.00	2.00

Notes: 1962: 3 unknown scorers v. Club de Tete in 3–3 draw

175.   **J. Pietersie**

Year	Caps	Subs	Total	Goals
1962	1	1	2	0

Summary of Games

Fixtures	P	W	D	L	F	A
Friendly Club	2	1	1	0	6	4
		50%	50%	0%	3.00	2.00

Notes: 1962: 3 unknown scorers v. Club de Tete in 3–3 draw

176.   **Terry Mills**

Year	Caps	Goals
1962	4	2

Summary of Games

Fixtures	P	W	D	L	F	A	GS
Friendly Club	2	1	0	1	4	5	2
Friendly Club "B"	2	1	0	1	2	3	0
	4	2	0	2	6	8	2
		50%	0%	50%	1.50	2.00	33.3%

Notes: 1962: 1 unknown scorer v. Salisbury Callies "B" in 1–3 defeat

177.   Haroon Karim

Year	Caps	Subs	Total	Goals
1962	1	1	2	0

Summary of Games

Fixtures	P	W	D	L	F	A
Friendly Club	2	1	1	0	6	4
		50%	50%	0%	3.00	2.00

Notes: 1962: 3 unknown scorers v. Club de Tete in 3–3 draw

178.   Peter West

Year	Caps	Goals
1962	4	0

Summary of Games

Fixtures	P	W	D	L	F	A
Oury Cup	1	1	0	0	2	1
Friendly Club	3	1	1	1	5	11
	4	2	1	1	7	12
		50%	25%	25%	1.75	3.00

179.   Tommy Ballantyne

Year	Caps	Goals
1962	1	0

Summary of Games

Fixtures	P	W	D	L	F	A
Friendly Club	1	0	0	1	0	4
		0%	0%	100%	0.00	4.00

180. **Don Mientjies**

Year	Caps	Goals
1962	4	0
1963	1	1
	5	1

Summary of Games

Fixtures	P	W	D	L	F	A	GS
Friendly Club	3	1	1	1	8	14	1
Friendly Club "B"	2	1	0	1	2	3	0
	5	2	1	2	10	17	1
		40%	20%	40%	2.00	3.40	10%

Notes: 1962: 3 unknown scorers v. Club de Tete" in 3–3 draw

1962: 1 unknown scorer v. Salisbury Callies "B" in 1–3 defeat

181. **B. Mcardle**

Year	Caps	Goals
1962	1	0

Summary of Games

Fixtures	P	W	D	L	F	A
Friendly Club "B"	1	0	0	1	1	3
		0%	0%	100%	1.00	3.00

Notes: 1962: 1 unknown scorer v. Salisbury Callies "B" in 1–3 defeat

182. **Jim Yiannakis**

Year	Caps	Goals
1962	2	0

Summary of Games

Fixtures	P	W	D	L	F	A
Friendly Club	2	1	0	1	2	3
		50%	0%	50%	1.00	1.50

Notes: 1962: 1 unknown scorer v. Salisbury Callies "B" in 1–3 defeat

183. **Dettmar**

Year	Caps	Goals
1962	2	0

Summary of Games

Fixtures	P	W	D	L	F	A
Friendly Club	2	1	0	1	2	3
		50%	0%	50%	1.00	1.50

Notes: 1962: 1 unknown scorer v. Salisbury Callies "B" in 1–3 defeat

184. **Hugh Smith**

Year	Caps	Goals
1963	1	0
1964	2	0
	3	0

Summary of Games

Fixtures	P	W	D	L	F	A
Oury Cup	2	0	0	2	2	4
Friendly Club	1	1	0	0	4	1
	3	1	0	2	6	5
		33.3%	0%	66.7%	2.00	1.67

185. **L. Ferguson**

Year	Caps	Goals
1963	2	0

Summary of Games

Fixtures	P	W	D	L	F	A
Oury Cup	1	0	0	1	1	2
Friendly Club	1	0	1	0	2	2
	2	0	1	1	3	4
		0%	50%	50%	1.50	2.00

186. **Chalmers**

Year	Caps	Goals
1964	2	0

Mario Antoine

Summary of Games

Fixtures	P	W	D	L	F	A
Oury Cup	1	0	0	1	1	2
Friendly Club	1	1	0	0	4	1
	2	1	0	1	5	3
		50%	0%	50%	2.50	1.50

187.	**Santokh Singh**	
Year	Caps	Goals
1964	1	1

Summary of Games

Fixtures	P	W	D	L	F	A	GS
Friendly Club	1	1	0	0	4	1	1
		100%	0%	0%	4.00	1.00	25%

Top Fives

Following are lists of the top five players in various segments. Players need to have played in five games minimum from 1935 to 1964 to be considered.

NFA "A" Team

Wins

Player	Games played	Percentage
Don Armstrong	6	83.3%
Godfrey Keys	6	83.3%
Jimmy Smith	8	75.0%
Tommy Allen	21	61.9%
Ricky Robertson	12	58.3%

Draws

Player	Games played	Percentage
Peter Lewis	5	40.0%
Colandria Lorenco	5	40.0%
Joaquim Cunha	6	33.3%
Michel Melotte	9	28.6%
George Trataris	7	28.6%

Losses

Player	Games played	Percentage
Don Armstrong	6	16.7%
Godfrey Keys	6	16.7%
Jimmy Smith	8	25.0%
Tommy Allen	21	38.1%
Peter Lewis	5	40.0%
Colandria Lorenco	5	40.0%
Cominas Yiannakis	5	40.0%

Average of Goals Scored Per Game:

Player	Games played	Average
Godfrey Keys	6	3.67
Don Armstrong	6	3.17
Jimmy Smith	8	2.75
Cominas Yiannakis	5	2.60
Jimmy Kongialis	12	2.58

Average of Goals Conceded Per Game

Player	Games played	Average
Godfrey Keys	6	1.50
Jimmy Smith	8	1.75
Micky Megraw	9	1.89
Archie Carver	5	2.00
Colandria Lorenco	5	2.00

Top Five Appearances

Player	Games played
Dennis Johnston	44
Brian Phillips	34
Brian Fox	33
Sergio Nicholas	32
Jackie Cottingham	26

Top Five Scorers

Player	Games played	Goals
Max Prien	13	13
Ken Mansfield	23	9
Brian Phillips	34	9
Bob Marrinan	7	6
John Patterson	10	6
Brian Fox	33	6

Top Clean Sheets

Player	Games Played	Clean Sheets
Sergio Nicholas	32	3
Harry Middleton	5	1

NFA "B" Team

Wins

Player	Games played	Percentage
Matt Hoyland	5	80.0%
George Trataris	7	71.4%
Peter Lewis	5	60.0%
Ken Thomson	6	50.0%
Alan Geldard	6	50.0%

Draws

Name of Players	Games played	Percentage
Jimmy Smith	5	20.0%
Alan Geldard	6	16.7%
Ken Thomson	6	16.7%
Costas Trataris	7	14.3%
George Trataris	7	14.3%

Losses

Player	Games played	Percentage
George Trataris	7	14.3%
Matt Hoyland	5	20.0%
Jimmy Smith	5	20.0%
Alan Geldard	6	33.3%
Ken Thomson	6	33.3%

Average of Goals Scored Per Game:

Player	Games played	Average
Alan Geldard	6	4.83
Matt Hoyland	5	4.80
Peter Lewis	5	4.80
George Trataris	7	4.43
Ken Mansfield	5	2.00

Average of Goals Conceded Per Game:

Player	Games played	Average
Jimmy Smith	5	1.20
George Trataris	7	1.29
Ken Thomson	6	1.33
Matt Hoyland	5	1.40
Costas Trataris	7	1.86

Top Five Appearances

Player	Games played
Costas Trataris	7
George Trataris	7
Ken Thomson	6
Matt Hoyland	5
Peter Lewis	5
Ken Mansfield	5
Jimmy Smith	5

Mario Antoine

Top Five Scorers

Player	Games played	Goals
Colin Findlay	4	5
Costas Trataris	7	5
Vic Moss	2	4
Rui Bastos	2	3
Peter Crossan	1	2
Bob Rodgers	2	2
Brian Phillips	3	2

Top Clean Sheets

Player	Games played	Clean Sheets
George Trataris	7	2
A. Gafforio	1	1
Stockman	3	1

CHAPTER TWELVE

ANALYSIS OF OUTSTANDING PLAYERS

Harry Middleton

Middlestone played in the historical first ever match on 16 February 1935 at Blantyre Sports Club v. Sport Lisboa e Beira in a 4–1 defeat. He played a further four games and managed a clean sheet in his last appearance three years later against the same opposition.

George Summers

History was made when Summers became the first ever international scorer in the 4–1 defeat against Sport Lisboa e Beira in 1935. He was elected president of the Nyasaland Football Association (NFA) in 1954, a position he held until his death in 1957. This led to the seeds being sown for the amalgamation of the two different associations as a benefit match was played between the European and African Leagues.

Forrest

Forrest is yet another player who featured in Nyasaland's first ever victory in 1936 by 3–1 against Alexandra Club from Southern Rhodesia, and his international career lasted fourteen years, during which time he won seventeen caps and scored 3 goals.

R. Grant

Grant also played in the first ever international win in 1936, marking his debut against Alexandra FC, and for eleven seasons he was a regular national player, earning sixteen caps and 3 goals scored. He was a regular Country Club Limbe member.

Russell-Jones

One of six changes in the second game saw Russell-Jones make his debut in 1936 v. Alexandra Football Club, and he then played in thirteen successive matches before bowing out in 1948, having earned a total of sixteen caps. He was a regular in Blantyre Sports Club League in its inaugural season in 1947–48.

John Patterson

Patterson was a debut scorer in the Oury Cup v. Sport Lisboa e Beira in a 2–1 defeat in 1948. He scored a further 5 goals and earned a total of ten caps during his six-year international career. John featured in many Blantyre Sports Club successes since the league was introduced in 1947, winning the title twice, in the 1947–48 and 1950–51 seasons. He also featured as a league title winner with

Zomba during the 1952–53 season and played for other clubs, such as Sunnyside Rovers (1951–52) and Corona (1955–56). John was a regular scorer in all the cup finals he was involved in.

Jackie Cottingham

Cottingham was a national player for both Southern Rhodesia (Zimbabwe), when he represented them against Israel in 1954, and Northern Rhodesia (Zambia), against English side Wolverhampton Wanderers, before arriving in 1957 as a twenty-four-year-old and joining his siblings Jim and Archie at Limbe Country Club (LCC).

He proved successful in his first season and was part of the Nyasaland squad before he made his debut on 29 March 1958 in a 2–0 win against Alexandra FC of Southern Rhodesia. He then followed this up by playing in the next twenty internationals.

He is one of five players that played against the three British teams that visited our shores in 1960: Blackpool (1–6), West Ham United (0–4 in 1962) and Dundee United (2–10 in 1963). The other players were veteran Dennis Johnston, Dennis Pritchard, Brian Fox, and Brian Phillips.

Cottingham also featured in the first ever proper international fixture that Nyasaland was involved with in 1960 when they lost their two matches by 4–3 and 13–3.

On the local scene, despite playing in over ten seasons, he never appeared in a title-winning side, but was a runner-up on five separate occasions with LCC (1959), Callies (1961), Olympia (1963), and Blantyre Sports Club (BSC) during 1965 and 1966. He was more successful in Cup competitions, as he twice appeared in the Royle Cup winning side for LCC in 1958 against Cholo (4–1) and in 1965 against his former club, LCC (2–1). In the Stanhope Cup, he was on the victory podium three times for different clubs. BSC were the first victims, by 1–0, as they completed a double in 1958. He then starred for BSC against Cholo in 1963, winning 6–3. And finally he won again with BSC when Chichiri Athletics in their first season were beaten 2–0 in 1966. The previous year, history was created when they shared this trophy with Wanderers after they drew 2–2 and no dates was available for a replay.

Jackie was twice nominated as Player of the Year, in 1961 and 1963.

Ken Mansfield

Mansfield's debut on 17 April 1954 against Sporting Lisbon e Beira in the annual Oury Cup saw him score twice in a 5–2 win, and he went on to play a further twenty games for Nyasaland during his eight years as a national player and a scorer of 9 goals, placing him third on the scoring chart.

He played for only two clubs, starting with Limbe Country Club (LCC) during the early fifties. He eventually played for Railways, where he was employed during the 1959–60 season. Local honours were very scarce, as he tasted victory for Railways only against his previous club, LCC, in the Franklin Trophy in 1965, 5–2, after a 5–5 draw. Railways reached yet another final in 1965 against Cholo in the Royle Cup, losing 2–1. The following year, they lost yet again by a similar score against Zomba.

Brian Phillips

Being the second-highest scorer, with 12 goals during a nine-year spell between 1954 and 1963, earned Phillips thirty-four caps. He is one of only four players to have scored a hat trick for Nyasaland, which was achieved in a 4–1 win against Sporting Lisbon e Beira in 1961.

On the local scene, Brian enjoyed a very successful career with Blantyre Sports Club between 1954 and 1962, winning the league title three times in 1956, 1959, and 1960. He appeared in fifteen cup finals and was on the winning side nine times and scored in five finals. He then transferred to Limbe Country Club in 1963 and grabbed two more league titles and played in a further six finals, being successful in three of those and scoring in two of them.

Wanderers FC

The seeds for the team that changed the landscape of local football were sown during the 1961–62 season when Rovers United were formed during the NFA era, though they played only friendly games and cup competitions.

Rovers, which was the first ever mixed-race team, started off with players such as Ibrahim Mojoo (later a successful FAM general secretary), Allaudin Osman, Basil Malila, Franco Bregger, Don Meintjies, George Antoine, and Patrick Silva, to mention a few.

Rovers successfully reached the semi-finals of the Royle Cup at the first attempt, which prompted them to join the NFA League the following year.

They ended their debut season in fourth place out of eight teams, hauled in 55 goals in fourteen games, and once more were beaten semi-finalists in the Royle Cup.

In the1963–64 season, the door was open for NAFA players to play in the NFA League, which eventually changed to City Suburban League under the guidance of the joint associations, now renamed as the Malawi Football Association (MFA).

What a pleasure it was to see such greats as legend James Kaminjolo, on his return from overseas studies, and Lameck Phiri, who had recently played for the NAFA National team in Northern Rhodesia, added to the squad.

Rovers were rewarded when Kaminjolo was a scorer in the 4–2 triumph against Limbe Country Club in the Franklin Trophy final, with forward Allaudin Osman the hat-trick hero.

The mixed-race Portuguese-speaking community, such as Manuel da Costa, Ignacio DeSouza, Ishmail Ibrahim, Jim Pinto, and other close friends, such as Miko Adelson, together with prominent Portuguese Club member Serafin Neto, decided to build a clubhouse behind the existing Portuguese Club for ease of membership gatherings, and by coincidence the folding up of Rovers United paved the way for Portuguese Wanderers to be born.

The club saw future stars such as Oliver Nakhumwa, already a Malawi National player since 1962; James Mkwanda; custodian Green Malunga; and the Nsewa brothers, to mention a few, added to the disbanded Rovers side.

At the end of the season, they disposed of NFA giants Blantyre Sports Club (BSC) by two points to grab the league title. Not satisfied with a single trophy, they shared the Stanhope Trophy after a 2–2 draw with BSC, with Henry Nsewa and Lameck Phiri on target.

The line-up that day was Green Malunga, Kirby Thomson, Oliver Nakhumwa, Wales Nsewa, Henry Nsewa, Lameck Phiri, Allaudin Osman, Joaquim Cunha, James Mkwanda, Smile Kampeza, and Basil Malila

Other players that featured for Wanderers that season were Januaro de Magalhaes, Damiano, Raleigh M'manga, Cullen Mwase, and young Yasin Osman at the tender age of sixteen.

It is not known why Wanderers and the Portuguese club split alliance, but rumours mention that when Clube Desportivo de Tete arrived to play in May 1965, the club wanted to feature most of its nationals with a few selected players from the actual team that did not go well with Wanderers. (However, I am undertaking ongoing research to establish the reasons behind this divorce.)

Although they failed to retain their league title the following season, they reclaimed it in the 1966–67 season and retained it to the end of the period covered in this publication, winning it during three successive seasons.

This was a record in this new era and equalled Limbe Country Club's achievement as the only club during the NFA to win during seasons 1961–62 to 1963–64.

In the cup competitions, they reached four finals, winning the Franklin Trophy in 1967 and defeating Bata Bullets after extra time by 3–2 in the inaugural Chibuku Cup.

In 1968, they created history by becoming the first football club to acquire sponsorship from Stansfield Motors, the agents of the French Peugeot Motor Cars and the Japanese Yamaha Motorcycles and Outboard Marine Engines; their name changed to "Yamaha Wanderers" as a result of this.

Wanderers became one of the modern era giants; to date they, have been crowned champions on sixteen separate occasions and have been winners of twenty-five cup competitions.

Bata Bullets

Standing: L to R; Allan Stuart, Iqbal Sheriff, Crighton Msiya, Mustafa Munshi, Charles Kagwa, Ernie Stuart, Paul Khamisa, Farid Osman
Front row: : L to R: Basil Malila, Dave Banda, Ralph Stanley, Bruce MacKenzie, Balraj Bouri, Prescot Magaleta

Disgruntled Wanderers fringe players and reserves, as well as the disbanding of the Chichiri Athletics team, was the genesis of Bata Bullets, who debuted the 1966–67 season as Blantyre City. The Stuart brothers, who played for disbanded Rovers United, initiated that move to create this new club, and in came youthful Mustafa Munshi, Prescott Magaleta, and stalwart Basil Malila from Chichiri Athletics; Balraj Bouri from Railways; and future Malawi national star Charles Kagwa. Farid Osman was elected team manager.

They ended that first season in third place on the log table, and despite reaching the Royle Cup final against Zomba, they ended trophyless. John Gilmore, who was unknown at that time, ferried his in-laws Basil Malila and Alex Paddy to the team's second annual general meeting, held in Kandjeza, and surprisingly was elected general secretary at the end of the event. This would mark the beginning of the long association and successes that Gilmore endured with the club.

The following season, they ended in mid table, and through their dynamic and hardworking club secretary, John Gilmore, they managed a lucrative sponsorship from Bata Shoe Company for the 1968–69 season under their new identity of Bata Bullets.That attracted new blood, and Yasin (Njinga) Osman was one of the early recruits in a record deal of £100. Some other notable new faces in the side were custodian Henry Kapalamula, already an established national player from Zomba, and Basil Malila, who was appointed captain of the side.

That season, they ended up in second place on the log table behind early giants Yahama Wanderers and were also victims to their rivals in the Chibuku Cup, 3–2, after extra time.

As a newly-formed club, that had existed for only three years and had no trophies to show for their efforts, they went on to become the future giants of Malawi football, with no fewer than twenty-three titles and fifty-four triumphs in cup competitions, earning them a grant total of seventy-seven honours in their fifty-two years of existence (the remainder of which will be covered in the next two volumes of this work).

Osman Siblings

The sequence begins with Allaudin, who was part of the newly-formed Rovers United in 1961, before playing for Wanderers when Rovers disbanded in 1964.

Whilst at Wanderers, he was joined by fifteen-year-old wonder boy Yasin.

However, the following season, when school team Chichiri Athletics joined the League, Yasin played for his school side, which unfortunately lasted only one year. His elder brother, Farid, was also on this team as a goalkeeper, making him the third Osman family member involved with football.

Yasin (nicknamed Njinga) returned to Wanderers and reunited with Allaudin for the 1966–67 season until he was transferred to Bata Bullets in 1968 for a then record fee of £100. Sattar was also a member of Bata Bullets at that time, making him a fourth sibling of the Osman clan.

Meanwhile, with the arrival of ex-Bristol City player Brian Griffin, the school team of Chichiri was revived in 1967–68 and Nazer became the fifth Osman family member to become a footballer in Malawi.But tragically, during the Easter weekend of 1968, on 12 April, en route to Mozambique to play friendly fixtures in Tete, they were involved in a fatal car accident in which Nazer, a student, and Francis Nseula, a schoolteacher, were killed, and two other students, Mustafa Munshi and Prescott Magaleta, suffered multiple injuries.

Meanwhile, Nazer's elder siblings, Allaudin and Yasin, had travelled to Southern Rhodesia to play friendly games there, and they had to cut their visit short to attend their brother's funeral.

Yasin also played for Michiru Castles for yet another record transfer fee of MK500, and after his retirement, he played for Seba Athletics (previously a social team, Dodo), who participated only in cup competitions and eventually replaced Combank (previously Chichiri Athletic) when they disbanded in the early '80s.

Yasin was also involved in coaching, and amongst his clubs were Michiru Blue Cross, Wanderers, Moneymen, Escom United, and Malawi National team. He was also FAM's general secretary on two separate occasions.

Dennis Johnston

An outstanding player during the NFA era, Johnston's Nyasaland International career kicked off in his first season that he played here in 1951.

He began his football sojourn in neighbouring Southern Rhodesia with Mashonaland in 1947, where he remained until 1950, when he captained both his club and national teams before embarking on another successful career in Malawi when he arrived in 1951.

His debut for Nyasaland came in Beira, where he featured in the Annual Oury Cup and was victorious in a 2–1 win and became a permanent member of the side until their second 10–0 trashing in 1955 (first inflicted in 1947, also in Beira) halted his twelve-game run.

He captained his country for eight successive years until his retirement was announced before the West Ham United match, although he played a further three games in 1963. Johnston earned a rare selection of 81 per cent, spanning twelve years, which topped the Nyasaland caps with a record forty-four caps from fifty-four games since his debut.

Although he never scored for Nyasaland, he was one of the few selected players that featured against the three visiting British sides (Blackpool, West Ham United, and Dundee United) that toured Nyasaland between 1960 and 1963. However, he was very unfortunate not to play in the only two proper international games against another country, Southern Rhodesia (his previous national team), in 1960.

His CV was upgraded when he became the first ever Malawi coach in Malawi's proper international games in 1962 against Ghana and Tanganyika—games that they lost by 12–0 and 6–2. Unconfirmed reports show that he might have been involved in another fixture against a Tanganyika club side beaten 9–0, prior to the main game during that country's republic celebrations.

His first venture in Nyasaland was with Zomba Gymkhana in 1951, and they were runners-up twice to then giants Blantyre Sports Club (BSC) in the Royle League and the Royle knockout competition, 3–1. He remained with them until the 1959 season, when transferred to BSC, at which time he led them to two league titles in 1953 and 1958. He won a further two League titles in successive years of 1959 and 1960 and won five knockout trophies of the Royle Cup (twice) and Stanhope (treble) before returning to his original club.

In 1960, he became the first Footballer of the Year and followed that by also becoming the first winner of the George Summers Memorial Trophy for the Sportsman of the Year in 1962. This trophy was in memory of the only official who died in office as the president of the NFA, not forgetting that he was the first ever scorer for the Nyasaland team in 1935.

Johnston was with the British South Africa Police (a police force of Rhodesia) between 1946 and 1951; he was transferred to Nyasaland to join the Nyasaland Police in 1951 to 1952. He was also a superintendent of Mpemba Boys Home and in the Ministry of Education and Social Development, which took him to various teaching assignments in Nepal, Kashmir, Ladakh, Pakistan, China, and New Zealand before he retired to Exeter, in his homeland, where he died in the early nineties whilst still able to speak fluent Nyanja.

Oliver Nakhumwa

Nakhumwa was one of the pioneers of today's second birth of the Flames in 1962 against Ghana. As noted in previous chapters in this book, the original seed was sown in 1949 when the first indigenous side travelled as Nyasaland to play Grupo Desportivo Robenta Fogo, a club side in Beira, Portuguese East Africa (now known as Mozambique).

However, the proper debut took place when Malawi faced another country for the first time ever on 15 October 1962, although they were trashed by Gold Stars of Ghana, 12–0. Nakhumwa went on to great heights, as he eventually captained new look Malawi on several occasions right up to the end of the period covered in this first volume, which ended his international career. He played an incredible twenty-two out of twenty-six matches—an 85 per cent appearance rate (which was higher against the NFA star Dennis Johnston).

He further appeared in nine games for either Malawi or a select XI against club sides including English side Oldham Athletic, narrowly losing by 3–2.

On the local scene, little is known of Nakhumwa, as he played his football in the Central Region in Dedza, and once in Blantyre, he became a founding member of Wanderers FC, which won the City and Suburban League title in their inaugural season in 1965. He was further decorated in three other Wanderers titles between 1967 and 1969. The latter year saw them achieve the Double by winning the newly introduced Chibuku knockout trophy against rising and future giants Bata Bullets 3–2 after extra time.

Overton Mkandawire

Mkandawire made his debut in the early stages of Malawi's introduction to the international football scene, as he was featured in only Malawi's fourth game against Southern Rhodesia. For the first time ever, the game did not end in defeat as they trod off at the end of the game with a respectable 2–2 draw.

He retained his place in the next eight matches that saw the Flames victorious for the first time ever on 12 November 1967 against Rhodesia in Salisbury (now Harare) by 1–0, courtesy of his strike that made him joint top scorer with Solomon Mkwapatira on 3 goals after a total of nine games.

However, his lethal prowess in front of goal was revealed in nine other fixtures against club sides, as he registered 10 goals that included a hat-trick—a rare feat for Malawi against Desportivo Clube de Tete at the Central Stadium (now Kamuzu Stadium, originally known as Rangely Stadium when first built in the late '50s). He also twice scored a brace, as well as scoring a goal against English side Oldham Athletic in a narrow 3–2 defeat.

Regrettably, his international football career was cut short as a result of him pursuing further studies overseas in England.

On the local scene, he was a prominent member of Zomba Gymkhana Club and featured successfully in the treble victorious side of 1966 when they grabbed the City and Suburban League title, followed by a resounding triumph against debutants Chichiri Athletics, 4–0, in the Franklin Trophy, and 2–1 in the Royle Cup against Railways at the fourth time of asking.

The following year witnessed them following another successful season as they retained the Royle Cup, defeating yet another debutant club, Blantyre City, who were later to be sponsored and renamed Bata Bullets, by a crushing score of 5–2. A new trophy was displayed on their cabinet when the Stanhope Trophy was won with a record-breaking score of 6–1 against rising giants Wanderers, a team that, however, prevented them from achieving a second successive treble as they lost the Franklin Trophy 3–1.

Nyasa United

The president of the NFA, Eric Ortton, officially announced the great news about a proposed multiracial professional national league for Southern and Northern Rhodesia, as well as Nyasaland, on 17 November 1960.

Southern Rhodesia (Zimbabwe) would contribute eleven teams: four from Copperbelt, two each from Salisbury and Bulawayo, and one each from Umtali, Gatooma, and Gwelo.

Northern Rhodesia (Zambia) would feature two teams from Lusaka and Ndola, whereas Nyasaland would have one team from Blantyre.

The league's rules and regulations stipulated that each team should have no more than eight players of any race.

The ongoing dialogue did not go down well in the Nyasaland camp. Divided interest in the NFA Council centred on choosing between professional and amateur players, which would disrupt their local league.

There were also objections from the political African Nationals, citing the league's wording of "Multi-Racial" football. The wording did not go down well, especially with the leader of the

Malawi Congress Party, Dr. Hasting Kamuzu Banda, who pointed out that even in Britain, of which Nyasaland was a colony, they had never mentioned their league as being multiracial, despite various races being featured in it.

In addition, Kamuzu Banda also said that the country was fighting imperialism and colonialism and should wait until after the elections before allowing indigenous Malawians to participate.

This was all happening just short of two months before the proposed commencement of the league, which was to start in April 1961 under the revised name of "Rhodesia and Nyasaland Football League."

Despite all these hiccups, including travelling arrangements of hiring a chartered flight, which was dealt a blow owing to a shortage of planes, the team travelled in two lots to play a friendly against a Salisbury City / United XI that was to curtain-raise the Durban v. Salisbury City / United first team on 9 April 1961, played at the Glamis Stadium.

The line-up that day was George Trataris, Vic Moss, Mann, Matt Hoyland, Sergio Nicholas, Vic Rodkin, Hassam, Mike Davis, Jackie Cottingham (capt.), Dennis Pritchard, and Ikram Sheriff.

Nyasa United lost that game 3–1, with Dennis Pritchard as the scorer.

The official opening fixture took place two weeks later at the Rangely Stadium in Chichiri, where Nyasa United were playing hosts to Lusaka City. Despite taking the lead with a Max Prien strike, Nyasa lost that fixture 2–1 in a match played on a miserable wet day. Though they had further travel arrangements, they unfortunately had to call it a day; this was also experienced by visitors Lusaka City.

Only five players were retained from the first match, with the others being replaced by Peter Parker, Max Prien, Costas Trataris, Brian Philips, and the two Malikula players believed not to be related.

APPENDIX A

RESULT TABLES

Malawi International Complete Results

1	15 Oct. 1962	Blantyre	Friendly	Ghana	0–12	
2	08 Dec. 1962	Dar Es Salaam	Friendly	Tanganyika	2–6	G. Kalitsiro, S. Thipa
3	13 Oct. 1963	Ndola	Friendly	Northern Rhodesia	1–5	S. Bweya
4	20 Jun. 1964	Blantyre	Friendly	Southern Rhodesia	1–3	W. Juma
5	21 Jun. 1964	Blantyre	Friendly	Southern Rhodesia	2–2	E. Gondwe, R. M'manga
6	04 Jul. 1964	Blantyre	Friendly	Northern Rhodesia	0–5	
7	06 Jul. 1966	Blantyre	Friendly	Zambia	0–6	
8	07 Jul. 1966	Blantyre	Friendly	Madagascar	1–6	O. Mkandawire
9	08 Jul. 1966	Blantyre	Friendly	Zambia	1–5	P. Chisasa
10	02 Oct. 1966	Maseru	Friendly	Basutoland	3–4	S. Mkwapatira
11	25 Mar. 1967	Blantyre	Friendly	Rhodesia	3–6	O. Mkandawire, Y. Osman, A. Osman
12	26 Mar. 1967	Blantyre	Friendly	Rhodesia	2–5	O. Mkandawire, B. Griffin
13	11 Nov. 1967	Salisbury	Friendly	Rhodesia	1–1	B. Bouri
14	12 Nov. 1967	Salisbury	Friendly	Rhodesia	1–0	O. Mkandawire
15	06 Jul. 1968	Blantyre	Friendly	Kenya	2–2	S. Chibambo, R. Cook
16	06 Sep. 1968	Mbabane	Friendly	Botswana	8–1	Y. Osman (3), R. Cook (3), J. Chauluka, S. Chibambo
17	07 Sep. 1968	Mbabane	Friendly	Swaziland	0–2	
18	31 Jan. 1969	Blantyre	Friendly	Rhodesia	0–0	
19	01 Feb. 1969	Lilongwe	Friendly	Rhodesia	2–2	R. Cook (o/g)
20	02 Feb. 1969	Blantyre	Friendly	Rhodesia	0–1	
21	08 Feb. 1969	Salisbury	Friendly	Rhodesia	0–4	
22	09 Feb. 1969	Salisbury	Friendly	Rhodesia	1–1	Y. Osman (p)
23	04 May 1969	Bulawayo	Friendly	Rhodesia	1–4	S. Chibambo
24	27 Jun. 1969	Tananarive	Friendly	Madagascar	0–3	
25	06 Jul. 1969	Blantyre	Friendly	Swaziland	3–0*	S. Chibambo (2), R. Cook
26	09 Jul. 1969	Blantyre	Friendly	Swaziland	1–1	S. Chibambo
27	30 Aug. 1969	Lusaka	Friendly	Zambia	0–4	
28	31 Aug. 1969	Ndola	Friendly	Zambia	0–5	
29	02 Sep. 1969	Kitwe	Friendly	Zambia	0–7	

Match abandoned after 55 minutes due to power failure

	Countries	P	W	D	L	F	A	W %	FPG	APG
1	Rhodesia	12	1	5	6	14	29	8.3%	1.2	2.4
2	Zambia	7	0	0	7	2	37	0.0%	0.3	5.3
3	Swaziland	3	1	1	1	4	3	33.3%	1.3	1.0
4	Madagascar	2	0	0	2	1	9	0.0%	0.5	4.5
5	Basutoland	1	0	0	1	3	4	0.0%	3.0	4.0
6	Botswana	1	1	0	0	8	2	100.0%	8.0	2.0
7	Ghana	1	0	0	1	0	12	0.0%	0.0	12.0
8	Kenya	1	0	1	0	2	2	0.0%	2.0	2.0
9	Tanganyika	1	0	0	1	2	6	0.0%	2.0	6.0
	Total	29	3	7	19	36	104	10.3%	1.2	3.6

Notes:
FPG: Goals For per game
APG: Goals Against per game
Rhodesia also includes Southern Rhodesia
Zambia also includes Northern Rhodesia

Malawi International, Select XI, Complete Results against Clubs

1	18 Jun. 1949	Beira	Friendly	Grupo Desportivo Rebenta Fogo	2–4	E. Thondoya, G. Jonas
2	19 Jun. 1949	Beira	Friendly	Grupo Desportivo Rebenta Fogo	1–2	
3	08 Jun. 1950	Blantyre	Friendly	Grupo Desportivo Rebenta Fogo	?	
4	10 Jun. 1950	Zomba	Friendly	Grupo Desportivo Rebenta Fogo	2–0	S. Menewa, S. Thipa
5	? 1952	Blantyre	Friendly	Southern Rhodesia	?	
6	? 1952	Blantyre	Friendly	Southern Rhodesia	?	
7	? 1954	Umtali	Friendly	Southern Rhodesia	W	
8	? 1954	Gweru	Friendly	Southern Rhodesia	W	
9	? 1954	Salisbury	Friendly	Southern Rhodesia	L	
10	? 1954	Bulawayo	Friendly	Southern Rhodesia	L	
11	? Nov. 1957	Johannesburg	Friendly	Pick Up 1st XI	1–4	
12	? Nov. 1957	Johannesburg	Friendly	Litsitsili Bugs	2–2	
13	? Nov. 1957	Johannesburg	Friendly	Pick Up 2nd XI	3–2	
14	? Nov. 1957	Johannesburg	Friendly	Coloured Community	4–7	
15	? Nov. 1957	Bulawayo	Friendly	White Army 1st XI	2–6	
16	? Nov. 1957	Bulawayo	Friendly	White Army 2nd	2–2	
17	? Nov. 1957	Blantyre	Friendly	Pick Up 1st XI	2–6	
18	? 1958	?	Friendly	Salisbury Yellow Peril		
19	10 Dec. 1960	Blantyre	Friendly	Mashonaland African		
20	13 Apr. 1963	Blantyre	Friendly	Malawi Stars	3–2	R. Banda (2), J. Sangala

21	11 Oct. 1963	Luanshya	Friendly	Copperbelt XI	4–5	E. Gondwe (2), J. Sangala, ?
22	15 Oct. 1963	Lusaka	Friendly	Midlands	2–8	M. de Thipa, R. Banda
23	10 May 1965	Blantyre	Friendly	Ferroviario de Beira	1–5	P. Bradley
24	30 Apr. 1967	Blantyre	Friendly	Sporting Club de Tete	4–1	O. Mkandawire (2), B. Griffin (2-1p)
25	11 Jun. 1967	Blantyre	Friendly	Desportivo Club de Tete	4–1	O. Mkandawire (3), A. Osman
26	06 Jul. 1967	Blantyre	Friendly	Oldham Athletic	2–3	O. Mkandawire, Y. Osman
27	15 Jul. 1967	Blantyre	Friendly	Salisbury City	3–0	S. Kapalamula (2), B. Griffin
28	16 Jul. 1967	Blantyre	Friendly	Salisbury City	0–0	
29	21 Oct. 1967	Blantyre	Friendly	Salisbury Callies	0–0	
30	22 Oct. 1967	Blantyre	Friendly	Salisbury Callies	2–3	O. Mkandawire. S. Chibambo
31	02 Mar. 1968	Blantyre	Friendly	Wankie	1–3	(o/g)
32	10 Mar. 1968	Blantyre	Friendly	Wankie	3–1	O. Mkandawire, R. Cook
33	02 Dec. 1968	Blantyre	Friendly	Salisbury Dynamos	3–1	B. Griffin, A. Mpinganjira, Y. Osman
34	17 May 1969	Blantyre	Friendly	West Ham Youth	0–1	

Malawi International, Select XI, Unknown Results against Clubs

	Teams	P	W	D	L	UN
1	S. Rhodesian Clubs	6	2	0	2	2
2	G. D. Rebenta Fogo	1	0	0	0	1
3	Mashonaland African	1	0	0	0	1
4	Salisbury Y. Peril	1	0	0	0	1
	Total	9	2	0	2	5

Malawi International, Select XI, Known Results against Clubs

	Teams	P	W	D	L	F	A	W %	FPG	APG
1	G. D. Rebenta Fogo	3	1	0	2	5	6	33.3%	1.7	2.0
2	Salisbury Callies	2	0	1	1	2	3	0.0%	1.0	1.5
3	Salisbury City	2	1	1	0	3	0	50.0%	1.5	0.0
4	Wankie	2	1	0	1	4	4	50.0%	2.0	2.0
5	Coloured Community	1	0	0	1	4	7	0.0%	4.0	7.0
6	Copperbelt XI	1	0	0	1	4	5	0.0%	4.0	5.0
7	Desportivo de Tete	1	1	0	0	4	1	100.0%	4.0	1.0
8	Ferroviario de Beira	1	0	0	1	1	5	0.0%	1.0	5.0
9	Litsitsili Bugs	1	0	1	0	2	2	0.0%	2.0	2.0
10	Malawi Stars	1	1	0	0	3	2	100.0%	3.0	2.0
11	Midlands	1	0	0	1	2	8	0.0%	2.0	8.0

		P	W	D	L	F	A	W %	FPG	APG
12	Oldham Athletic	1	0	0	1	2	3	0.00%	2.0	3.0
13	Pick Up 1st XI (SA)	1	0	0	1	1	4	0.00%	1.0	4.0
14	Pick Up 1st XI (Rhod)	1	0	0	1	2	6	0.00%	2.0	6.0
15	Pick Up 2nd XI (SA)	1	1	0	0	3	2	100.0%	3.0	2.0
16	Salisbury Dynamos	1	1	0	0	3	1	100.0%	3.0	1.0
17	Sporting C. de Tete	1	1	0	0	4	1	100.0%	4.0	1.0
18	West Ham Youth	1	0	0	1	0	1	0.0%	0.0	1.0
19	White Army 1st XI	1	0	0	1	2	6	0.0%	2.0	6.0
20	White Army 2nd XI	1	0	1	0	2	2	0.0%	2.0	2.0
	Total	25	8	4	13	53	69	32%	2.1	2.8

Regionals Complete Results

1	04 Mar. 1968	Lilongwe	Friendly	Wankie	4–6	E. Gondwe (2), S. Mkwapatira, Katanga
2	06 Mar. 1968	Zomba	Friendly	Wankie	2–1	D. Malefula, S. Kapalamula
3	08 Mar. 1968	Chikwawa	Friendly	Wankie	1–2	Mhango
4	26 Nov. 1968	Cholo	Friendly	Salisbury Dynamos	2–6	Mboga, B. Malila
5	28 Nov. 1968	Zomba	Friendly	Salisbury Dynamos	2–7	?

Zomba

	Countries	P	W	D	L	F	A	W %	FPG	APG
1	Salisbury Dynamos	1	0	0	1	2	7	0.0%	2.0	7.0
2	Wankie	1	1	0	0	2	1	100.0%	2.0	1.0
	Total	2	1	0	1	4	8	50.0%	2.0	4.0

Chikwawa

	Countries	P	W	D	L	F	A	W %	FPG	APG
1	Wankie	1	0	0	1	1	2	0.0%	1.0	2.0

Cholo

	Countries	P	W	D	L	F	A	W %	FPG	APG
1	Salisbury Dynamos	1	0	0	1	2	6	0.0%	2.0	6.0

Lilongwe

	Countries	P	W	D	L	F	A	W %	FPG	APG
1	Wankie	1	0	0	1	4	6	0.0%	4.0	6.0

Malawi Schools' Complete Results

1	26 Aug. 1967	Blantyre	BAT Cup	Zambia Schools	1–7	
2	28 Aug. 1968	Livingstone	Friendly	Southern Province	1–4	K. Kamwendo
3	2 Sep. 1967	Blantyre	BAT Cup	Zambia Schools	3–2	O.Mkandawire (2) (O/G)
4	2 Sep. 1968	Ndola	BAT Cup	Zambia School	0–7	
5	5 Sep. 1968	Kitwe	BAT Cup	Zambia Schools	1–2	D. Malefula
6	8 Sep. 1968	Lusaka	BAT Cup	Zambia Schools	0–6	
7	09 Sep. 1968	Luanshya	Friendly	Western Province	0–3	
8	18 May 1969	Blantyre	Friendly	West Ham Youth	1–4	K. Kamwendo
9	31 Aug. 1969	Lilongwe	BAT Cup	Zambia Schools	1–2	B. Phoya
10	02 Sep. 1969	Blantyre	BAT Cup	Zambia Schools	1–6	K. Kamwendo
11	07 Sep. 1969	Blantyre	BAT Cup	Zambia Schools	1–2	T. Kazembe

Malawi Schools

	Countries	P	W	D	L	F	A	W %	FPG	APG
1	Zambia Schools	8	1	0	7	6	32	12.5%	0.8	4.0
2	Southern Province	1	0	0	1	1	4	0.0%	1.0	4.0
3	Western Province	1	0	0	1	0	3	0.0%	0.0	3.0
4	West Ham Youth	1	0	0	1	1	4	0.0%	1.0	4.0
	Total	11	1	0	10	8	43	9.1%	0.7	3.9

Lilongwe Schools complete results

1	30 Aug. 1969	Lilongwe	Friendly	Zambia Schools	1–6	S. Bweya

Lilongwe Schools

	Countries	P	W	D	L	F	A	W %	FPG	APG
1	Zambia Schools	1	0	0	1	1	6	0.0%	1.0	6.0

NFA international complete results

1	15 Oct. 1960	Rangeley Stadium	Southern Rhodesia	3–4	B. Phillips, P. Crossan (o/g)
2	16 Oct. 1960	BSC	Southern Rhodesia	3–13	B. Phillips, B. Rodgers, P. Parker (jnr)

NFA

	Countries	P	W	D	L	F	A	W %	FPG	APG
1	Southern Rhodesia	2	0	0	2	6	17	0.0%	3.0	8.5

Oury Cup Complete Results

Oury Cup		Sport Lisboa E Beira		
No.	Date	Venue	Result	Scorers
1	28 Mar. 1937	CCL	0–1	
2	16 Apr. 1938	Beira	1–0	R. Grant
3	08 Apr. 1939	BSC	0–6	
4	23 Mar. 1940	Beira	3–2	Forrest (2),?
5	1941 or 1944	BSC/CCL	Draw	
6	31 Mar. 1945	Beira	1–4	C. Allin
7	20 Apr. 1946	BSC	2–3	C. Allin, R. Grant
8	05 Apr. 1947	Beira	0–10	
9	28 Mar. 1948	BSC	1–2	J. Patterson
10	16 Apr. 1949	Beira	3–3	Forrest (p), J. Patterson, Imlah
11	08 Apr. 1950	CCL	5–4	D. Armstrong (2), J. Patterson (2), D. Nock
12	24 Mar. 1951	Beira	2–1	G. Sophos, D. Nock
13	12 Apr. 1952	CCL	1–2	J. Patterson
14	04 Apr. 1953	Beira	1–0	Dipple
15	28 Mar. 1954	CCL	5–4	K. Mansfield (2), B. Marrinan, J. Patterson (o/g)
16	09 Apr. 1955	Beira	0–10	
17	31 Mar. 1956	BSC	5–0	C. Trataris (2), L. Doran, A. Taylor, K. Mansfield (p)
18	21 Apr. 1957	Beira	4–1	T. Allen, B. Phillips, K. Mansfield, G. Keys
19	05 Apr. 1958	CCL	3–2	A. Marr, K. Mansfield, L. Doran
20	29 Mar. 1959	Beira	0–2	
21	16 Apr. 1960	Rangeley (BT)	0–2	
22	02 Apr. 1961	Beira	4–1	B. Phillips (3), P. Lewis
23	21 Apr. 1962	BSC	2–1	D. Pritchard, B. Fox
24	14 Apr. 1963	Beira	1–2	B. Rodgers
25	27 Mar. 1964	CCL	1–2	D. Pritchard

NFA Oury Cup

	Countries	P	W	D	L	F	A	W %	FPG	APG
1	Sport Lisboa e Beira	25	11	2	12	45	65	44.0%	1.8	2.6

Trataris Trophy Complete Results

Trataris Trophy		Alexandra FC			

No.	Date	Venue	Result	Scorers
1	02 Oct. 1954	BSC	1–4	J. Patterson
2	19 Mar. 1955	CCL	3–2	B. Marrinan (3)
3	24 Mar. 1956	Salisbury	0–2	
4	30 Mar. 1957	BSC	4–1	J. Smith (2), B. Phillips, R. Robertson
5	29 Mar. 1958	Salisbury	2–0	J. Hawthorne, A. Marr
6	10 Oct. 1959	BSC	2–5	B. Phillips, D. Pritchard (p)
7	26 Mar. 1960	Salisbury	1–3	M. Prien (p)
8	25 Mar. 1961	Rangeley Stadium	3–1	M. Prien (3)

NFA Trataris trophy

	Countries	P	W	D	L	F	A	W %	FPG	APG
1	Alexandra FC	8	4	0	4	16	18	50.0%	2.0	2.3

NFA Friendlies "A" Complete Results

No.	Date	Venue	Opponent	Result	Scorers
1	16 Feb. 1935	BSC	Sport Lisboa e Beira	1–4	G. Summers
2	1936	BSC	Alexandra	3–1	G. Summers, Bemister, R. Neil
3	1936	BSC	Alexandra	3–5	R. Neil, R. Grant, L. Hayes
4	10 Jul. 1937	BSC	Alexandra	?	
5	11 Jul. 1937	BSC	Alexandra	?	
6	17 Apr. 1938	Beira	Beira Select XI	1–3	Russell
7	09 Apr. 1939	Zomba	Sport Lisboa e Beira	0–3	
8	24 Mar. 1940	Beira	Sporting C. de Beira	1–3	
9	01 Apr. 1945	Beira	De Sportivo e Beira	?	
10	06 Apr. 1947	Beira	Sport Lisboa e Beira	0–3	
11	17 Apr. 1949	Beira	Beira Select XI	1–5	?
12	13 Apr. 1952	Zomba	Sport Lisboa e Beira	4–3	?
13	05 Apr. 1953	Beira	Beira Select XI	0–1	
14	18 Apr. 1954	Zomba	Sport Lisboa e Beira	4–3	B. Marrinan (2), B. Phillips, K. Mansfield
15	03 Oct. 1954	Zomba	Alexandra	1–3	K. Mansfield
16	20 Mar. 1955	Cholo	Alexandra	5–2	B. Fox (3), A. Muir, K. Mansfield
17	10 Apr. 1955	Beira	Beira Sporting Club	2–1	A. Muir (2)
18	25 Mar. 1956	Salisbury	Alexandra	1–2	D. Harper
19	01 Apr. 1956	Zomba	Sport Lisboa e Beira	1–2	K. Mansfield
20	31 Mar. 1957	Zomba	Alexandra	1–8	?

21	22 Apr. 1957	Beira	Beira Select XI	2–0	R. Robertson (2)
22	06 Apr. 1958	Zomba	Sport Lisboa e Beira	1–2	Marr
23	30 Mar. 1959	Beira	Beira Sporting Club	3–3	A. Cottingham, (2 o/g)
24	11 Oct. 1959	Cholo	Alexandra	1–2	?
25	27 Mar. 1960	Salisbury	Salisbury Select XI	3–2	B. Phillips (2), P. Crossan
26	17 Apr. 1960	Rangeley (BT)	Sport Lisboa e Beira	2–2	B. Phillips, M. Prien
27	14 May 1960	Rangeley (BT)	Quelimane	4–4	M. Prien (4)
28	15 May 1960	Rangeley (BT)	Quelimane	2–2	Colley, M. Bowery
29	31 May 1960	Rangeley (BT)	Blackpool	1–6	M. Prien
30	26 Mar. 1961	Zomba	Alexandra	6–1	M. Prien (3), ?
31	03 Apr. 1961	Beira	Beira Sporting Club	0–3	
32	22 Apr. 1962	CCL	Sport Lisboa e Beira	4–1	B. Fox (2), Mills (2)
33	26 May 1962	BSC	Salisbury Callies	1–1	R. Bastos
34	27 May 1962	Cholo	Salisbury Callies	0–9	
35	06 Jun. 1962	Rangeley (BT)	West Ham United	0–4	
36	16 Jun. 1962	Tete	Clube de Tete	3–3	
37	17 Jun. 1962	Tete	De Sportivo Tete	3–1	J. Ruprecht, J. Cunha, S. Nicholas
38	15 Apr. 1963	Beira	Beira Railways	2–2	D. Pritchard, L. Ferguson
39	19 May 1963	Rangeley (BT)	De Sportivo Tete	0–1	
40	19 Jun. 1963	Rangeley (BT)	Dundee United	2–10	D. Meintjies, A. Osman
41	28 Mar. 1964	BSC	Sport Lisboa e Beira	4–1	S. Singh, I. Sheriff, B. Keddie, J. de Magalaes

	Countries	P	W	D	L	F	A	W %	FPG	APG
1	Sport Lisboa e Beira	10	4	1	5	21	24	40.0%	2.1	2.4
2	Alexandra FC	8	3	0	5	21	24	37.5%	2.6	3.0
3	Beira Select XI	4	1	0	3	4	9	25.0%	1.0	2.3
4	Sporting Club Beira	4	1	1	2	6	10	25.0%	1.5	2.5
5	Quelimane	2	0	2	0	6	6	0.0%	3.0	3.0
6	Salisbury Callies	2	0	1	1	1	10	0.0%	0.5	5.0
7	De Sportivo Tete	2	0	1	1	1	2	0.0%	0.5	1.0
8	Beira Railways	1	0	1	0	2	2	0.0%	2.0	2.0
9	Blackpool	1	0	0	1	1	6	0.0%	1.0	6.0
10	Clube de Tete	1	0	1	0	3	3	0.0%	3.0	3.0
11	Dundee United	1	0	0	1	2	10	0.0%	2.0	10.0
12	Salisbury XI	1	1	0	0	3	2	100.0%	3.0	2.0
13	West Ham United	1	0	0	1	0	4	0.0%	0.0	4.0
	Total	38	10	8	20	71	112	26.3%	1.9	2.9

NFA Friendlies

Notes:
Three unknown results: two versus Alexandra in 1937, and one against De Sportivo Beira in 1945

	Countries	P	W	D	L	F	A	W %	FPG	APG
1	Sport Lisboa e Beira	35	15	3	17	66	89	42.9%	1.9	2.5
2	Alexandra FC	16	7	0	9	37	42	43.8%	2.3	2.6
3	Beira Select XI	4	1	0	3	4	9	25.0%	1.0	2.3
4	Sporting Club Beira	4	1	1	2	6	10	25.0%	1.5	2.5
5	Quelimane	2	0	2	0	6	6	0.0%	3.0	3.0
6	Salisbury Callies	2	0	1	1	1	10	0.0%	0.5	5.0
7	De Sportivo Tete	2	0	1	1	1	2	0.0%	0.5	1.0
8	Beira Railways	1	0	1	0	2	2	0.0%	2.0	2.0
9	Blackpool	1	0	0	1	1	6	0.0%	1.0	6.0
10	Clube de Tete	1	0	1	0	3	3	0.0%	3.0	3.0
11	Dundee United	1	0	0	1	2	10	0.0%	2.0	10.0
12	Salisbury XI	1	1	0	0	3	2	100.0%	3.0	2.0
13	West Ham United	1	0	0	1	0	4	0.0%	0.0	4.0
	Total	71	25	10	36	132	195	35.2%	1.9	2.7

Complete NFA Fixtures versus Club Sides

Bruss Cup Complete Results

Bruss Cup		Alexandra Football Club			
No.	Date	Venue	Result	Scorers	
1	02 Oct. 1954	BSC	2–1	C. Trataris, A. Taylor	
2	20 Mar. 1955	Cholo	1–4	B. Phillips	
3	24 Mar. 1956	Salisbury	0–0		
4	31 Mar. 1957	Zomba	6–1	C. Findlay (5), A. Muir	
5	29 Mar. 1958	Salisbury	3–5	Carver, L. Colandria, K. Mansfield	
6	11 Oct. 1959	Cholo	2–5	P. Crossan (2)	
7	26 Mar. 1960	Salisbury	3–1	C. Trataris, I. Grilli, K. Mansfield	
8	26 Mar. 1961	BSC	9–1	V. Moss (4), R. Bastos (3), B. Rodgers (2)	

Bruss Cup

	Countries	P	W	D	L	F	A	W %	FPG	APG
1	Alexandra FC	8	4	1	3	26	18	50.0%	3.3	2.3

NFA Friendlies "B" Complete Results

1	03 Oct. 1954	Zomba	Alexandra FC	0–2	
2	19 Mar. 1955	CCL	Alexandra FC	2–0	B. Phillips, D. Nock
3	25 Mar. 1956	Salisbury	Alexandra FC	3–1	C. Trataris (3)
4	30 Mar. 1957	BSC	Alexandra FC	2–2	?
5	10 Oct. 1959	BSC	Alexandra FC	2–3	?
6	25 Mar. 1961	Rangeley (BT)	Alexandra FC	8–0	?
7	26 May 1962	BSC	Salisbury Callies	1–3	?
8	27 May 1962	Cholo	Salisbury Callies	1–0	M. Hoyland

NFA "B" Friendlies

	Countries	P	W	D	L	F	A	W %	FPG	APG
1	Alexandra FC	6	3	1	2	17	8	50.0%	2.8	1.3
2	Salisbury Callies	2	1	0	1	2	3	50.0%	1.0	1.5
	Total	8	4	1	3	19	11	50.0%	2.4	1.4

NFA "B" Complete Results

	Countries	P	W	D	L	F	A	W %	FPG	APG
1	Alexandra FC	14	7	2	5	43	26	50.0%	3.1	21.9
2	Salisbury Callies	2	1	0	1	2	3	50.0%	1.0	1.5
	Total	16	8	2	6	45	29	50.0%	2.8	1.8

APPENDIX B

SUMMARY OF DOMESTIC TOURNAMENTS

Blantyre and Other League Champions

No.	Sponsors/Region	Year	Champions	Runners-Up
1	Royle	1947–48	Blantyre SC	Mlanje
2		1948–49	Mlanje	Blantyre SC
3		1949–50	Mlanje	Blantyre SC
4		1950–51	Blantyre SC	Zomba GC
5		1951–52	Blantyre SC	Zomba GC
6		1952–53	Zomba GC	Limbe Wanderers
7		1953–54	Corona	Blantyre SC
8		1954–55	Corona	Blantyre SC
9		1955–56	Blantyre SC	Sunnyside Rovers
10		1956–57	Limbe CC	Blantyre SC
11		1957–58	Zomba GC	Cholo SC
12		1958–59	Blantyre SC	Limbe CC
13		1959–60	Blantyre SC	Olympia
14		1960–61	Olympia	Callies
15		1961–62	Limbe CC	Blantyre SC
16		1962–63	Limbe CC	Olympia
17		1963–64	Limbe CC	Corona
18	City & Suburban	1964–65	Portuguese Wanderers	Blantyre SC
19		1965–66	Zomba GC	Blantyre SC
20		1966–67	Wanderers	Zomba Town
21	BDFL	1967–68	Yamaha Wanderers	Zomba Town
22		1968–69	Yamaha Wanderers	Bata Bullets
	LDFL	1967–68	Flashers	Police

Castle Cup Final

No.	Year	Teams	Result	Scorers
1	1968	Chichiri Athletics v. Blantyre SC	3–2	B. Griffin (2), I. Sheriff, D. Douglas, Macauley
2	1969	University v. Yamaha Wanderers	2–0	Mphande (2p)

Chibuku Cup Final

No.	Year	Teams	Result	Scorers
1	1969	Yamaha Wanderers v. Bata Bullets	3–2	R. Cook, S. Kampeza, A. Osman, Y. Osman, M. Munshi

BAT Cup Final

No.	Year	Teams	Result	Scorers
1	1969	Malawi Police v. Yamaha Wanderers	2–1	Mboga, R. Kalembo, S. Chibambo

Royle Cup Final

No.	Year	Teams	Result	Scorers
1	1950	Blantyre SC v. Mlanje	2–1	Kirby, J. Patterson, Dickie
2	1951	Blantyre SC v. Zomba GC	3–1	J. Patterson (2), Harvey, Coleman
3	1952	Sunnyside Rovers v. Blantyre SC	1–0	Bridle
4	1953	Corona v. Zomba GC	3–0	J. Smith (2), M. Megraw
5	1954	Blantyre SC v. Corona	2–1	J. Patterson (2), ?
6	1955	Corona v. Blantyre SC	5–3	B. Marrinan (3), A. Taylor, A. Muir, M. Megraw (2), J. Patterson
7	1956	Blantyre SC v. Zomba GC	4–1	B. Marrinan (2), B. Phillips, Shergold, Freeman
8	1957	Blantyre SC v. Cholo SC	4–1	G. Barley (2), F. Taylor (2), L. Doran
9	1958	Limbe CC v. Cholo SC	4–1	P. Kelly (2), K. Mansfield, D. Pritchard, A. Vatteroni
10	1959	Blantyre SC v. Corona	2–2	M. Bowery (2), Acconci, Preen
	Replay	Blantyre SC v. Corona	5–1	M. Bowery (2), T. Donaldson (2), B. Phillips, Preen
11	1960	Olympia v. Blantyre SC	2–1	M. Prien (2), T. Allen (p)
12	1961	Blantyre SC v. Olympia	4–1	Hamilton (2), B. Power, G. Keys (p), Stellious
13	1962	Olympia v. Callies	5–2	R. Bastos (3), M. Prien, J. Cunha, J. Hawthorne, McDonald
14	1963	Limbe CC v. Railways	4–3	Chalmers, D. Pritchard, B. Phillips, J. Lowery, I. Sheriff (2), S. Singh
15	1964	Limbe CC v. Blantyre SC	4–3	D. Pritchard, P. Isham, B. Rodgers (o/g), P. Bradley (2), J. Brown (p)
16	1965	Blantyre SC v. Limbe CC	2–1	H. Wrigley (jnr), Wood, B. Phillips
17	1966	Zomba Town v. Railways	2–1	P. West, O. Mkandawire, P. Crossan
18	1967	Zomba Town v. Blantyre City	5–2	

Franklin Cup Final

No.	Year	Teams	Result	Scorers
1	1954	Sunnyside Rovers v. Blantyre SC	4–3	F. De Vito, C. Trataris, D. Robertson, Morgado, B. Philips, M. Megraw, J. Patterson
2	1955	Corona v. Blantyre SC	5–3	B. Marrinan (3), J. Smith, T. Allen (p), B. Phillips, M. Megraw, J. Kongialis

3	1956	Blantyre SC v. Limbe CC	5–1	B. Marrinan (2), Shergold (2), F. Taylor, L. Doran
4	1957	Blantyre SC v. Limbe CC	5–1	A. Taylor (2), B. Phillips, G. Keys (o/g), R. Ingram
5	1958	Limbe CC v. Blantyre SC	1–0	A. Cottingham
6	1959	Blantyre SC v. Cholo SC	3–1	T. Donaldson (2), A. Carver, Harvey
7	1960	Blantyre SC v. Cholo SC	2–1	K. Thomson, T. Allen, Grilli
8	1961	Olympia v. Callies	8–1	R. Bastos (4–1p), M. Prien (3), Wimberger (o/g)
9	1962	Blantyre SC v. Callies	2–1	B. Power (p), A. Carver, T. Allen
10	1963	Olympia v. Cholo SC	6–3	O. Kalitsiro (3), M. Prien (2), C. Trataris, Dettmar (2), T. Mills
11	1964	Limbe CC v. Blantyre SC	5–2	D. Pritchard (3), B. Phillips (2), T. Mills, P. Bradley
12	1965	Port. Wanderers v. Blantyre SC	2–2	L. Phiri, H. Nsewa, Rosenast (2)
13	1966	Blantyre SC v. Chichiri Athletics	2–0	?
14	1967	Zomba Town v. Wanderers	6–1	?

Trophy shared as unavailable date

Stanhope Cup Final

No	Year	Teams	Result	Scorers
1	1962	Olympia v Blantyre SC	2–1	McIntosh, L. Colandria, B. Rodgers
2	1963	Railways v Cholo SC	2–1	S. Singh, M. Melotte, Dettmar
3	1964	Rovers v Limbe CC	4–2	A. Osman (3), J. Kaminjolo, J. Pieterse (2)
4	1965	Railways v Limbe CC	5–5	I. Sheriff (2), G. Antoine, P. Crossan, K. Mansfield, M. Prien (2), P. Yiannakis (2), P. Isham
	Replay			
5	1966	Zomba Town v Chichiri Athletics	4–0	?
6	1967	Wanderers v Zomba Town	2–1	

Champions v. the Rest (Known Results Only)

1	1949	Mlanje v. The Rest	1–1	Eggington, J. Patterson
2	1951	Blantyre SC v. The Rest	5–1	G. Sophos, J. Patterson, ?
3	1952	Blantyre SC v. The Rest	1–2	M. Megraw, A. Muir, J. Patterson
4	1953	Zomba GC v. The Rest	1–3	A. Muir, M. Megraw (2), Dipple
5	1954	Blantyre SC v. The Rest	3–3	?
6	1955	Corona v. The Rest	2–2	L. Doran, K. Mansfield, ?
7	1956	Blantyre SC v. The Rest	4–3	F. Taylor (3), B. Marrinan, C. Trataris (2), F. de Vito
8	1957	Limbe CC v. The Rest	1–4	(o/g), T. Allen (2), C. Findlay, G. Keys
9	1958	Zomba GC v. The Rest	3–0	Pagel, Webb, J. Hawthorne
10	1960	Blantyre SC v. The Rest	4–2	B. Phillips (2), A. Muir (2), M. Prien, J. Hoatson
11	1962	Limbe CC v. The Rest	2–1	J. Pieterse, Mann, T. Mills
12	1963	Limbe CC v. The Rest	1–1	J. Pieterse, F. Rodgers
13	1964	Limbe CC v. The Rest	2–2	D. Pritchard, Chalmers, P. Bradley, H. Karim

| 14 | 1965 | P. Wanderers v. The Rest | 3–1 | A. Osman (2), J. Cunha, P. Bradley |
| 15 | 1969 | Yahama Wanderers v. FAM Select | 0–2 | D. Quennell, ? |

Scotland v. England or the Rest (Known Results Only)

1	1949	Scotland v. England	2–2	Imlah (2)–Kirby, R. Grant
2	1950	Scotland v. The Rest	4–1	D. Armstrong (3), J. Patterson, Taylor
3	1955	Scotland v. The Rest	0–0	
4	1956	Scotland v. The Rest	0–3	A. Taylor (2), C. Trataris
5	1959	Scotland v. The Rest	0–1	K. Mansfield
6	1960	Scotland v. England	4–3	J. Hawthorne (2), P. Crossan, A. Muir, P. Lewis, L. Doran, Crawford (p)
7	1961	Scotland v. The Rest	1–0	P. Crossan
8	1962	Scotland v. The Rest	5–5	J. Allan (4), Watt, R. Bastos (3), D. Pritchard, French
9	1963	Scotland v. The Rest	3–3	A. Muir (2), P. Crossan, M. Prien (2), C. Trataris
10	1964	Scotland v. The Rest	2–5	P. Crossan, L. Ferguson, S. Singh (2), P. Isham, B. fox, ?
11	1965	Scotland v. The Rest	5–3	P. Crossan (3), B. Keddie (p), J. Gallacher, P. Bradley (2), M. Prien
12	1969	Scotland v. England	4–2	B. Phillips, McDonald, McKenzie, C. Campbell, D. Quennell, D. Douglas

Vic Rodkin 6-a-Side from 1962 (Known Results Only)

1	1958	Limbe "A" v. Limbe "B"	7–2	K. Mansfield (4), B. Rodgers, A. Cottingham, Lorimer, Reid (2)
2	1962	Olympia v. Zomba GC	4–1	M. Prien (3), ?
3	1963	Olympia v. Blantyre SC	3–1	M. Prien (2), G. Kalitsiro, T. Mills
4	1964	Corona "A" v. Railways "A"	8–1	H. Nsewa (5–1p), M. Prien (2), J. Cottingham, J. Cunha
5	1965	Blantyre SC v. Railways	3–1	

Europeans v. Africans (Known Results Only)

1	1950	Blantyre: Europeans v. Africans	6–1	?
2	1954	Lilongwe: Europeans v. Africans	0–4	?
3	1958	NFA XI v. NAFA XI	6–4	T. Allen (3), J. Hawthorne (2), G. Barley, Nguruwe (2), S. Thipa, J. Kaminjolo
4	1960	Multiracial: Zomba GC/ Zomba African FA v. Olympia/SHAFL	2–1	Daudi, Botha–Mwatinamba
5	1960	Olympia v. SHAFL XI	5–5	Grilli (2), C. Trataris (2–1p), M. Prien, R. Banda (2), S. Thipa (2), D. Thipa
6	1962	NFA XI v. SHAFL XI	2–2	M. Prien, Dettmar, R. Banda (2)

Footballer of the Year

1	1960	Dennis Johnstone
2	1961	Jackie Cottingham
3	1962	Godfrey Keys
4	1963	Jackie Cottingham
5	1964	Bill Keddie

Governor's Cup (Kamuzu Cup From 1963)

1	1957	S. Province v. Central Province	9–1	
2	1958	N. Province v. S. Province	3–2	
3	1962	S. Province "A" v. C. Province	3–2	G. Kalitsiro (3), F. Chitenje, Zimba
4	1963	N. Region v. S. Region (NS)	2–1	S. Gondwe (2), R. Banda
5	1964	S. Region (SS) v. S. Region (NS)	3–1	G. Kalitsiro (2), A. Osman, S. Kapalamula
6	1965	C. Region		
7	1966	C. Region v. S. Region (NS)	2–1	R. Kalembo (2), O. Mkandawire
8	1967	C. Region v. S. Region "B"	2–1	
9	1968	N. Region v. S. Region (SS)	3–0	C. Munde, C. Nyirongo, ?
10	1969	N. Region v. S. Region	?	

Abraham Shield (Known Results Only)

1	1939	Ndirande Welfare (WD) v. ITC (ED)	5–0	T. Mittoche (2), B. Matenje, F. Sazuze, D. Sazuze
2	1946	Abrahams (B) v. Ntenjela	?	
3	1947	Kapeni v. Black Bombers	?	
4	1953	African Urban (L) v. Abrahams (B)	?	
5	1955	Ndirande Lions (winner)		

King's Birthday Cup (Known Results Only)

1	1941	Ndirande Welfare (WD) v. ITC (ED)	0–0	
2	1953	Kapeni (L) v. Abrahams (B)	?	
3	1955	Ndirande Lions v. Lime Makers	3–1	D. Thipa, Sangala, Byson, Salimu
4	1961	Red Army v. Ndirande Welfare	2–1	J. Sangala, G. Sembereka, N. Chikoko
5	1964	NESCOM v. Red Army "A"	3–1	R. Kapote, J. Zefa, Dave (p), ?

United Tobacco Cup—Champions of Blantyre v. Zomba (Known Results Only)

1	1946	Zomba Athletics v. Abrahams	2–1	Chisomo, Kaminjolo, T. Sazuze
2	1947	Kapeni (L) or Abrahams (B) v. African Athletics	?	

3	1953	Zomba v. Blantyre	5-0	?
4	1955	SHFL v. Zomba		?
5	1956	Zomba win against Cholo		?

Lilongwe Football League Cup Final—Likuni Final (Known Results Only)

| 1 | 1952 | Black Bombers v. Mbabzi | 2-0 | ? |

Coronation Cup (Known Results Only)

| 1 | 1961 | Limbe beat Cholo | ? | |
| 2 | 1962 | Shire Highlands AFL v. Limbe AFL | 9-1 | R. Banda (6-1p), W. Sangala (2), J. Sangala, Karoh |

Chilembwe Cup (Known Results Only)

| 1 | 1962 | Shire Highlands AFL v. Limbe AFL | 2-1 | J. Sangala, S. Thipa—C. Msiya |

Coca Cola Cup (Known Results Only)

1	1962	Ndirande Welfare winners	?	
2	1963	Ndirande Welfare v. Abrahams	5-1	D. Thipa (2), W. Sangala (2), J. Sangala, R. Banda
3	1964	Red Army "A" v. Ndirande Welfare	1-1	E. Mtawali, J. Sangala

Amazon Cup Final (Known Results Only)

| 1 | 1964 | Shire Highlands AFL v. Limbe AFL | 4-2 | W. Juma (3), Kagwa, C. Msiya, Dama |

Gallagher Cup Final (Known Results Only)

| 1 | 1967 | Kanjedza Rios beat ITC | ? | |

Inter Districts Cup Final (Known Results Only)

| 1 | 1962 | Blantyre v. Dowa | 7-0 | W. Sangala (3-1p), R. Banda (2), S. Thipa, J. Sangala |

I.O. Adam Shield (Known Results Only)

1	1957	Postals v. Ntondwe	2-1	(?-?)
2	1961	Red Bombers winners		
3	1962	Red Bombers winners		
4	1967	Farmers Marketing Board (FMB) v. Kanjedza Rios	3-1	A. Mpinganjira (2), Kalulu, S. Kamwendo

ABOUT THE AUTHOR

Mario Antoine's involvement in administration, professional and experiential contributions, and management across a multitude of sporting disciplines laid the foundation for his interest in producing this book.

Born and bred in Malawi, Mario served as a board member of the Malawi National Council of Sports, a board member for Malawi's top-flight league giants Silver Strikers from 2006 to 2008, a team manager for the Malawi National Snooker Team in Mauritius in 1994, the Hockey Malawi vice president from 1998 to 2008, and team manager for the Malawi National Hockey Team in 1999 at the All-Africa Games in Johannesburg, South Africa.

His romance with football dates back to 1964, when he was a pre-teenager whilst studying abroad in Mauritius, beginning with his love for the English football team Chelsea Football Club. On his return to Malawi, Mario joined Chichiri Athletics as a goalkeeper, playing for the reserves from 1971 to 1973 under Coach Brian Griffin (a former Bristol City Football Club player during the early '60s and Malawi National Football Coach in 1967, prior to the arrival of Ray Batchelor). Players such as Zorro Msiska, Jack Chamangwana, Peter Tsinabuto, Mustafa Munshi and Charles Satha were his work colleagues at Mobile Motors Limited (now Toyota Malawi Limited).

Mario played for a social football team at Country Club Limbe with Ken Mansfield, Paul Morin, and Jackie Cottingham. He was among the founders of Dodo Football Club, which later changed to Seba Athletics between 1979 and 1982 and also included Malawi football superstars Yasin Osman, Frank Wadabwa, Harold Chiwaya, Montfort Pemba, Mustafa Munshi, and the late Basil Malila.

Mario's sporting interests were diverse. In 1989, he achieved his first international accolade with Malawi National Hockey in the Africa Cup Five Nations Tournament, earning a bronze medal. In 1990, Mario again represented Malawi as national goalkeeper in their participation at the Zone VI Tournament, which included Zimbabwe and Namibia, where the team won gold.

Mario also played darts at both club and international levels, and helped Malawi attain gold medals in the Zone VI tournaments in 2000 and 2001.

Being a collector of all information statistical, informational, and historical relating to Chelsea Football Club garnered Mario's interest in producing something similar for Malawi. The authors of similar books for the Chelsea Football Club, Scott Cheshire and Ron Hockings, assisted in developing Mario's desire to produce this book. Mario has been a member of the Rec.Sport. Soccer Statistics Foundation (RSSSF, founded in 1994) since 2018 and is also a member of the International Federation of Football History and Statistics (IFFHS) and contributes towards the National Team websites for both Malawi and Mauritius.

Mario and his wife emigrated from Malawi to the UK in 2009.